An American Teacher in Early Meiji Japan

Asian Studies at Hawaii, No. 17

An American Teacher in Early Meiji Japan

Edward R. Beauchamp

ASIAN STUDIES PROGRAM
UNIVERSITY OF HAWAII
THE UNIVERSITY PRESS OF HAWAII

Library of Congress Cataloging in Publication Data

Beauchamp, Edward R   1933–
   An American teacher in early Meiji Japan.

   (Asian studies at Hawaii; no. 17)
   Originally presented as the author's thesis,
University of Washington, 1973, under title:
William Elliot Griffis: an American yatoi in Meiji.
Japan.
   Bibliography: p.
   1. Griffis, William Elliot, 1843–1928.
2. Education—Japan—History. 3. Japan—History—
Meiji period, 1868–1912. I. Title. II. Series.
DS3.A2A82 no. 17 [LA2317.G66]   915′.03s
ISBN 0–8248–0404–X   [370′.952]   75–45222

Series cover design by Janet Heavenridge

Reproduction of William Elliot Griffis' signature on page 148 courtesy of *Monumenta Nipponica.*

TO NANCY AND KEVIN

Entrance to Kai-sei Gak-ko, where William Elliot Griffis taught in Tokyo. From Edward Warren Clark, *Life and Adventure in Japan* (New York: American Tract Society, 1878).

Contents

Griffis as Historian; Griffis' View of Japan's Past;
Griffis in America, 1874–1928; A Grateful Japan Honors
Its *Yatoi*; Summing-Up

Foreword

The global outlook of the twentieth century is so much with us that we tend to overlook earlier periods when the geographical and mental horizons of mankind were greatly expanded. The sixteenth and seventeenth centuries were a period for active exploration by Europeans of unfamiliar cultures as well as climes. In the nineteenth century again, many men and women gained experience in far continents through trade, missionary work, emigration, even travel for pleasure.

The opening of Japan is a particularly dramatic episode in nineteenth-century history. For over two centuries that country had deliberately cut itself off from contact with all but a few traders and officials, mostly Dutch in nationality. Then through the efforts of Commodore Perry, Townsend Harris, and their diplomatic counterparts from other western powers a culturally rich and attractive corner of the world was rather quickly opened to view and normal international relationships. Even more strikingly, after the accession of the Meiji Emperor in 1867 the Japanese reached out actively for cultural and technical exchange. Hundreds of Japanese went abroad to study in schools and colleges in America and Europe. Several thousand westerners were employed as teachers, technical specialists, and advisers.

The true variety, importance, and dynamics of these cultural contacts can only be understood and appreciated through consideration of individual cases. In this book Edward Beauchamp studies the experience of William Elliot Griffis, a young American who taught science in Japan from 1871 to 1874.

For several reasons Griffis is a particularly interesting subject for a case study. He taught both in the remote feudal domain of Fukui and in the new national capital at Tokyo. A long series of letters written on the spot to members of his family have luckily survived, along with many other personal papers now in the library of Rutgers University. While still in Japan, Griffis also began to write for publication. His book *The Mikado's Empire*, published two years after his return, was in successive expanded editions perhaps the most widely read American book on Japan for a quarter of a century or more. Finally, throughout his long subsequent career as clergyman and writer Griffis was consciously interested in the role of foreigners in Japan, wrote biographies of several of them, and collected much more material about the *yatoi*—the employed foreigners.

In the afterglow of reminiscence Griffis may sometimes have attributed undue romance and importance to his own experiences. One corrective perspective is probably irretrievably lost to us: how the Japanese—high and low—viewed the earnest young man from Philadelphia and New Brunswick. But by carefully detailing and analyzing those experiences, primarily on the basis of statements that Griffis made at the time, Beauchamp recaptures some of the uncertainty and confusion, along with the excitement, inherent in a period of political and cultural transition in Japan. To this task he successfully applies his own strong interests in education, in crosscultural communication, and in Japan.

Robert S. Schwantes
The Asia Foundation
San Francisco, California

Preface

"William Elliot Griffis: An American Yatoi in Meiji Japan" was originally presented as my doctoral dissertation to the University of Washington in
1973. Since that time I have continued my investigations into the career of
William Elliot Griffis and have found nothing to necessitate substantial
changes in my original manuscript. Several minor changes, primarily
stylistic, have been made to provide for greater clarity.

In common with many other Americans of my generation, I owe my
earliest interest in Japan and the Japanese to my military service during
the Korean War. Again, like most Americans I did not come to that
experience with my mind as a *tabula rasa*; indeed, I shared with millions
of my countrymen the serious disadvantage of an ethnocentric education
in which the nonwestern world was viewed as merely a somewhat sinister
shadow on the periphery of "real" history. An unintended consequence
of my military service in East Asia, however, was the falling away of many
of the stereotypes about Japan that were the legacy of my early miseduca-
tion. Several years later, I had the opportunity of living and teaching at an
American high school in Okinawa while that Japanese island was still
under American military occupation. It was during this period that I
became seriously interested in the Japanese past and determined to enter
graduate school to pursue that interest.

As a doctoral candidate in the history of education and Japanese studies
at the University of Washington, however, I became increasingly interested
in the role played by western advisors and experts during the modernizing

efforts of early Meiji Japan. The idea of studying the *yatoi* in general, and William Elliot Griffis in particular, resulted from my fortuitous reading of Dr. Robert Schwantes' outstanding book, *Japanese and Americans: A Century of Cultural Relations* (New York: Harper and Brothers, 1955). This pioneering study should be read by anyone seriously interested in Japanese-American cultural relations, particularly graduate students in search of a thesis topic. Schwantes' book is a treasure chest of suggestive material.

The *yatoi* of early modern Japan command our attention not only because of their intense interest as political, economic and educational "missionaries," but also because they were the precursors of today's Peace Corps volunteers in developing nations throughout the world. Their story is instructive in another, perhaps more profound, sense. Their attitudes toward Japan, its people, and its institutions enable us to see nineteenth-century American values and attitudes in sharp relief. There is truth to the oft-repeated statement that one can understand his own society with greater clarity by standing outside of it and looking back from a foreign perspective. William Elliot Griffis' experience tells us a great deal about what it meant to be a Christian man in the United States during the last half of the nineteenth century.

There are many people who contributed to the completion of this study, but I am solely responsible for all errors of fact, omissions or failure to draw correct conclusions. To list all who helped is not possible, but I would be remiss if I did not particularly acknowledge the invaluable assistance of Charles Burgess of the Department of Educational Policy Studies of the University of Washington who served as friend, critic, and advisor during the research and writing of this study. I feel especially fortunate to have been able to draw upon the rich resources of that university's superb history department. I am especially grateful to Kenneth Pyle who introduced me to the intricacies of modern Japanese history and served as my conscientious stylistic taskmaster. Also, thanks must go to W. Stull Holt and Max Savelle in whose seminars I learned much of what it means to be an historian.

Thanks also go to *Asian Profile* (Hong Kong) and *Monumenta Nipponica* (Tokyo) for allowing me to reprint portions of this study which appeared in those journals in slightly different form.

Finally, my wife, Nancy Junko Beauchamp, and my son, Kevin Kenji Beauchamp, to whom this book is dedicated in appreciation for their patience and understanding during its research and writing. The typing was done by my wife who also served as my efficient and patient editor. There is no one to whom I would rather give my love and my first drafts.

A brief note about the Japanese names used in this study. They are presented in the manner in which the Japanese use them, that is, family name first.

Honolulu, Hawaii

Fukuwi Sept. 9 1871.

Dear Maggie,

Being still in the dark as to what news or letters may await me, I send off a few lines by the mail which leaves to-day. School opened on Monday and I have felt the invigorating influences of pedestrian and mountain travel in excellent health, and have enjoyed the delicious September weather. To-morrow week, you know, I shall enter on my 28th year. I little expected on my sixth birthday, (for that to me is the full conscious beginning of my life, though I recollect several incidents before that time) which was 22 years ago, that I should have seen so much of the world, and experienced such a chequered life both as to country, family and self, and yet with some sad lessons of experience, I cannot but thank God for what I may yet become, and that things are on the whole, what they are. I keep plodding here, day after day, sometimes home-sick, heart-sick and discouraged, but with the strengthened determination to do my Japanese work well, to fight it out on one line, and try to leave my mark ineffaceable on the Japan of the future. I expect no sudden results, but I ground my hopes on the rising generation, and expect the bread cast forth to come back after many days. Just now, the two chief men of this local government have been called to Yedo by the Imperial Government, to take part in the discussions of the National Parliament or Council and I have had long and interesting discussions with them concerning civilization and reform in Japan, and I think they will ventilate their newly gained ideas in influential places.

In school, I have organized new classes, setting two assistants to work at teaching, gave private lessons to the smartest and best students in German & French respectively, and set them to teaching in the school, and introduced largely, the blackboard system of instruction and set Mr. Sasaki, the recently appointed one of the two chief officers of the school (instead of the six sinecures jolly do-nothings) to teach drawing, as he is a good draughtsman. As soon as the apparatus comes, I shall begin to teach Nat. Philosophy. No less than six students left the school this week. One, to go to the

German School in Tokio, and five more go to seek
their fortunes in Yokohama, to learn more English,
get into business &c; I do not wonder at anyone
leaving their dull provincial city for the gay capital or the new and lively Yokohama. For the
reason that the grown-up young men are liable
thus to break off study and go to business
&c, I care more for and place my hopes on the
smaller boys, many of them bright and quick.
In my own household, I have had another change
the young girl of 18, whom I took for a servant to
wait specially upon me proved to be very faithful,
diligent and pleasant in every way, anticipated
my every want, and made my house almost as comfortable as a home, I liked her very much. All of
which to a sometimes weary and home-sick young man
must necessarily be a strong temptation in this lonely
house, I found after two weeks, that she made too
much comfort for me, and was too attractive herself. After having her 11 days, I sent her away,
before temptation turned into sin. I could in
simple justice, pay her salary, for a few months $13, and
now, though with less comfort, and a more lonely
house, I can let all my inner life be known to you,
without shame. In my new house, I hope not to be so
lonely, as my two assistants, my friend Honda, fra.
Yedo, now to live in Fukui six months, will breakfast
me, and Iwabuchi will dine & take supper with
us; and we shall talk, alternately in Japanese
& English. Besides with plenty to do in the house &
in school, and with letters regularly coming, I
hope to be kept from the bitterness of home-sickness, by
this mail, I send to Clarkie, all the details of his
future place of labor, and half envy him the
fine "position" I have obtained for him; he is quite
near Yokohama, I expect him to leave for Japan
Dec. 1st from San Francisco. Good bye! send plenty of
letters! Willie

Letter, William Elliot Griffis to Maggie Griffis, Sept. 9, 1871. Courtesy of the Griffis Collection, Rutgers University Library.

Introduction

It seems likely that the historian of education in the twenty-first century will look back on the post-World War II world with a good deal of interest at the role played by the American advisors, technical experts, and teachers in spreading modern western concepts of technology and values throughout much of Asia, Africa, and Latin America. The case studies provided by the experiences of these men and women will illuminate not only their professional impact on developing societies and tell a great deal about their own societies, but will also vividly illustrate the stresses and strains resulting from the conflict of cultures.

Contemporary historians of education, however, can mine a rich lode of materials of a similar nature stretching back to at least the middle of the nineteenth century. One example of the possibilities of this type of study is the American educational impact on Japan during the early days of the Meiji period. Emerging from almost three centuries of isolation in 1868, the young Meiji Emperor's promulgation of the Imperial Charter Oath best illustrates the new internationalism of the "Mikado's Empire." This proclamation laid down the aims of the new government, called on the people to eschew old-fashioned ways, and insisted that "Knowledge shall be sought throughout the world." In response to this, many Japanese students journeyed, at government expense, to the United States and western Europe seeking to learn the secrets of western power and prestige so that Japan could join the ranks of the modern and powerful nations of the world. A slightly different manifestation of the Emperor's charge was the employment of foreign specialists as teachers, technicians, and experts by both the new government in Edo (soon renamed Tokyo, or eastern capital) and several of the *han* (fief) governments in order to foster rapid development. The Japanese employed several thousand foreign helpers, or *yatoi*, in the first two decades of the Meiji era (1868–1912).

Of these so-called *yatoi*, one of the earliest, most influential and interesting was a young American graduate of Rutgers University, William Elliot Griffis. Born in Philadelphia in 1843, Griffis, very early in his life established close personal contacts with Japan and the Japanese. Several intersections with things Japanese highlighted his otherwise conventional childhood. At an early age he witnessed from his father's wharf the construction and launching of Commodore Perry's future flagship, the U.S.S. *Susquehanna*; in the streets of Philadelphia he personally viewed the first Japanese diplomatic mission to visit the United States, and while studying at Rutgers, he befriended and tutored several of the earliest Japanese students to study in the United States prior to the Meiji Restoration. In addition, the institution which he attended, Rutgers College, had very close ties to the Dutch Reformed Church whose missionaries had been active in Japan at least a decade prior to his graduation. Finally, one of his Rutgers' classmates was the son of Robert Pruyn, a former American diplomatic representative in Japan. These experiences whetted his interest in Japan and appear to have been instrumental in his being offered the opportunity to teach in Japan in September of 1870. After declining the original offer, he reconsidered and decided that it was his duty to go to Japan. In many ways, the approximate three-and-one-half years that Griffis spent in Japan was the highlight of his life, and provided him with the seeds from which he fostered his long-time reputation of being one of our earliest "Japan hands." In Japan, he was a visible actor on the periphery of the historical stage, and he savored every moment of it.

Griffis claimed that he was the first of the several thousand *yatoi* who were employed as a direct result of the Charter Oath, and the only white man to have actually lived under the feudal system in the interior of Japan. As a result of his relatively high status in developing Japan, and his sharp instincts which drew him toward important people, Griffis was able to make the acquaintance of a wide variety of influential men—both westerners and Japanese—in Japan during 1870–1874. These elements, then, both shaped and informed his writing and lecturing on Japan and the Japanese problems for the remainder of his life.

Griffis' life and his experiences as a teacher and observer of modernizing Japan are instructive. Jonathan Spence, writing about the role of western advisors in China, asked "What were the basic motives of these men, what did they hope to achieve? What was the personal cost of their type of service? and by what right did they go?"[1] His answers to these questions could be applied to William Elliot Griffis with only slight modifications.

One motive certainly, was to help; to bring improvement . . . either spiritual or material. . . . Help meant making [Japan] more like the West, bringing change that was understood (by definition) to be constructive. It therefore did not matter that they were initiating a series of events whose outcomes they would be unable to determine. But implicit in most of their actions is a more complex motive, a desire not so much to help [Japan] as to help themselves. . . . [Japan] seemed to offer them freedom of maneuver, a chance to influence history by the force of personality, and thus to prove their own significance.

Many of the advisors did indeed find a measure of psychological fulfillment, but the cost of the experience was, not surprisingly, high. Even if some [Japanese] received them warmly, there were always more who met them with indifference, deception or hostility. Each advisor, in a way, had sought to control [Japan's] destiny; the dawning realization that such would not be the case was a serious disappointment. Sensing that they were being used by the [Japanese] rather than using the [Japanese], that they were being swallowed by their own technique. . . . The answer to the third question—by what right did they go? is more difficult. A clue to the answer surely lies in the fact that the advisors did not think of posing the question. They were confident. They were sure that their own civilization, whatever its shortcomings, had given them something that [Japan] lacked. They had the right because they had the ability, the faith, the drive. They were, quite literally, on top of the world.[2]

On a more personal level Griffis, like many contemporary Peace Corpsmen, missionaries (both educational and religious), and others with similar functions, grappled with culture shock soon after his arrival in the interior of Japan. This led him to go to great lengths to secure a position in the more cosmopolitan capital when the loneliness and his perceived cultural deprivation became too much for him to handle. Ironically, however, his relations with his Japanese hosts were at their highest level when he was lonely and isolated in Fukui, exposed to all kinds of alien cultural influences which he could not accept. When he finally received a position in Tokyo, these relations with the Japanese officialdom rapidly deteriorated. After a very brief, initial period of good relations in the capital, several incidents and domestic problems began to follow one upon the other, leading to Griffis' departure from Japan in July 1874.

Griffis' educational contributions to Japan were not inconsequential. He established the first chemical laboratory in the interior of Japan and advocated western political and social ideals in informal settings, both to his students and to leading governmental figures of the day. Among his students were two Japanese prime ministers, several ambassadors, foreign ministers, and successful businessmen and scholars.

Although this phase of Griffis' career was an extremely interesting and productive one, it could be argued that he had a greater impact on both Japan and the United States after he left Japan in 1874 for America. He did not return to Japan's shores until just a few months before his death in 1928, but he kept in close touch with friends and correspondents in Japan for a half century, and freely gave his hospitality to anyone from Japan who happened to his doorstep. He was a prolific writer, and Japan was the focus of much of what he wrote. These writings included several major books on Japan or on the western impact on Japan, and literally hundreds of magazine and newspaper articles, which he produced at the drop of a *fude* (calligraphy brush), and sent to outlets all over the country. In addition, he was a tireless lecturer who journeyed throughout the East and Midwest informing Americans about Japan and the Japanese.

Soon after returning home in 1874, Griffis entered the Union Theological Seminary, and in 1877 entered the ministry. While serving congregations in Schenectady, Boston, and Ithaca for the next quarter of a century, he managed to devote a good deal of his time to historical pursuits. In 1876 he published what was to be his most important and lasting work, *The Mikado's Empire,* which went through twelve editions between its original publication and 1913.

By 1903, tired of dividing his time and interests between his ministerial duties and his historical inclinations, Griffis resigned his Ithaca pastorate in order to devote all his time to writing and lecturing. His prolific writings include fifty books (eighteen on Japan) and several hundred articles. Although this study deals only with Griffis and Japan, it ought to be pointed out that he wrote widely on numerous other diverse subjects including the Netherlands, New England, Puritanism, art, literary matters, Korea, China, the Philippines, and international affairs. His work appeared in such influential and distinguished journals as *Harper's, Century, Nation, North American Review,* and *Scribner's* in addition to numerous religious publications and leading newspapers. His lecture engagements were as prolific.

Twice decorated by the Japanese government for his services to the nation, Griffis consciously styled himself as an interpreter of Japan to his fellow countrymen and attempted, at every turn, to foster better understanding between his native and adopted lands.

It is clear that William Elliot Griffis, almost a century before Point Four, AID, and the Peace Corps, was playing a comparable role in a developing nation. His sense of mission in wanting to help the Japanese develop not only fulfilled a psychological need in Griffis, but helped to shape the growth of several important and influential Japanese politicians, statesmen, businessmen, and scholars. His experiences in Japan and his compulsion to share them with other Americans informed two generations of scholars and intelligent laymen. Borrowing Harold Issac's perceptive phrase, we can appreciate that William Elliot Griffis placed some of the first "scratches on the minds" of the American people about Japan and the Japanese.[3]

NOTES

1. Jonathan Spence, *To Change China: Western Advisors in China, 1620–1960* (Boston: Little, Brown and Company, 1969), p. 292; hereafter cited as Spence, *To Change China.*
2. Spence, *To Change China,* pp. 292–293.
3. Harold R. Issacs, *Scratches on Our Minds* (Cambridge: MIT Press, 1958).

Griffis' house in Fukui. Courtesy of *Monumenta Nipponica*.

Chapter 1

The Years of Preparation, 1843–1870

INTRODUCTION

When William Elliot Griffis died in February 1928,[1] the respected liberal journal, *The Nation,* eulogized him as "an authority on things Japanese," and the "first, if not the only, American to live in the interior of Japan during the feudal days, [where] he helped to lay the foundations of the existing Japanese school system."[2]

The Nation thus paid tribute to a man who for over sixty years had devoted much of his energy to the study of Japan and her people. For most of that time, at least since 1874, he consciously viewed himself as a bridge of understanding between the United States and Japan. His work in the "Mikado's Empire" was in a very real sense a religious calling. Shortly before his death, he wrote:

> Providence so ordered that I should see, when almost a baby, the launching, in 1850, of Commodore Perry's (sometime) flagship, the frigate *Susquehanna*; that I should have as a classmate the son of our American Minister, Pruyn, who had been in Japan; that I should during my four years at Rutgers College . . . teach the first Japanese students in America; that I should spend another four years in educational work in the interior and capital of Dai Nippon; that my sister Margaret Clark Griffis, should be principal of the first government school for girls; and that I should remain on constant terms of intimacy with Nippon's sons and daughters ever since meeting them at my home, at the Asiatic society, and in a hundred ways.[3]

The words contain in a significant measure the essence of William Elliot Griffis; he was a man secure in his belief that he was God's chosen instrument to assist in bringing the blessings of western civilization—material and spiritual—to Japan, and of explaining Japan and the Japanese to his fellow Americans. He saw America as a model nation, and in order to become modern, Japan needed to acquire the characteristics of America; Griffis was a modernizer who would accomplish his goal by helping to export these things to the less fortunate Japanese.

FAMILY ROOTS

In the summer of 1727, a determined young Englishman in the borough of Worksop, Nottingham, of central England reached an important decision. The reasons behind any man's decision to emigrate from his homeland to a distant land are always difficult to unravel. The motives of twenty-seven-year-old George Eyre are shrouded in mystery. They might well have been connected in some way with his Quaker faith, for the life of a Quaker in early eighteenth-century England was not easy. Or perhaps his fortunes were adversely affected by the pricking of the "South Sea Bubble" in 1721 resulting in a dilemma where, in the words of Sir Winston Churchill, "The porters and ladies' maids who had bought carriages and fineries found themselves reduced to their former station. Clergy, bishops, poets, and gentry found their life savings vanish overnight. There were suicides daily."[4]

In any event, upon arriving in the New World, Eyre made his way to Burlington, New Jersey, a center of Quaker sentiment, where he established himself, quickly adapting to local conditions. Shortly thereafter, in the spring of 1729, he took as a bride Mary Smith, the daughter of a local Quaker notable who was to bear him eleven children. Five years and two babies later, Mary presented her husband with twins, Sarah and Samuel, both of whom lived far beyond the brief life expectancy of the era.

Samuel Eyre, at an unknown age, married a Burlington girl, Elizabeth Folwell, of whom little is known except that she produced six children. The youngest of this brood, Hannah, married a Devonshire seafarer named Captain John Griffis "for which," we are told, "she was read out of the Friends' Meeting."[5]

John Griffis possessed the blood of his seafaring ancestors, and as a young man came to America as supercargo aboard an English merchantman to seek his fortune in the New World with the intention of returning to England to enjoy its fruits. Establishing himself in Philadelphia's tea trade, he quickly decided to cast his lot with the colonials and married the daughter of his patron. Sometime during these years, he had struck up a friendship with another Philadelphian, Benjamin Franklin, with whom he now shares a quiet corner of Philadelphia's Arch Street cemetery.[6]

The oldest son of this union, John Limeburner Griffis (1804–1879), was one of five children. He met, courted, and on April 11, 1837, married Anna Maria Hess in the Philadelphia church of the Reverend John Chambers. The young couple made their home in Philadelphia with John the respected operator of a coal business, probably willed to him by his father-in-law. Little else is known of him except that as a young bachelor, he had seen much of the world, traveling widely in Europe, Africa, the Philippines, and China before returning to Philadelphia and choosing a wife.

His bride Anna was a pious young woman who taught Sunday School and reflected the simple virtues of her sturdy Swiss-German forebears. This marriage produced seven children, including the subject of this study, William Elliot Griffis (1843–1928).

MIDCENTURY PHILADELPHIA

Urban historians often refer to the three decades between 1830 and 1860 as Philadelphia's "Golden Age,"[7] a time when Philadelphia emerged from "a place where manners followed the familiar paths of English and American provincial towns . . . [and became]. . . . something new to the world and to America—a modern big city."[8] The forces of social change were clearly at work in Philadelphia during this period, and as C. E. Black, among others, have cogently argued, rapid social change and violence are two sides of the same coin.[9]

Thus, Philadelphia, in the words of historian Samuel Bass Warner, experienced the effects of "the interaction of the most important elements of the big-city era: industrialization, immigration, mixed patterns of settlement, changing styles of leadership, weakness of municipal institutions, and shifting orientations of politics."[10] Complicating this already complex situation were social and economic confusion resulting from the Panic of 1837, and a volatile nativist movement which plagued the city until it was overshadowed by the Civil War.

The Panic of 1837 resulted in serious economic dislocations that had lasting effects. In the summer of 1837, Horace Greeley wrote that "one-fourth of all connected with mercantile and manufacturing interests are out of business with dreary prospects for the winter," and a few months later, he claimed that ninety percent of eastern factories were closed down.[11] In 1840, Philip Hone of New York confided to his diary that "Business of all kinds is completely at a stand . . . and the whole body politic sick and infirm, and calling aloud for a remedy."[12] By 1843 Sidney Fisher, a prominent Philadelphian wrote in his diary,

The natural consequences of a diminished currency and a ruined credit are now occuring. Specie is flowing in from all quarters to supply the place of exploded bank paper and business is conducted by cash payments or with

cautious regard to security. Prices are . . . going up . . . & I suppose we
shall run thro [sic] a similar career of speculation and extravagence to that
from which the country has just emerged with heavy loss.[13]

Fisher's pessimism was based on solid evidence as the Bank of the United
States, the nation's largest, was forced to shut its doors a year earlier
"bringing the state of Pennsylvania into temporary bankruptcy."[14]

In addition to this economic uncertainty, Philadelphians were experiencing unstable relations with both the large black community as well as
with increasing numbers of Roman Catholics. At least as early as 1830,
Philadelphia could lay claim to a black ghetto on her south side, and "in
respect to Negro caste practices, Philadelphia was a southern city" in
which black men "knew their place."[15] Racial tensions were exacerbated
by rapidly increasing immigrant numbers, mostly Irish Catholics, who
poured into the city between 1835 and 1850.[16] The established ethnic elements greeted the Catholic influx with suspicion, and as the Irish grew in
numbers and in influence, the Protestant majority often clashed with them
over issues such as which versions of the Bible should be used in the recently established public school system.[17]

It is probably fair to say that between 1834 and 1849 the "City of Broth-
erly Love" was a community in almost constant turmoil as an increasingly serious series of riots and mob actions shook the city. Blacks and
Catholics were most often the targets of this violence, but there were a
number of cases involving struck workers, abolitionists, and political
opponents of the established power.[18]

GROWING UP

This then was the milieu into which at 7:30 A.M. on Sunday, September 17,
1843, William Elliot Griffis was born. Scant evidence exists about the first
two decades of his life, but it appears that his childhood was comfortable,
albeit uneventful.

"Willie," as his family and friends called him, acquired his earliest
education on his mother's knee, and between 1848 and 1850, attended a
local dame school before entering one of Philadelphia's recently established elementary schools. The Griffis family fortune might have declined
in the mid-1850s, causing an economic squeeze,[19] but Willie continued his
schooling at Central High School, graduating in 1859.

Central High School, in the judgment of a leading educational journal
of the day, was in "the discipline and course of study . . . superior to any
institution of this grade with which we are acquainted."[20] Its principal,
Mr. John S. Hart, was a firm advocate of "the indispensable necessity of
the teacher's raising the pupil himself to decided cooperation and activity,

in order to his making acquisitions of permanent value."[21] If Griffis' later deportment and intellectual interests are any indication, these lessons were well learned.

Even though not fired with scholarly enthusiasm as a youngster, Griffis compiled a respectable academic record at Central. He was also an avid and voracious reader with wide-ranging interests that foreshadowed his future pursuits. Years later, he confessed to his sister Margaret that "I hardly know now whether to be glad or sorry that I neglected Cooper and Scott and Dickens when I was a boy. You know I never was a bookworm, but I wish that the best works of fiction had been put into my hands, instead of the acres of trash which I grazed on in the *New York Ledger*."[22] However, he satisfied his romantic imagination, which years later would both help and hinder his historical writing, by reading "all of Mayne Reid's books about wood rangers, scalp hunters and white chiefs."[23]

Willie's father and older brother, Mont, may have fueled this romantic streak, for they no doubt told him of their foreign experiences. Both had traveled widely, his father to Europe on frequent occasions, in addition to Africa, the Philippines, and China, while Mont had joined the merchant marine at sixteen years of age and sailed to Europe, South America, and the West Indies.[24]

Earlier in this chapter, Griffis referred to his attendance at the launching of Commodore Perry's flagship, the *Susquehanna*. His father, having "followed the sea from 1816 to 1836," had a number of acquaintances at the Navy Yard and indeed knew the Commanding Officer at the time who allowed the Griffis boys a great deal of freedom in the shipyard.[25] As a result, young William saw the ship being constructed on his frequent visits. Reflecting on his youth, he later wrote, "My father, his coal yard being next to the United States Navy Yard—built a platform over his pile of coal, for his friends to witness at 9 AM [April 7, 1853] the launching of the U.S.S.S. [*sic*] 'Susquehanna'—the flag-ship of Commodore Perry . . . ."[26]

Almost ten years later on June 9, 1860, Griffis witnessed the first Japanese Embassy to this country as they arrived in Philadelphia to visit the Mint, the Gas Works, an iron foundry, and other points of technical and historical interest. It was while in Philadelphia that the Embassy first learned of Ii Naosuke's assassination, but "whatever their feelings about the news . . . [they] plunged head and shoulders into all that Philadelphia had to offer them. They were seen in bookstores buying atlases and school books, and in optical shops investigating the instruments available."[27]

We do not know precisely when Griffis first saw the delegation, but he later wrote that "From the first, I took the Japanese seriously. In many respects our equals, in others they seemed to be our superiors.[28] This was a judgment which he maintained to the end of his long life, although he would later become disillusioned with the Japanese, for example, in their treatment of Korea.

William Griffis was above all a deeply religious young man. His first religious experiences were as a Presbyterian in the flock of the Reverend John Chambers' First Independent Church of Philadelphia. By the age of twenty, he had, in his words, "sat for years under John Chambers' preaching so long as to be saturated with his ideas."[29] It was perhaps because of this saturation that he broke with Chambers at the outset of his third decade over the moral issue of slavery. This issue split the congregation with Chambers taking a pro-Southern position.

It is clear from the record that Griffis' views toward slavery had undergone a transformation during the years just prior to his break with Chambers. He later wrote that at the age of ten, he had viewed the abolitionist as a "kidnapper, a fiend, the embodiment of all evil," but at twenty, he saw them as "saints, patriots, and 'beginners of a better time.' "[30]

Following his rupture with Chambers, Griffis gravitated to the Reverend Thomas D. Talmage's Second Reformed Dutch Church where, on May 24, 1863, he heard a sermon that he credited with giving his life a direction that had earlier been lacking. Rutgers' president, William Henry Campbell, had delivered it and inspired Griffis "to enter the ministry, to study at Rutgers, and eventually to go to Japan."[31] Interestingly enough, his mother, twenty years earlier, had attended a commencement at Rutgers and was so moved she vowed that should one of her boys be called to the ministry, he would study at Rutgers.[32]

With his future plans settled, the young Griffis answered his nation's call and enlisted in the Union Army in June of 1863. He was duly sworn in as a private in "H" Company of the 44th Pennsylvania Regiment and shipped off to war; on July 6 he was promoted to color corporal, and missed seeing action at the Battle of Gettysburg only because his unit, fortunately, arrived a few days too late to participate in the carnage. Upon the completion of his ninety-day enlistment on August 28, 1863, he received an honorable discharge and began to prepare himself for college.

THE RUTGERS YEARS

Shortly after receiving his discharge from the Union Army, in the late summer of 1863, Griffis became with George H. Hartman coeditor of *Our Sabbath School Messenger,*[33] a Philadelphia organ of the Dutch Reformed Church. A few months later, he engaged a tutor and assiduously prepared himself to take Rutgers' entrance examinations.

The entrance requirements to the college, described in the Rutgers *Catalogue* of 1865–1866, fell into four categories—Latin, Greek, mathematics, and geography. In the spring of 1865, during the college's Commencement Week activities, Griffis presented himself at the President's Room and easily hurdled the examination obstacle, being accepted into the class of 1869.

In the autumn of 1865, Rutgers was a small institution recovering from a series of financial crises. Housed in a handful of buildings of varying quality, it boasted a total enrollment of eighty-one students and twelve faculty members. Taking advantage of the Morrill Land Grant Act (1862), Rutgers added a new Scientific School to become New Jersey's land-grant institution. Created in 1864, the Scientific School induced a great deal of innovative ferment, and change was in the air when Griffis arrived to pursue his higher education in 1865.[34]

Although planning to study for the ministry, Griffis interestingly enough chose to follow the new scientific curriculum rather than the more traditional classical path to a degree.[35] This decision was typical of Griffis; he possessed a lively curiosity and always resisted pressures to confine his interests within narrowly proscribed channels of specialization. This indeed may have been a contributing factor to the shallowness of much of his later works. While an undergraduate, he studied a wide range of subjects including mathematics, astronomy, chemistry, physics, botany, Latin, Greek, Greek philosophy, German, French, Hebrew, and history.

Despite an extremely active extracurricular schedule, his academic performance was outstanding; he graduated fifth in his class with a 93.6 percent. He regularly attended chapel services, Bible classes, and taught Sunday School in New Brunswick. In addition, he received and accepted in 1866 an invitation to join Delta Upsilon Fraternity. Moreover, he became a member of Phi Beta Kappa and served as vice-president of the Rutgers' Chapter in 1869-1870 as a seminary student.

He won a total of six academic prizes as an undergraduate including the Schermerhorn Prize for Composition in 1868 for his paper, "The Relationship of Oliver Cromwell, to the Death of Charles the First." Others included the Suydam Prizes for Sciences and Composition in 1869. He was runner-up in the 1867 Myron W. Smith Oratory Contest, causing the *Christian Intelligencer* to remark of his "Spartacus to the Gladiators,"

> Without the advantage of a fine natural voice, the orator nevertheless acquitted himself with such power and knowledge of the orators' art, that it really seemed the veritable gladiator, Spartacus, stood on the college rostra.[36]

Finally, he was active in the Philoclean Literary Society, and with fellow student Robert C. Pruyn, conceived, planned and published a monthly college magazine, *The Targum*.[37] It was at about this time that his work first appeared in print. During his junior and senior years he published a total of nineteen articles in *The Targum, Our Sabbath School Messenger*, and various newspapers.

Despite the very busy schedule that all of these activities must have required of him, Griffis appears to have been a voracious reader. A compulsive record-keeper and "pack rat," Griffis maintained a list of the books he read while at Rutgers. The subjects of his reading are very broad, but include some of the best writings of the time. His historical taste, for example, ran toward the grandiose and panoramic—he devoured Gibbon's *Decline and Fall of the Roman Empire,* John Lothrop Motley's *The Rise of the Dutch Republic,* Prescott's *Conquest of Mexico* and *Conquest of Peru,* Macauley's *History of England,* and Buckle's *History of Civilization.*[38] Conspicuous by its absence from his list is George Bancroft's multivolume *History of the United States* which, in many ways, seems to have influenced his own later writings. While in Japan, however, he became acquainted with Bancroft's work. Surprising also is the absence of any serious work on Japan, for example, Richard Hildrith's early contribution, which was undoubtedly available to Griffis.

An interesting sidelight to Griffis' college career is his participation in the first American intercollegiate football game in 1869, in which Rutgers defeated her Princeton neighbors by a score of 6 to 4. There exists, in fact, a photograph taken almost fifty years later of the remaining members of that 1869 Rutgers team which included Griffis.[39]

The annual expenses of Griffis at Rutgers included forty-five dollars for tuition and thirteen dollars for other fees. During his senior year, these increased to sixty and twenty dollars respectively, and this may have had an influence on his taking part-time teaching and tutoring jobs. Since he was, however, preparing himself for the ministry, Griffis was eligible to live in Hertzog Hall, the theological student's residence for only five dollars per year, plus approximately eight dollars annually for fuel and electricity.[40] There were also a number of private homes near the campus which provided board for a reasonable price. During his senior year, perhaps because of his teaching position, Griffis moved from Hertzog Hall to a nearby rooming house.

Whatever the reason, it is clear that Griffis welcomed the opportunity to teach at Rutgers Grammar School. In addition to teaching Latin and Greek, he gave frequent lectures on all kinds of subjects from Greek mythology to political economy. He also tutored several students at this time including some of the first Japanese to study in this country.

The historical ties between Rutgers and Japan are unique. Perhaps because of the college's connections with the Dutch Reformed Church, the New Brunswick institution was in a position to have an interest in Japan as well as to take appropriate actions in behalf of this interest.[41]

The Dutch had had a foothold in Japan for centuries and, even during the long two-and-one-half-century period of foreign exclusion, managed to maintain a small trading station on Deshima, in Nagasaki Harbor, which in some respects, resembles the current British position in Hong Kong vis-á-vis the People's Republic of China. As a result of this historical fact, the Dutch, including many who emigrated to America, often possessed both an interest in and a knowledge of Japan. Finally, among the first missionaries to arrive in Japan, after Commodore Perry's opening of the country in 1853, were four representatives of the Reformed Church in America, including the Reverend Guido Verbeck, who stepped ashore in 1859.[42]

Since Christianity was still officially proscribed in Japan, one of the major activities of the missionaries was education. Verbeck, for example, taught a number of bright, young "progressive" students from all over the nation. In June 1866, he sent to Rutgers "the two nephews of Yokoi Heishiro[43] 'Ise' and 'Numagawa' . . . the first of a host . . . . who with Mr. Verbeck's introduction were helped in various ways, when in America, by the Reformed Church and Mission Board."[44]

These two young men who had stowed away on an American ship arrived in New York in the fall of 1866 and presented to the Reverend John Ferris, Secretary of the Board of Foreign Missions of the Reformed Church, a letter from Verbeck testifying "that they were of good faith and worthy of attention."[45] Upon questioning the boys, Ferris learned that they had come to America "to study navigation, to learn how to build 'big ships' and make 'big guns' to prevent European powers from taking possession of their country."[46]

Several weeks later, when Griffis met these young men, he "was surprised and delighted to find these earnest youth equals of American students in good breeding, courtesy and mental acumen."[47] Two years later a young student from Echizen *han,* Kusakabe Taro, entered Rutgers and received Latin instruction from Griffis. Unfortunately, Kusakabe died before his graduation, but when Griffis learned that he was going to Japan, he personally delivered the deceased youth's Phi Beta Kappa key and personal effects to the Kusakabe family in Echizen.[48]

Life for the Japanese students in New Brunswick was often difficult. Griffis later observed that "Boarding-house keepers were afraid to lose their guests and the maids of Erin gave immediate notice that they would 'lave' if those 'nagurs' were taken under the same roof.'[49] He did see in this attitude, however, a personal benefit. He noted, "To what happy deliverance from local, ethnic and sectarian prejudices and religious bigotries they helped lead me, as I discerned the Heavenly Father's methods of education and endowment of his children."[50]

Despite these affronts, Japanese students still came to America, and

Richard Demarest, in his standard history of Rutgers, estimates that between 1866 and 1876, approximately forty Japanese students were sent to
Rutgers, with thirteen actually attending the college and four graduating.
The remainder studied at Rutgers Grammar School (today Rutgers Preparatory School whose history dates back to 1766) to acquire competency
in the English language.[51]

During Griffis' busy college years he solidified many of the habits of his
youth and acquired new interests which he would nurture for the rest of
his life. The solid Christian teachings, learned from his mother were, by
the late 1860s, part of his every thought and action: he also began his
writing career at the same time and took the first steps toward his ultimately prolific output.

EUROPEAN EXPOSURE

Following his graduation from Rutgers in the late spring of 1869, Griffis
embarked with his sister Maggie on a long-planned visit to Europe.[52]
A close college friend, Edward Warren Clark, had left earlier to study
theology at the famous École de Théologie in Geneva, and had promised
to meet the Griffis party on the continent. Neither Maggie Griffis nor Ed
Clark could suspect that Willie, within a few short years, would go to Japan and be instrumental in securing attractive teaching positions for both
of them in that country.[53]

Prior to keeping their rendezvous with Clark, the Griffises spent several
weeks touring Britain, Holland, Belgium, and Germany. Finally, the trio
had a happy reunion in Paris where Clark had journeyed to meet his
friends. After spending a few days in the French capital, they decided to
split up with Maggie accompanying Clark back to Geneva and his studies
while Willie journeyed to Italy to satisfy his desire to experience the rich
cultural life of that country. After wandering among the cultural and
artistic artifacts of Italy for several weeks, Willie rejoined his companions
in Geneva. Comfortably situated at the bourgeoise Pension Picard in that
city, Maggie and Willie satiated themselves in its old world atmosphere.
Bidding farewell to Clark, Willie and Maggie set out for Austria exploring
much of Switzerland on the way. Leaving the land of the Hapsburgs, the
two travelers made their way back to Britain before catching the ship that
returned them to American shores.

By the relatively young age of twenty-six, William Griffis had been exposed to a quality and quantity of experiences that would have done credit
to a man twice his age. Individually, these experiences may not have made
a great impact, but cumulatively, it appears that they were instrumental in
shaping many of his attitudes, and important in making him susceptible to
the lure of Japan. As a young boy, he listened to the stories of far away

places told by his father and brother Mont both of whom had traveled widely to many ports throughout the world. Recall too that Griffis witnessed the launching of the U.S.S. *Susquehanna,* and as a teenager saw the first Japanese embassy to the United States as it passed through the streets of Philadelphia. He also served with the Pennsylvania militia during the Civil War, and although he missed seeing combat, he did have the opportunity to see part of the upper South and talk with those who had seen action. After the war ended, Griffis entered Rutgers where he engaged in a wide variety of academic and extracurricular activities, including tutoring and teaching some of the first Japanese students to come to the United States. One of his Rutgers' classmates, Robert Pruyn, was the son of a former American diplomatic minister to Japan, and Griffis learned much of Japan from the illustrious father. Given this kind of background, it is difficult to visualize Griffis leading a conventional, home-oriented life before satisfying his urge to build upon these experiences.

NOTES

1. The William Elliot Griffis Collection, housed in the Rutgers University Library, contains a vast amount of material dealing with Dr. Griffis, his work, and Japan. Very little of this material, however, deals with Griffis' youth and only a little more deals with his years at Rutgers. As a result, this chapter is based on fragmentary documentary evidence and secondary sources; hereafter this collection will be referred to as GCRUL.

2. "Obituary," *The Nation,* no. 126 (February 22, 1928): 199.

3. William Elliot Griffis, "Japan at the Time of Townsend Harris," in W. E. Griffis and Hugh Byas, *Japan: A Comparison* (New York: Japan Society, 1923), p. 12. Griffis maintained a long-standing friendship with young Pruyn whose father, Robert H. Pruyn, served as United States Minister to Japan under President Abraham Lincoln (1861–1865). The younger Pruyn was with his father during his Japan service. Griffis visited the Pruyn residence in Albany (see William Elliot Griffis Diary, November 28, 1870, GCRUL), and borrowed a large sum of money from him in order to finance his trip to Japan (see his "Fukui Scrapbook," GCRUL).

4. Winston Churchill, *A History of the English Speaking Peoples,* 3 vols., *The Age of Revolution* (London: Cassell and Company, 1957), 3: 93–94.

5. Katherine Johnson, "Paternal and Maternal Ancestors and Relatives of William Elliot Griffis" (paper prepared for private use), GCRUL. There is no evidence indicating the reason for Hannah being "read out of the Friends' Meeting."

6. William Elliot Griffis, "British and American Cooperation in Asia," *Landmark,* 7, no. 9 (1925): 553–556.

7. Sam Bass Warner, *The Private City; Philadelphia in Three Periods of Its Growth* (Philadelphia, Penna.: University of Pennsylvania, 1968), p. 49; hereafter cited as Warner, *The Private City.*

8. Warner, *The Private City,* p. 49.

9.   Cyril E. Black, *The Dynamics of Modernization: A Study in Comparative History* (New York: Harper and Row, 1966), especially pp. 26–34.
10.   Warner, *The Private City,* p. 125.
11.   Samuel Rezneck, "The Social History of an American Depression, 1837–1943," *American Historical Review* 40, no. 4 (1935): 662–687; hereafter cited as "The Social History."
12.   Rezneck, "The Social History."
13.   Nicholas B. Wainwright, ed., *A Philadelphia Perspective: The Diary of Sidney George Fisher Covering the Years, 1834–1871* (Philadelphia, Penna.: Historical Society of Pennyslvania, 1967), p. 134.
14.   Warner, *The Private City,* p. 137.
15.   Warner, *The Private City,* p. 126.
16.   Warner, *The Private City,* pp. 137–138.
17.   Vincent P. Lannie and Bernard C. Diethorn, "For the Honor and Glory of God: The Philadelphia Bible Riots of 1840 [*sic*]," *History of Education Quarterly,* 8, no. 1 (Spring, 1968): 44–106.
18.   For details see, among others, John Higham, *Strangers in the Land* (New Brunswick, N. J.: Rutgers, 1955); J. Thomas Scharf and Thompson Walcott, *A History of Philadelphia,* I (Philadelphia, Penna.: L. H. Everts Co., 1884); and W. E. G. Dubois, *The Philadelphia Negro: A Social Study* (New York: Shocken Books, 1889).
19.   Mrs. Katherine Johnson to Edward Beauchamp, February 15, 1969.
20.   *Connecticut Common School Journal* 3, no. 3 (1941): 162.
21.   *The American Journal of Education* 5, no. 13 (1858): 95.
22.   Letter, Margaret Clark Griffis to William Elliot Griffis, Fukui scrapbook, Dec. 24, 1871, GCRUL, quoted in Frances Yeomans Helbig, "William Elliot Griffis: Entrepreneur of Ideas" (M.A. thesis, University of Rochester, 1966), p. 9; hereafter cited as Helbig "William Elliot Griffis: Entrepreneur." Helbig's thesis has been helpful in presenting an outline of Griffis' life and thoughts, but was completed before a large amount of new materials were deposited in the William Elliot Griffis Collection in 1965.
23.   A handwritten note with an obituary notice of Mayne Reid in Griffis' "Authorship" scrapbook, GCRUL.
24.   Ardath Burks, "William Elliot Griffis, Class of 1869," *The Journal of the Rutgers University Library,* 19, no. 3 (1966): 93; hereafter cited as Burks, "William Elliot Griffis."
25.   William Elliot Griffis, "The Launching of Commodore Perry's Flagship, 1850," (unpublished longhand draft), GCRUL; hereafter cited as Griffis, "The Launching."
26.   Griffis, "The Launching."
27.   Lewis Bush, *77 Samurai: Japan's First Embassy to America* (Tokyo: Kodansha International, 1968), p. 198; hereafter cited as Bush, *77 Samurai.*
28.   Ardath Burks, "Reflections on 100 Years of Cultural Exchange," (paper delivered before the Japan Society's Meiji Centennial Lectures series, Rutgers University, November 13, 1967), p. 10; hereafter cited as Burks, "Reflections."
29.   William Elliot Griffis, *John Chambers: Servant of Christ and Master of Hearts and His Ministry in Philadelphia* (Ithaca, N. Y.: Andrus and Church, 1903), p. 3.
30.   William Elliot Griffis, "Britain and America in Africa," *Landmark* 12 (October, 1925): 614.

31.   Burks, "Reflections," p. 9.
32.   William Elliot Griffis, "Intimate Glimpse," *Rutgers Alumni Quarterly* 2 (April, 1916): 134.
33.   A monthly journal published by the First Dutch Reformed Church of Philadelphia, which issued only twelve editions in its brief existence from 1864 to 1865.
34.   See Richard Demarest, *A History of Rutgers College 1766–1924* (New Brunswick, N. J.: Rutgers College, 1924); hereafter cited as Demarest, *A History of Rutgers College.*
35.   Burks, "William Elliot Griffis," p. 94. Frances Helbig contends that Griffis was enrolled in the Classical Department during his Rutgers years. Burks presents a listing of the courses Griffis took, and from the nature of these courses, it seems reasonable to conclude that Griffis, indeed, studied in the Scientific Curriculum.
36.   *Christian Intelligencer* (March 7, 1867), also quoted in Helbig, p. 29
37.   Rutgers' monthly newspaper.
38.   Griffis carefully listed all the books he had read in college in his "College Life" scrapbook. GCRUL.
39.   Demarest, *A History of Rutgers College,* p. 137.
40.   Helbig, "William Elliot Griffis: Entrepreneur," p. 20.
41.   Until the post-Civil War era, Rutgers was closely tied to the Dutch Reformed Church and to this day its theological school is housed across the street from the School of Education. Dutch traders, scholars, and missionaries have played an important part in Japan's history; in fact, Guido Verbeck, a Dutch-American missionary worked in Japan from the late-1850s and was indirectly responsible for Griffis being offered a position in Japan in 1870.
42.   William Elliot Griffis, *Rutgers Graduates in Japan* (New Brunswick, N. J.: Rutgers College, 1916), p. 1. A reprint of a speech that Reverend Griffis delivered to the Student Body on June 16, 1885, in Kirkpatrick Chapel.
43.   Yokoi Heishiro (1810–1869) according to David Earl "was an outstanding thinker, influential in political affairs during the late Tokugawa and early Meiji periods." David Earl, *Emperor and Nation in Japan: Political Thinkers of the Tokugawa Period* (Seattle, Wash.: University of Washington, 1964), p. 122. He was also a man who had "a practical bent that had made him much interested in the West and an advocate of foreign trade," and in 1869 was cut down by assassins' swords. See John K. Fairbank, Edwin O. Reischauer, and Albert M. Craig, *East Asia: The Modern Transformation* (Boston, Mass.: Houghton Mifflin Company, 1965), p. 215.
44.   William Elliot Griffis, *Verbeck of Japan: A Citizen of No Country* (New York: Fleming H. Revell Company, 1900), p. 124; hereafter cited as Griffis, *Verbeck of Japan.*
45.   Griffis, *Rutgers Graduates in Japan,* pp. 32–33.
46.   Griffis, *Rutgers Graduate, in Japan,* p. 33.
47.   William Elliot Griffis, *The Mikado's Empire* (New York: Harper and Brothers, Publishers, 1876), p. 8. Hereafter all references to *The Mikado's Empire* are to the 12th ed., 1913, vol. 2, unless otherwise specified.
48.   Burks, "William Elliot Griffis," p. 95.
49.   William Elliot Griffis, "The Japanese Students in America," *The Japanese Student* 1, no. 1 (1916): 13.
50.   Griffis, "The Japanese Students in America."

51.   Demarest, *A History of Rutgers College*, p. 440.
52.   Frances Helbig speculates that perhaps Griffis was interested in exploring the possibility of attending theological school in Europe as he "was having doubts about the theology taught at Rutgers." Helbig, "William Elliot Griffis: Entrepreneur," pp. 25–26.
53.   Even before leaving for Japan, Griffis spoke about this possibility on several occasions. During his period in Japan Griffis was instrumental in helping Clark secure an excellent position teaching physical science at Shizuoka. Edward W. Clark, *Life and Adventure in Japan* (New York: American Tract Society, 1878); hereafter cited as Clark, *Life and Adventure in Japan*. Griffis also secured a position for his sister Margaret who was one of the first two instructors in the first school established for Japanese girls. Griffis, *Verbeck of Japan*, p. 222.

Chapter 2

The Call to Japan

Upon returning to the United States from his European sojourn, Griffis paid a short visit to his family in Philadelphia before returning to New Brunswick, the scene of his undergraduate years, enrolled in the Rutgers Theological Seminary, and reclaimed his teaching position with the Rutgers Grammar School. While at the seminary, Griffis came into contact with Professor James Woodbridge whose lectures on church history fired his imagination and Professor Joseph F. Berg whose lectures on philosophy led Griffis to write,

> My soul being in the midst of great strife, I faced that which is great and shouted from the bottom of my heart, "Lord, Grant me your assistance; otherwise I shall die." I shall go out into the great and spacious world of God; furthermore, I welcome as the voice of God to do some contemplation by myself on a huge rock in the midst of the solitude of the oceans and of Japan, in other words, to seek out Jesus Christ.[1]

At the grammar school he most enjoyed teaching English and natural science, but also taught natural philosophy, familiar science, chemistry, geology, American literature, mythology, and elocution. He judged the several Japanese in his class as "bright and gentlemanly."[2] Even though he was kept busy with his teaching responsibilities and his own studies, Griffis found time to preach and to give lectures in a number of small towns in the vicinity. Despite this however, he seemed uncertain of what he really wanted to do with his life. Much of this self-doubt can be seen in his letters to Maggie in which he worried about his ability to pay off his debts. At one time he planned to complete his course of study as quickly as possible so as to become economically sufficient. He sought out Professor Berg, a man in whom he placed great trust, and was persuaded that to do it would be "a loss to me all my life."[3]

This juncture in his life appears to have been a particularly difficult one for him to cope with; his ambitions were high, but he was in debt, and the finanical situation of his family was, if anything, more tenuous than his own. His position at the Rutgers Grammar School was not a happy one, and he felt compelled to complain to the principal, Professor D. T. Reilley, about his low salary and Reilley's attitude toward the faculty, several of whom Griffis felt were incompetent. To further compound his state of mind, Griffis was smitten with a young lady, Ellen G. Johnson, whom it seems he rather expected to marry. Her intentions, however, were not as certain. When Ellen decided to leave the country for a trip to England, he asked Maggie to "[c]omfort me, for my love is going to Europe. . . . All her friends told her to go, and she wanted me to say *yes* too. It was hard for me to do so, but how could I withhold my blessing?"[4] Finally his theological studies forced him into a "grappling with doctrines that shake my old faith to the very foundation and demand of me all my power of mind to meet them."[5]

With the completion of his first year of theological study, Griffis plunged into a summer position preaching at New York City's Knox Memorial Chapel which he described as "exceedingly tasteful and beautiful in the true Methodist style."[6] He participated in as much of the church program as he could, including "preaching twenty-nine sermons, giving twenty prayer meetings and Sunday School addresses, editing six articles . . . and doing a great deal of pastoral visiting."[7]

THE CALL TO JAPAN

It was in the early days of September 1870 that the opprtunity to go to Japan first came to Griffis. During that summer, the *daimyō* ("lord") of Echizen *han*, Matsudaira Shungaku,[8] requested Guido Verbeck, the well-known Dutch-American missionary educator in Japan, to recommend a qualified person "to establish a scientific school on the American principle and teach the natural sciences" in his provincial capital of Fukui facing the Sea of Japan.[9] Verbeck, anxious to secure a fellow member of the Dutch Reformed Church for this position, passed on this request to Reverend John M. Ferris, secretary of the Board of Foreign Missions of the Dutch Reformed Church in New York City. Ferris, in turn, passed it on to friends at Rutgers,[10] and it finally found its way to Professor D. T. Reilley, principal of the grammar school.

Verbeck told Ferris that whoever was sent out would be expected to teach chemistry and physics at an annual salary of $2,400 plus a house and a horse. He added that under these conditions a single man could live adequately on about $800 per year. He warned, however, that the conditions would be trying and the temptations great; the country was filled with those who had fallen into a dissolute way of life.[11]

Sometime during the first week of September, Reilley wrote a note to Griffis offering him the position. Why Reilley chose to ask Griffis is not completely clear. There appears to be little doubt that Griffis had compiled a distinguished academic record at Rutgers, was religiously committed, and had a reasonable amount of teaching experience. Indeed, Reilley's offer to Griffis may have been based on these factors, but reading the few letters that passed between Reilley and Griffis leaves one with a twinge of doubt. In a curious postscript to the letter in question, Reilley went to considerable length to rebut Griffis' complaints about his low salary and his charge of faculty incompetence in the grammar school. Somewhat defensively, Reilley told Griffis, "I want you of course [to return and] I cannot recall [doing] anything to hurt your feelings." This is particularly interesting since in the body of the letter Reilley wrote that "difficult as it would be for me to supply your place yet it is so tempting a thing . . . that I cannot help asking you if you want it." Sensitive to Griffis' desire for acquiring more money, he concluded by suggesting that "I should think that you could bring back in three years nearly $6,000."[12]

The offer forced Griffis to weigh the obvious economic and travel advantages that it offered against his feelings for Ellen Johnson who, two weeks prior to her departure for Europe, "promised freely all that I could desire,—not to forget me, to love me more, and to be my wife." Although tempted by Japan, Griffis' heart and thoughts were with this "radiant, glowing creature . . . [who] thinks no home brighter and happier than a ministers."[13] In the end, he turned down Japan in favor of Ellen but was soon besieged by his Japanese students and several of his friends to reconsider. He spent the night of September 15 with the Pruyn family in Albany, and the former American minister to Japan "spent almost all evening with me showing what a splendid offer I had received . . . and urged me strongly to take it." The elder Pruyn's arguments bore fruit as Griffis concluded that "In point of money and travel advantages, society, health, knowledge, usefulness & good to be accomplished, the prospect is dazzling and if the position is again offered me, I shall reconsider it."[14]

It is apparent that sometime between Reilley's offer during the first

week in September and Griffis' conversation with Pruyn on the evening
of September 15, his relationship with Ellen Johnson changed, and it seems
that a crucial meeting with Ellen took place between noon of September
16 and the evening of September 17 at Red Hook, New Jersey.[15] There is
record of what transpired between the two, but that *"there is no present
likelihood, that E.[llen] and I, will ever be husband and wife."*[16] After admitting that he had "an almost broken heart" as a result of that fateful meeting, he was able to rationalize his change of mind relative to going to
Japan on grounds other than his lost affair of the heart. He told of how
Reverend Ferris "so laid it before me that it seemed *duty* to God, the
church, my country and to Japan to go."[17] He sought the advice of President Campbell and several of his Rutgers professors who, with few
exceptions, urged him to go to Japan. Professor Woodbridge provided him
with the unassailable argument that he could take his books with him and
continue his theological studies in Japan. Griffis embraced this idea and
wrote his sister,

> *I can study and be ordained there, and God willing, return to my native land,
> only one year later than if I staid* [sic]. Beside the grand opportunities and
> culture, travel and good climate, and being under the special protection of
> the prince of the province, I can not only study on my theology, but collect
> materials to write a book. I can support my family at home, at least, *pay
> the rent, and carpet the floors, and send handsome sums home, too.*[18]

This explanation is revealing of Griffis. It demonstrates his long-term
commitment to doing the work of God, improving his financial status, and
using his literary talents to secure a reputation for himself. "I feel a call
there," he added, with a primary motive "in preaching the gospel . . . in
an indirect way, and help prepare the country for the gospel"[19] One week
later in a letter to Maggie, Griffis confirmed his decision by informing her,
"I have decided to go to Japan . . . [and] I go forth to my new duties with
conscience clear, and the path as plain, as when I first started in the
work of the ministry."[20] This may have been the result of a bit of positive
reinforcement from Reverend J. H. Ballagh who, in response to Griffis'
request for his opinion, wrote that "the whole project meets my hearty
approval. You need have no hesitancy from fears of personal safety in
Japan [as it] is vastly more in the interest of the Japanese Gov't. to preserve
your life than lose it not only in view of your service to them but in view
of the heavy indemnity they have to pay in case it was lost."[21]

FAMILY REACTION

His decision did not win full support in the Griffis household. One sister,
Mary, wept openly. Her "tears flowed so copiously that she appeared to

disolved [*sic*]." Another sister, Martha, "fled to her chamber there in secret to give vent to her grief." Mrs. Griffis, however, told Willie that "the fact that you believe yourself called of him is sufficient to me."[22] Maggie, challenging her brother's motives, blamed Willie's grief at losing Ellen for his decision to go to Japan. "If she [Ellen] had only made you understand her feelings while she was away . . . perhaps this offer would not have affected you, but coming as it did at such a time you have determined to go away . . . to a land without God, without the Bible, without a Holy Sabbath."[23] In almost the next breath, however, she recovered her poise sufficiently to ask Willie to forgive her and Martha's debt to him since "We know no other way to meet the rent [and] even then we are left penniless."[24] She concluded by reminding Willie that the Griffis home was badly in need of new carpets, suggesting that since he was borrowing $800 to finance his trip to Japan, "it would be just as well to get $1,000 [and] thus furnish our carpets."[25] This rather severe demand on Willie's finances were not without precedent, and indeed, would continue throughout his sojourn in Japan.

There is no evidence detailing the reactions of Willie's father and brothers to his decision to journey to Japan. His brothers, however, probably saw their brothers' opportunity as an opportunity for them also. Americans of that time commonly imagined Japan to be a place where a westerner could make a great deal of money while living very well. Almost as soon as Willie announced that he was going to Japan, references began to appear in his correspondence with Maggie about the possibility of one or more of his brothers joining him in Japan. The only thing that remained was for Willie to find them positions.

It seems that the Griffis menfolk were of relatively little help in supporting the family at this time. The elder Griffis was advancing in years and had not held a steady job since he had lost his coal yard years earlier. Willie's brothers were either living away from home or more interested in spending money than in earning it. The sisters Maggie and Martha contributed to the family's narrow financial base by teaching in Philadelphia schools, but while in Japan, Willie would bear the brunt of the family's financial burden. In addition to being a major source of support for the family, Willie also felt morally obliged to repay the church the money it had given to him to finish his education at Rutgers. Finally, Willie had borrowed several hundred dollars to enable him to get to Japan and to live until he received his first salary payment. Money matters would be on his mind the entire period that he was in Japan.

In the slightly less than two months between his decision to go to Japan and his actual departure, Griffis busily wound up his affairs. On Saturday, October 1, he traveled to New York to inform Reverend Ferris of his decision to go to Japan. Returning from the offices of the Board of Missions, he stopped at a bookstore to buy a copy of J. J. Hoffman's *A Japanese Grammar* (Leiden, 1868), which he used as a text in his study of the Japanese language. Several of his Japanese friends at Rutgers helped him in this endeavor.

On October 22, Samuel Lockwood of the Monmouth County, New Jersey Office of Public Instruction responded to Griffis' letter asking for his help in brushing up on practical geology. After warmly congratulating Griffis on his decision to go to Japan, Lockwood expressed disappointment at the short time remaining before Griffis' departure, but offered to come to New Brunswick in order to "spend a day with you . . . [working] in the college [geology] cabinet."[26]

One of the last things Griffis did before leaving for Japan was to arrange for a Japanese student to board with the Griffis family, clearly specifying to Maggie that Tegima Seiichi "will occupy the 3rd story room, and pay $8 per week for board, light, fuel and washing," and promising that "If I can get another one, I shall let you know. . . . "[27] This scheme was purely economic on Griffis' part; it was to secure his family's financial condition before his departure.

He informed Maggie that he was able to secure insurance on his person only at great expense. "I paid $155 for [a] policy and travel permit, on $5,000, and expect to pay $25 to my Newark policy of $2500."[28] American businessmen seemed surprised that "an intelligent young man should trust people like the Japanese to keep a financial agreement."[29]

CROSSING THE CONTINENT

His preparations finally completed, the time for farewells arrived. On the evening before his departure for San Francisco, at a gathering in the Second Dutch Reformed Church in Philadelphia, it appears that Griffis successfully ignored his recent romantic entanglement with Ellen Johnson. The following morning's newspaper commented simply that "The brother goes forth . . . burning with the desire to proclaim Jesus to the millions sitting in the darkness."[30]

Late the following morning, he bid adieu to his mother and Martha on the steps of the family home, and proceeded with other family members and friends to the railroad depot located at Market and Thirty-first streets. At 12:30 P.M. he boarded the train that was to carry him on the first stage of his long journey.[31] His brother Mont accompanied him as far as the suburban station at Parkensburg where he left Willie to return to Philadelphia. Griffis continued to Altoona, arriving at 8:15 P.M. that evening. He thus began his cross-country journey, broken by several stopovers, notably at Chicago and Omaha. He awakened from a deep sleep on the morning of November 17 shortly before arriving in Chicago, and confided to his diary that he had "dreamed that I had brought E. G. J. [Ellen G. Johnson] home, and all thought her lovely."[32] Griffis began to become more and more involved in his new activites, as from this point on, references to Ellen in his diary and letters become increasingly infrequent. As her memory faded into the background, life began to focus more on Japan, and his writings on that country, its people and history increased sharply.

After spending several days exploring Chicago, Griffis resumed his westward journey arriving in Omaha on November 22. He wrote that while waiting for the train to leave Omaha, a city of "150,000 people, fine hotels, etc.," he felt that he "must *barberize*" himself for the long ride across the empty prairie, and to do this, he "purchased a basket of provisions, roast chicken, canned oysters, pickles, rolls, biscuit, plate, cup for hot coffee, sausage, cheese, apples, etc."[33] It was this leg of his continental journey that taught him a great deal about the reality of the American West. He was surprised that "There were no stations, though plenty of drinking places, between Omaha and Ogden, so I laid in four or five days' cooked provisions before leaving Nebraska. . . . I saw plenty of wild Indians with scalp locks, one or two scalped white men, others that wanted to 'rub out' all the red men, and squaws that not knowing what a nickel coin was, but not ashamed to beg, would throw away as a joke and fraud, the money fresh from the mint at Philadelphia."[34]

Prior to leaving Philadelphia, Griffis, with an eye to the future, had arranged to write articles for several newspapers and magazines. While crossing the United States he reminded Maggie that with all of his writings "I want you to cut them out, and begin the scrapbook I spoke of. . . . you will carefully preserve all I write."[35]

Finally, at 6:45 on the evening of November 26, 1870, Griffis saw "the waters of the Pacific gleaming into view, the Golden Gate in sight." Taking a ferry from Oakland across the bay to San Francisco, he registered at the Russ House, and "slept, to dream about home."[36] The following day Griffis began a pleasant sojourn in San Francisco in which he visited family and college friends, toured Chinese schools, shops, and tenements, browsed in bookstores and wandered around the city. On the morning of December 1, accompanied by gift-bearing well-wishers, Griffis boarded the steamer *Great Republic* which sailed for Yokohama punctually at noon.[37]

A few days preceding the sailing, Griffis had examined the vessel with care and described its great size and luxurious appointments to Maggie and concluded that he doubted "that there are finer steamers afloat." Almost as soon as the vessel cleared the harbor and faced the open sea, his diary recorded that perennial problem of sea voyagers: "Sea sick all day, ate only a cracker at noon, but could not retain it."[38]

Despite this, Griffis seems to have enjoyed the long twenty-seven-day voyage to Yokohama, and he spent much of his time studying Japanese and chemistry, writing letters, conducting religious services, and as much time as he could with the ship's captain. He wrote that Captain Freeman "has taken quite a fancy to me, and I use his room as I please, while he always pays much attention to me at the table."[39] This generally pleasant relationship, however, did not extend to the rest of the passengers toward whom Griffis' "indifference or dislike [daily] becomes deeper."[40] Unfortunately, Griffis' letters home do not detail the reasons for his reactions to his fellow voyagers.

If he felt uneasy with the majority of the ship's passengers, he often thought of his family in Philadelphia and exhibited a good deal of concern over his brothers Clarence and Montgomery. On Christmas Day, 1870, he confided to Maggie, "[i]t always has, and does now, grieve me more than words can express, that my brothers should be as they are . . . bound down by galling poverty."[41] From the start of his Japan experience, he attempted to secure positions for them in Japan, which he viewed as a land of opportunity for the ambitious American with an adventurous heart but in this he failed.[42]

ARRIVAL IN THE MIKADO'S EMPIRE

Excited over the prospects which awaited him in Japan, Griffis slept little during the night of December 28–29, 1870. The following morning he "awakened early, and from our state-room window saw by the gray light of the morning the eye-gladdening land." Describing the scene in some detail, he tells how "imperial over all" stood fabled Mount Fuji.[43] A contemporary described the entry into Tokyo Bay as "a sail that the visitor will never forget."[44] Soon the *Great Republic* had reached her anchorage and was swarming with visitors anxiously searching for friends and the latest news from home. On hand to meet the newcomer were the Reverend and Mrs. James C. Ballagh and Reverend and Mrs. J. C. Hepburn who were to begin a lifelong friendship with Griffis. They helped him to clear customs quickly and to carry his luggage ashore.[45]

In 1870 Yokohama was "a cosmopolitan place. In the harbor lie a hundred vessels floating a dozen different flags. On the land Americans have their stores, their newspapers and their chapel. England is represented by merchants, soldiers and a church and building. Eight hundred British troops are encamped on the bluff. Two companies of French troops garrison their quarter. The number of foreigners cannot fall short of three thousand."[46] Another dimension of the treaty port can be seen in the comments of the Bishop of Hong Kong following a visit ten years earlier. He charged the Japanese with making Yokohama "an attractive locality for young unmarried foreigners by establishing. . . one of those infamous public institutions. . . containing its two hundred female inmates dispersed over a spacious series of apartments and all under government regulation."[47]

Griffis spent several days in Yokohama, attending a reception given on New Year's Day by the American Minister to Japan, Charles E. De Long, and preaching a sermon, "One is your master, even Christ," at the Presbyterian Chapel in Yokohama.[48] After an early breakfast on the morning of January 3, 1871,[49] Griffis boarded the Tokyo stage for the forty-mile journey on the famous Tōkaidō (highway connecting Kyoto and Tokyo).[50]

Arriving in Tokyo, Griffis made his way across the city to the grounds of the Imperial College where he presented his credentials to the college's superintendent, the Reverend Guido Verbeck, with whom he would stay for six weeks while the arrangements with the Fukui authorities were being concluded.[51]

Guido Verbeck, who exerted a powerful influence over the young Griffis, was a fascinating figure in his own right. Born in Holland, he became an American citizen prior to going to Japan as a missionary of the Dutch Reformed Church. He arrived in Nagasaki in 1859 where he spent five years spreading his religious message before being called to Tokyo to take charge of the Imperial College. One student of the period credits Verbeck with having "the greatest impact upon the Japanese in their period of awakening."[52] Griffis was impressed with his considerable abilities, and later wrote a laudatory, but useful, biography of Verbeck.[53]

Griffis put to good use the several weeks he spent in the capital prior to leaving for Fukui. The curious newcomer filled his hours exploring the city and its environs, sometimes with Verbeck guiding him, studying Japanese, reading, and teaching in the college. He also began collecting those details of Japan and the Japanese that were to intrigue the readers of his articles in American publications. His relationship to Verbeck gave him access to many of the most prominent Japanese leaders of the day whom he mined for materials for his writings. Some of the more prominent people he became acquainted with were Iwakura Tomomi, whose son he had taught at Rutgers, Ōkubo Toshimichi, Mori Arinori, Fukuzawa Yukichi, and Matsudaira Shungaku, the daimyō of Echizen han.[54]

The excitement and vitality of Tokyo was not a good preparation for the reality of provincial Fukui, located two hundred miles west of the capital in one of the most remote parts of Japan. While Fukui was still a feudal castle town, Tokyo was described by a contemporary as a place where

> Something was always going, on, and pleasant society was not wanting, whenever one felt the need for it. Evening parties and entertainments were frequent among the foreign residents, and the elegance and style seen on such occasions reminded one more of the fashionable life at home than residence in a foreign city.[55]

Perhaps the highlight of Griffis, initial sojourn in Tokyo was the dinner given him by Matsudaira on the eve of Griffis' departure for the Prince's domain. Griffis described the European style feast with its "gorgeous table," and the "10 or 12 courses" with accompanying "ale, sherry, claret and champagne."[56] Griffis was impressed that the Prince was "evidently used to foreign dinners," but commented that at least two of his staff were not, for they "made loud noises in eating their soup, and one of them took a drink out of the finger bowls." Their adventure was climaxed with the serving of the cheese course which they described as "stinking stuff."[57]

Despite the genteel aspects of a cultivated foreigner's life in Tokyo during the 1870s, it must be pointed out that it also had its unsavory side. Griffis summed up this aspect when he suggested that "it is doubtful whether vice in [Tokyo] was ever more rampant than in the third quarter of the nineteenth century. . . . life was held to be cheaper than dirt by the swash-bucklers, *rōnins* [masterless *samurai*] and other strange characters and outlaws . . . infesting Tokyo."[58] Indeed, antiforeign feeling ran so high among the *rōnin* that they felt it was an act of the highest patriotism to cut down a "barbarian" in the street. Griffis had been forewarned of this danger by his Japanese friends at Rutgers, and it seems that insurance companies were also aware of it as he had a very difficult time arranging for life insurance.[59] Upon the advice of his Rutgers students, he purchased a Smith and Wesson revolver before leaving New Brunswick, and was "not certain that the mere gesture of putting my hand into my bosom was more than once a means of impressing upon some scowling patriot that he had better not draw."[60]

Although one wonders how much embellishment this situation received with Griffis' romantic imagination, the reality of the danger was demonstrated shortly after his arrival in Tokyo. Early in the evening of January 13, 1871, two teachers named Dallas and Ring, of the Imperial College, dismissed the bodyguards who had been assigned to escort the teachers whenever they left the campus. While walking down the famous Tōkaidō, "suspicious of nothing," they were attacked from the rear by two sword-wielding *rōnin*.[61] Dallas suffered a severe wound, from his right ear to his left shoulder, "about 8 inches long and three inches deep." Ring's assailant cut him "across the neck and shoulder," and when Ring tried to escape, slashed his back "severing one of the ribs and touching the spine."[62] In a letter to Maggie, he assured his family that the incident would be exaggerated at home, but if one took reasonable precautions, there was little danger. He had little synpathy, he continued, for those who "deliberately reject all guards, [and] go unarmed."[63]

Verbeck also felt that the two teachers were to blame since they were fully aware of the dangers involved, but their passions led them to pursue women. "If they lived a moral life," Verbeck preached, "they would have been safe enough that night."[64] Griffis concurred, but spent several nights sitting up with them after taking the news to Yokohama on the morning after the incident had occurred. The attack on the two foreigners was the source of several articles he wrote for American publications.[65]

Finally, on February 3, 1871, Griffis received his contract from the Echizen authorities. His duties were to consist of the principalship of Echizen College in addition to teaching both chemistry and natural science. In return, the authorities promised to build him a European-style house, provide a horse (including its food and care) and pay Griffis a salary of $3,600 per year for the first two years of the contract and $3,900 for the third and final year. Moreover, he was to receive one month vacation per year and the privilege of free postage.[66]

Griffis confided to Maggie that he was actually offered a choice of going to Fukui as planned or remaining in Tokyo with Verbeck, but he chose the former because it would not have been "fair to disappoint Prince Echizen" who had been responsible for his coming to Japan.[67] He did not protest, however, when Verbeck interceded with the Prince to obtain for him $3,600 per year rather than the original $2,400 which had been offered to him in New Brunswick.[68] On February 6 he received a payment of $525 from the Prince as "payment for travelling expenses and 12 days salary."[69]

With his contract settled, his relations with Verbeck solidified, and the Fukui officials anxiously awaiting his arrival, Griffis wound up his affairs in Tokyo in preparation for his departure to the interior. Although he had journeyed several thousand miles from home and had thrown himself into his new environment with characteristic enthusiasm, his family and "home" remained a continuing source of concern for him in those hectic and exciting days. His concern and worry focused around the ne'er-do-well male members of his family, and the resulting financial bind that the family constantly found itself facing. Griffis felt obliged to assist as much as he could, but at the same time, resented the unfair burden that he felt he was carrying. His letters are replete with warnings to Maggie to make do with what he could send her and not to ask for more money. He was also deeply concerned over the debts he had incurred as a student at Rutgers and as a result of his coming to Japan. He was determined to allow nothing to prevent him from paying these off at the earliest moment.

Even while weighing his decision to accept the Japan position, Griffis had "thought deeply" about the possibility of taking his brother Clarence with him,[70] but decided that it was best not to do so. However, one of the first things he did upon arriving in Japan was to try to find a suitable position for his other brother Mont but was frustrated in this attempt. He wrote to Maggie that other family members would have to be patient for "there is simply a plethora of men in need of situations," and they must wait until a suitable vacancy occurred.[71]

NOTES

1.   William Elliot Griffis, *Sunny Memories of Three Pastorates* (Ithaca, New York: Andrus and Church, 1903), p. 8.
2.   William Elliot Griffis (hereafter cited as WEG) to Margaret Clark Griffis (hereafter cited as MCG), January 20, 1870, GCRUL.
3.   WEG to MCG, February 10, 1870, GCRUL.
4.   WEG to MCG, April 8, 1870, GCRUL.
5.   WEG to MCG, March 30, 1870, GCRUL.
6.   WEG to MCG, April 7, 1870, GCRUL.
7.   Helbig, "William Elliot Griffis: Entrepreneur," p. 26.
8.   Matsudaira Shungaku, alias Yoshinaga or Keiei (1829–1890), was a feudal lord of Echizen and one of Japan's major political figures in the late Tokugawa and early Meiji periods. For interesting details see Marius Jansen, *Sakamoto Ryōma and the Meiji Restoration* (Princeton, N. J.: Princeton University Press, 1961), especially pages 69–71, 126–128, 143–145, 162–166, 289–294, and a brief biographical sketch on page 401; hereafter cited as Jansen, *Sakamoto Ryōma*. Other pertinent facts about Matsudaira and his family background are found in E. Papinot, *Historical and Geographical Dictionary of Japan* (Yokohama: Kelly and Walsh, Ltd., 1910. Tokyo: Charles E. Tuttle, 1972), pp. 355–360.
9.   Foster Rhea Dulles, *Yankees and Samurai: America's Role in the Emergence of Modern Japan* (New York: Harper and Row, 1965), p. 156.
10.   Although it later became a land-grant college, in its early days Rutgers had very close ties with the Dutch Reformed Church and was the site of a theological school which still exists.
11.   Guido Verbeck to J. W. Ferris, July 21, 1870, GCRUL.
12.   D. T. Reilley to WEG, n. d., GCRUL. Internal evidence indicates it was written in early September, 1870.
13.   WEG to MCG, n. d., GCRUL. Internal evidence indicates it was written in April, 1870.
14.   WEG to MCG, September 21, 1870, GCRUL.
15.   WEG to MCG, September 21 and September 26, 1870, GCRUL.
16.   WEG to MCG, September 21 and September 26, 1870, GCRUL.
17.   WEG to MCG, September 21 and September 26, 1870, GCRUL.
18.   WEG to MCG, September 21 and September 26, 1870, GCRUL.

19. WEG to MCG, September 21 and September 26, 1870, GCRUL.
20. WEG to MCG, October 3, 1870, GCRUL.
21. Reverend James Ballagh to WEG, September 28, 1870, GCRUL.
22. Anna Marie Griffis to WEG, October 10, 1870, GCRUL.
23. MCG to WEG, October 10, 1870, GCRUL.
24. MCG to WEG, October 10, 1870, GCRUL.
25. MCG to WEG, October 10, 1870, GCRUL.
26. Samuel Lockwood to WEG, October 22, 1870, GCRUL.
27. WEG to MCG, November 2, 1870, GCRUL.
28. WEG to MCG, November 2, 1870, GCRUL.
29. Griffis, *Verbeck of Japan*, pp. 217–218.
30. Clipping, *Christian Intelligencer*, n. d., in Griffis, "Fukui Scrapbook," p. 144, GCRUL.
31. William Elliot Griffis, "Diary," November 15, 1870, GCRUL.
32. Griffis, "Diary," November 17, 1870, GCRUL.
33. WEG to MCG, November 21, 1870, GCRUL.
34. Griffis, *Verbeck of Japan*, p. 218.
35. WEG to MCG, November 18, 1870, GCRUL.
36. WEG to MCG, November 27 or 28, 1870 [illegible], GCRUL.
37. WEG to MCG, November 28, 1870; November 30, 1870. Also Griffis, "Dary," November 27, December 1, 1870, GCRUL.
38. Griffis, "Diary," December 1–3, 1870, GCRUL.
39. WEG to MCG, December 13, 1870, GCRUL.
40. WEG to MCG, December 19, 1870, GCRUL.
41. WEG to MCG, December 25, 1870, GCRUL.
42. See chapter 1, note 53.
43. William Elliot Griffis, "First Glimpses of Japan," *Christian Intelligencer*, March 2, 1871, n. p. Also see William Elliot Griffis, *The Mikado's Empire*, 2 vols. (New York: Harper & Brothers, 1913), 2: 327–332.
44. Arthur C. Maclay, *A Budget of Letters from Japan: Reminiscences of Work and Travel in Japan* (New York: A. C. Armstrong & Son, 1886), p. 17.
45. Griffis, *Verbeck of Japan*, pp. 218–219.
46. Griffis, "First Glimpses of Japan," Also see Harold S. Williams, *Tales of Foreign Settlements in Japan* (Tokyo: Charles E. Tuttle, 1958), pp. 37–63; hereafter cited as Williams, *Tales of Foreign Settlements*.
47. Williams, *Tales of Foreign Settlements*, p. 41.
48. Griffis, "Diary," January 1, 1871, GCRUL.
49. Griffis, "Diary," January 3, 1871, GCRUL.
50. See description in Griffis, *The Mikado's Empire*, pp. 353–362.
51. Griffis, *Verbeck of Japan*, pp. 217-239.
52. Robert S. Schwantes, *Japanese and Americans: A Century of Cultural Relations* (New York: Harper and Brothers, 1955), p. 154; hereafter cited as Schwantes, *Japanese and Americans*.
53. See Griffis, *Verbeck of Japan*.
54. Iwakura Tomomi was a court noble who led the 1872–1873 government mission on a world diplomatic tour (the Iwakura Mission) and who held numerous important governmental positions.
     Ōkubo Toshimichi was a leading Satsuma *samurai* who was instrumental in putting down rebellions in Saga and Satsuma in the 1870s. He was assassinated in 1878 by his political enemies.

Mori Arinori was Japan's minister to Washington and later Minister of Education. A proponent of progressive ideas in his early years and a fervent nationalist later, he was assassinated by a disgruntled youth in 1889. An excellent study of the life, thoughts, and times *of* Mori is Ivan Hall, "Mori Arinori: A Reconsideration," 2 vols. (Ph. D. dissertation, Harvard University, 1969).

Fukuzawa Yukichi was probably Japan's foremost interpreter of the West who traveled to the United States and Europe, wrote numerous influential articles and books and founded one of Japan's most prestigious private universities—Keio University. Invaluable sources on Fukuzawa are Carmen Blacker, *The Japanese Enlightenment: A Study of the Writings of Fukuzawa Yukichi* (Cambridge: Cambridge University Press, 1964); Eiichi Kiyooka, ed., *The Autobiography of Fukuzawa Yukichi* (New York: Columbia University Press, 1966); and Sir George Sansom, *The Western World and Japan: A Study in the Interactions of European and Asiatic Cultures* (New York: Alfred A. Knopf, 1950), pp. 427–451; hereafter cited as Sansom, *The Western World and Japan.*

Matsudaira Shungaku was the feudal lord of Echizen *han*, see chapter 1, note 8.

55. Clark, *Life and Adventure in Japan* p. 147.
56. WEG to MCG, February 15, 1871, GCRUL.
57. WEG to MCG, February 15, 1871, GCRUL.
58. Griffis, *Verbeck of Japan*, p. 245.
59. Griffis, *Verbeck of Japan*, p. 217.
60. Griffis, *The Mikado's Empire*, p. 377; and Griffis, *Verbeck of Japan*, p. 237.
61. It seems that the two men had left their compound with their normal armed escort in the early evening. They dismissed their guards at about 7:15 P.M. and were attacked while walking on the road at about 8:15 P.M.
62. WEG to MCG, January 15, 1871, GCRUL.
63. WEG to MCG, January 15, 1871, GCRUL.
64. Griffis, *Verbeck of Japan*, p. 249.
65. See, for example, Griffis, "In the Heart of Japan," *The Christian Intelligencer,* April 27, 1871, n. p.
66. WEG to MCG, February 3, 1871, GCRUL.
67. WEG to MCG, February 3, 1871, GCRUL.
68. WEG to MCG, February 3, 1871, GCRUL.
69. Griffis, "Diary," February 6, 1871.
70. WEG to MCG, October 30, 1870, GCRUL.
71. WEG to MCG, January 15, 1871, GCRUL.

Chapter 3

Teaching in Feudal Fukui

FUKUI IN 1870

The Fukui which greeted William Elliot Griffis on March 4, 1871 offered sharp contrast to both the relatively sophisticated Tokyo which he had recently left, and his anticipated image of Fukui. After an arduous journey of twelve days and several hundred miles, "escorted by twelve knights on horseback,"[1] Griffis entered the ancient capital of Matsudaira Shungaku's Echizen fief, "amid wind, light showers, and fitful flakes of snow alternating with rays of sunlight."[2]

One student of the period described Fukui at the time of Griffis' arrival in 1871 as "a typical provincial city of its time, containing some 12,000 inhabitants, 2,849 homes, 25 inns and 34 streets along the center of which clear mountain water was conducted through stone channels [in which] the citizens washed their dishes and their clothes."[3] Nearby were both an important paper mill, famous throughout Japan, and a prosperous silk industry which Griffis described in a letter to his sister Margaret.[4]

In his often fertile imagination, Griffis had envisioned Fukui as an opulent Asian city, indeed, "the ideal Fukui was a grand city."[5] As he "rode through its streets," however, "expecting at last to emerge into some splendid avenue . . . the scales," he wrote, "fell from my eyes." Suffering from nothing more serious than "culture shock,"[6] Griffis wrote that "I was amazed at the utter poverty of the people, the contemptible houses, and the tumble-down look of the city, as compared with the trim dwellings of an American town . . . . I realized what a Japanese—an Asiatic city—was [and] I was disgusted."[7]

In an article written a few days later, and subsequently published in *The Christian Intelligencer*, he rhetorically asked, "How *could* a nineteenth century New Yorker live in the twelfth century?" After a full week in Fukui, Griffis, a nineteenth-century Philadelphian, managed to adjust, a fact he attributed to his missionary impulse; "it is," he wrote, "no loss to live in a social desert, if [one] can help the people upward to God."[8] As is not uncommon, the passage of time mellowed Griffis' early opinion of Fukui. Years later, in a more generous mood, he claimed, "I was proud and delighted that my lot was cast in Fukui, a city which in eminence and intellectual and moral progress was set, as it were, upon a hill."[9]

This later judgment was, at least in an objective sense, partially accurate. Fukui was the capital of Echizen *han* whose *daimyō*, Matsudaira Shungaku was one of Japan's wisest and most progressive leaders. Adamantly opposed to the western challenge at the outset, he quickly came to see the futility of that position and reversed himself.[10] Sir George Sansom, perhaps the most distinguished western student of Japanese history, has written that even prior to Matsudaira's change of heart in 1863, "foreign studies had made good progress"[11] in Echizen, and Marius Jansen has described Matsudaira as "one of the outstanding lords" of his era.[12]

Assuming the position of *daimyō* of Echizen in 1838, Matsudaira set out to rebuild the *han*'s shaky financial structure and to strengthen its military posture.

In 1848 cannon on Western models were cast at Fukui. Echizen sent some of the young men to study medicine of the Dutch at Nagasaki, and, without ordering, advised European practice. To stay the ravages of smallpox he petitioned the Shogun to have general vaccination attempted throughout the country. Failing in this, in 1850 he opened at Fukui an office at which his own people could receive the pure vaccine virus. The next year he introduced the Dutch artillery, drill and infantry tactics. In 1852 he abolished archery, as the Samurai's accomplishment, and ordered rifle shooting at the butts.[13]

EDUCATIONAL REFORM IN FUKUI

Education was not neglected in this burst of reform-oriented energy. Several years after Matsudaira became *daimyō*, Yokoi Shōnan, a Kumamoto *samurai* and a well-known scholar, paid his first of several visits to Fukui in 1847. Although Matsudaira was in Tokyo at the time of this visit, Yokoi met with a number of the *daimyō*'s advisors whom he impressed with his great knowledge. Yokoi's views on education were largely shaped by his conviction that, in Sir George Sansom's words, "the modern samurai were taken up, besotted almost, with art over letters, to the neglect of political and social studies which the times demanded; and the aim of his teaching was described as the encouragement of real, practical learning."[14] He felt that education and politics were inseparable as young men pursued formal education to better prepare themselves for political activities. This type of "imaginative and politically conscious education" was attractive to Matsudaira and his advisors.[15]

As a result of the enthusiasm generated by Yokoi's ideas, a school was established on May 2, 1855, called the Meidōkan ("School of enlightened methods"). At first the Meidōkan taught the Confucian classics, military arts, national history, Chinese philosophies other than Confucianism, ceremonial affairs, poetics, writing—arithmetic—calendar reading, medicine and Dutch Studies,"[16] Hashimoto Sanai, son of a prominent Fukui doctor, had been studying in Tokyo since 1854 and returned to Fukui in the summer of 1856 "as an instructor in charge of Dutch studies at the new *han* academy . . . and by February 1857, he had become the school's headmaster." During his tenure he encouraged "a new and more utilitarian curriculum."[17] On May 6, 1857, "a foreign literature training department, with a curriculum of study, with textbooks based on the Dutch model, was established."[18]

Sanai was anxious to have the Meidōkan's effectiveness increased and he wrote,

> The appointment of able men is important in any age. It is especially important now when the *han* government is being reformed and the organization of the han is being reestablished. At present, men of ability have been appointed, but this is as yet insufficient. Thus we need to educate the young people and cultivate their talent. The school should hold fast to educational policy and provide for the future of the han government. . . . In order to achieve this educational policy of the unification of study and politics, it is not enough to do our best for school education. The *han* authorities have to appoint men of ability positively and in large numbers, giving great encouragement to general students. Otherwise, without a proper place for themselves, men of talent would lose all hope, complain and be dissatisfied. In the end, this educational policy would create a damaging effect on the school education itself.[19]

In order to lend "encouragement to general students," Hashimoto arranged for the establishment of four schools outside the castle walls to serve as a branch for training in the martial arts.[20]

Between the time of Yokoi's first visit to Fukui in 1847 and the 1870 decision to invite foreign teachers to Fukui, the major goal of education in the *han* had shifted from the training of hereditary warriors loyal to the Prince, to the training of men of ability who would serve in positions of governmental power and responsibility. This shift was reflected in a proclamation issued by the Prince in December 1869, suggesting that since all were now, more than ever, subjects of the Emperor, "the school has to bring up men of talent who would be useful to the Imperial Government by widening the students' knowledge and improving their morality."[21] Thus, western teachers were welcomed for the knowledge and skills they could transmit to the Emperor's subjects.

THE ARRIVAL OF THE YATOI

Riding through the crowded streets and surrounded by curious people trying to get a look at the blue-eyed foreigner from across the seas, Griffis was greeted by "several officers, all in their best silks, swords, sandals, and top-knots, with bows, and such awkward but hearty handshaking as men unused to it might be supposed to achieve."[22] After these formalities, Griffis was quickly escorted to his temporary quarters, "an old mansion, nearly 150 years old, once belonging to an ancient Japanese family, and still bearing the crest of the Tokugawa family on the lofty painted gable."[23] The house contained western furnishings and was heated by Fukui coal.

Griffis admitted that he was "agreeably surprised . . . to find how comfortable they had my own house."[24] These first quarters were actually the *yashiki* ("residence") of a *han* officer, and contained "a large and handsome canopied iron bedstead and mattress, bureau, and cheerful little stove, all fitted with pipe, set in a stove basin, and sending out a cheerful glow with the coal recently discovered in Fukui."[25] He informed his sister Maggie of his complete satisfaction with the treatment he had received and exclaimed that his hosts, so far at least, had "acted so generously *above* their contract, that it sometimes moves me almost to tears."[26] Somewhat suspiciously he attributed this treatment to the fear of the Japanese hosts that he would "be disgusted with the loneliness and uncivilized condition of the country and leave."[27]

His hosts had had prepared a western-style dinner, complete with beer and wine, which they shared with him. After dinner and polite conversation, the Japanese departed, and he spent the remainder of his first night in Fukui unpacking his belongings before retiring at 11 P.M.[28]

Early the next morning, Sunday, March 5, Griffis was invited to the castle to meet Matsudaira Shungaku, the *daimyō* of Echizen. The formal ceremony, by Griffis' account, was quickly transformed as "Icy etiquette melted into good humor, and good humor flowed into fun."[29] Comparing Griffis' published account of the meeting with his diary entry for that date with his description of it in a letter to his sister makes one wonder why the published account is so much more florid than his private description. In writing to his sister, he dismissed the meeting in three brief sentences, and his diary reveals only that he "met the Prince and four chief officers," enjoyed his refreshments and "exchanged cards" during the one-hour conference.[30]

PREPARING TO TEACH

The day following his meeting with the Prince, Griffis began his educational work in earnest. Settled comfortably in his temporary quarters, he contemplated with satisfaction the western-style house that the authorities had promised to build for his comfort. Then he visited the school, met with the other teachers and began to plan for his classes and to set up his own classroom and laboratory. He wrote,

I was surprised to find it so large and flourishing. There were in all about eight hundred students, comprised in the English, Chinese, Japanese, medical, and military departments. A few had been studying English for two or three years, under native teachers who had been in Nagasaki. In the medical department, I found a good collection of Dutch books, chiefly medical and scientific, and a fine pair of French dissection models, of both varieties of the human body. In the military school was a library of foreign works on military subjects, chiefly in English, several of which had been translated into Japanese. In one part of the yard young men, book, diagram or trowel in hand, were constructing a miniature earthwork. The school library, of American and English books—among which were all of Kusakabe's—was quite respectable. In the Chinese school I found thousands of boxes, with sliding lids, filled with Chinese and Japanese books. Several hundred boys and young men were squatted on the floor, with their teachers, reading or committing lessons to memory, or writting Chinese characters.[31]

Griffis informed Maggie that the school stood in "the very heart of the old castle and lies inside the innermost of the three circuits of walls and moats." He went on to tell how "Some of the rooms are gorgeously decorated in golden and lacquered designs." The laboratory in which he initially worked, however, "was in the daimio's ladies boudoir."[32]

In honor of Griffis' first visit to the school, young men performed kendo, wrestling, and other physical-martial arts. Griffis admitted being "highly impressed with the display, and could not fail to admire the splendid, manly physique of many of the lads." Nevertheless, as Griffis returned to his quarters, he "wondered how long it would require to civilize such 'barbarians.' "[33]

March 7, 1872 saw him teach his first class in Fukui, which he felt "succeeded quite well." In appreciation of his efforts and in honor of the occasion, the director of the school made him a personal gift of a plump goose, and another officer, Sasaki Gonroku, made him a present of "two bottles of champagne and carved monkeys."[34]

Charged with enthusiasm, Griffis confided to his sister his major goal: "to make Fukuwi College the best in Japan, and to make a national textbook on Chemistry, to advocate the education of women, to abolish the drinking of sake, the wearing of swords, the promiscuous bathing of the sexes."[35] "I want the Prince to feel that I am more than a time-serving foreigner." He invited the Prince and other high-ranking officials and with them, he wrote, "I discuss my ideas for the welfare of Japan, and have every reason to believe they are deeply influenced. Various evidences that all I do for the people is appreciated and is leavening opinion, come to me in various ways."[36]

IWABUCHI: INTERPRETER AND FRIEND

To function effectively in the far interior of Japan where few, if any, people had ever heard English spoken, Griffis needed a good interpreter. To this need he was quite sensitive, admitting that in a place like Fukui "a tongue was more than a right arm."[37]

While still in Tokyo preparing for his journey to Fukui, Griffis had spent a good deal of time searching for an interpreter in whom he could place his complete confidence. His first choice for this important position had been Tateishi Tokujuro ("Tommy" in the American press), a first-rate interpreter who had won a favorable reputation as a fun-loving, young playboy in the United States. Lewis Bush, longtime student and amateur historian of Japan, has written that during "Tommy's" visit to Washington, D. C., he had "acquired a host of feminine admirers . . . [and it appeared] that he had already lost his heart to a certain young lady of society who was able to frequent the hotel."[38] Young "Tommy," however, did not want to abandon the flesh pots of Tokyo for life in a provincial backwater, not even for the generous (for a Japanese of the time) salary of $1,000 per year.[39]

Griffis' second choice for his interpreter was a young man of twenty years attached to the Imperial College in Tokyo, a certain Iwabuchi. Griffis described him as "a *ronin* samurai of secondary rank and rather well educated." Iwabuchi had a "broad, high forehead, luxuriant hair cut in foreign style, keen, dancing black eyes, and a blushing face." He seemed to Griffis to be "the very type of a Japanese gentleman of letters . . . . of delicate frame, his face lighted by intellect, softened by habitual meekness."[40]

Given Griffis' values and interests, the choice of Iwabuchi was probably a fortunate one. Although they sometimes clashed when, in Griffis' words, "American steel struck Japanese flint," Griffis was quick to admit that "Iwabuchi was invaluable to me."[41] Their relationship blossomed into friendship and they spent a great deal of time with one another. They rode together in the countryside in the afternoons following the close of school, went on weekend excursions to the seashore and shared many meals. When Iwabuchi informed Griffis that he would be taking a wife, Griffis bemoaned to Margaret that this event "taking away much of his close connection with me, leaves me more lonely than ever."[42] The workload

had increased to the point where Griffis required several additional interpreters, and since Griffis could not speak Japanese, Iwabuchi remained
with Griffis following his marriage to act as a necessary intermediary for
most of Griffis' instructions. Iwabuchi was not only Griffis' "tongue"
during his sojourn in Fukui, but was vital in explaining Japanese life and
culture to him.

FRENETIC ACTIVITY VS. LONELINESS

Griffis found in March 1871 that "my pupils at present number less than
90 divided into four classes,"[43] and that he was expected to teach four
hours per day, six days per week. Sunday was a free day in keeping with
his Christian conscience and the terms of his contract. Characteristically,
Griffis planned to throw himself completely into his work. He expected to
"have my hands full of all sorts of teaching and work . . . all of which
will be entirely voluntary outside of school hours,"[44] His typical inclination
to do more than expected of him was perhaps reinforced by his feeling
that his employers had been so generous toward him "that it sometimes
moves me almost to tears; not a day so far, but some present, which although small, testifies to a kind heart."[45]

The first few weeks of his teaching took on a routine form; he taught his
classes in the morning, received gifts of food from various people in both
the school and the town, worked on the plans for his new laboratory,
took afternoon rides and evening walks, and taught various subjects to
his students and the townspeople in the evening. "It is only by keeping
incessantly busy in school, at study, or at exercise," he confided to his
sister, "that I shall be able to drive off home-sickness and occasional
dejection."[46]

Griffis attempted to counter his isolation with a continual round of
activities. Only three weeks after arriving in Fukui, he announced that his
"heart and soul, body and mind are for the present given to Japan. From
early morn till near midnight, I am busy, and I go to bed, weared [sic]
out. I dare not have time to be homesick, or country-sick." He explained
why he did not mind doing more than his contract called for to remain
busy, but even with this extra work "I cannot tell you how much and how
often I think of and long for the one I left behind, on whom all my love
centered."[47]

During his first three weeks in Fukui, Griffis arranged voluntarily to
teach German for three hours per week to a class of six medical students.
He also planned to "begin evening classes for the study of History, Physiology, U. S. Constitution, the Bible" through his interpreter whom,
he admitted, "I like very much."[48]

Griffis avidly looked forward to receiving mail from home and often admonished Margaret for not writing often enough, and the rest of his family for leaving the correspondence to her. "I think it very unfair," he warned, "when none at home but you, write to me. When I get letters from others, I get a fuller and more vivid conception of things at home, and it will be *their fault*, not mine, if I lose interest and regard for home, by lack of knowledge of details."[49] In a less agitated moment he confessed that "You will find that I refer very little in my letters to matters at home. . . . I want to know everything about all of my relations. You don't know how dear they *all, every one* are to me. I mean especially those whose *past* have been closely connected with mine, and around whom the tender memories of childhood are entwined. *All* my aunts and uncles and their children will ever be dear to me, the new generation that comes in their place, I do not, cannot love so dearly, if at all. *I cannot spare any love.* . . . never fail to let me know that 'they miss me at home.' "[50]

Griffis made much of his isolation in Fukui. Without doubt, he was isolated, but it should be noted that he did not completely lack western companionship. Mr. Alfred Lucy, an English teacher and citizen of Great Britain whom Griffis had earlier met in Tokyo, had been teaching in Japan for five years and in Fukui for six months prior to Griffis' arrival in Japan. Lucy, Griffis wrote Margaret, "is rather a pale, quiet young man of about my own age, and is a smart fellow with a head packed full of information, and talks the Jap language fluently."[51] Despite their disagreement on many subjects, Griffis described his relations with Lucy as "pleasant and fruitful"[52] although he "is not specially sensitive or delicate in his feelings."[53] Griffis felt that their major difference was that Lucy's "view of civilization is entirely of the money-making kind. He has not the slightest interest in any of the historic, ethical or poetic side of Japan."[54] One cannot help but suspect, however, that Griffis' real differences with Lucy were based on the question of morality, for Lucy, "like the 99 of every hundred single men in Japan, had taken a temporary wife, but put her away just before I came."[55] Despite this, however, they shared many afternoon walks rides, and hunting expeditions. The gnawing loneliness and profound sense of isolation which Griffis described became unendurable when Lucy's contract was not renewed in the summer of 1872, and he left to seek his fortune in Tokyo.

THE JAPANESE VIEW OF THE YATOI

The general attitude of the Japanese authorities, both in Tokyo and in Echizen, toward the *yatoi* whom they hired to teach them the secrets of western power was the source of this frustration. The Japanese had no intention of allowing these foreigners to have any real control over actual policy-making functions. The "Japanese only look upon foreigners as schoolmasters. As long as they cannot help themselves, they make use of them; and they send them about their business."[56] To his credit, Griffis recognized this fact of life early in his tour in Echizen. Writing in the *Scientific American*, he warned those contemplating coming to Japan that this country was already overstocked.

Several letters from America and Europe have been directed to me by parties in search of employment. I can only say, very briefly, that this country is already overstocked with foreigners out of employment. I should advise no American to come to Japan, unless he has a position secured before he comes. A man can do well here if he comes to Japan having been appointed in America. It gives him *prestige* over those who are trying to get employment here . . . .

In regard to men appointed to offices with high sounding names and large salaries, I am afraid many people will be disappointed concerning Japan. The Japanese simply want helpers and advisers. They propose to keep the "bossing," officering, and the power all in their own hands. Some disappointment and a little profanity has been indulged in by certain people who deceived themselves by supposing the flattering Japanese to mean all their polite words said in America. All this "taking charge of," "being at the head of," "organizing," etc., is sheer daydreaming. People from America and Europe must remember that "there were brave men before Hector," and a few foreigners have been laboring in Japan for years, and with all the knowledge of the language, etc., have helped the Japanese help themselves. Many who come here to "organize," etc. find that things are already organized as much as they can be under the circumstances, and that all the newcomers can do is wait quietly until perchance they gain the confidence of the Japanese, and even then all they advise is by no means adopted. Nearly every appointee comes here "to revolutionize" his department, but the Japanese don't want that. They want the foreigners to get into the traces, and pull just so fast as, and no faster than, their mighty enterprises can bear. Let it not be forgotten that this country is an emphatically poor country now, and that millions of its people are very ignorant, and that it has just emerged from feudalism; and that therefore the rulers of Japan must go slowly and cautiously. Above everything else, it is not wise to put their soil or their enterprises too much into foreign hands, and to prove that Japanese nature is human nature, they like to do it themselves, to play with their own toys and to run their own machines. Therefore, if a man means real hard work that takes off his coat, and is willing to run the risk of going hungry occasionally, and if he has patience enough to wait until an experience taught people can trust him, and he isn't a born brigadier-general, and is willing to help without "taking charge" of everything, let him try Japan. If he expects that the Japanese people wish to make him a Secretary of State, or Minister of Education, or Postmaster General, etc., he had better stay at home, because the Japanese people like to be officers themselves, and are neither children nor weak-minded.[57]

Probably the most thorough research on the question of the *yatoi* in Meiji Japan has been done by Professor Hazel Jones whose dissertation, "The Meiji Government and Foreign Employees, 1868–1900," is a treasure chest of valuable information on the subject.[58] Elsewhere Dr. Jones has asked, "Were these foreign employees in any applicable degree creators? This would assume a leadership or decision-making role. Were they salaried helpers, even servants? Or was their role something else?"[59] She compares the views of Griffis and another prominent *yatoi*, the Englishman Basil Chamberlain, on the role of foreign employees in Meiji Japan. Briefly stated, Dr. Jones sees Griffis as advancing the position that "foreign employees were answering a specific call [The Imperial Charter Oath] and perceived their role as 'helpers and servants.' " Chamberlain, on the other hand, felt that "foreign employees were creators of New Japan."[60] Jones concludes her study by suggesting that the foreign employee "functioned in the technological phase of Japanese development as live machines and in the professional phase as living reference books."[61]

A third possibility, however, exists. Perhaps both Griffis and Chamberlain were correct. It is certainly true that Griffis judged correctly that the Japanese wished to retain control over the foreign experts and used them, in Griffis' phrase, as "helpers and servants." Could it also be true, however, that these foreign experts were the "creators of the new Japan" in the sense that without their particular contributions at this crucial time in Japan's history, Japan would not have modernized so quickly? Without this rapid modernization would Japan have developed a viable political, economic, and military system by the end of the century? Without these elements could Japan have defeated the Chinese in 1894 or the Russians in 1905? Even under the best of circumstances, historical "ifs" are dangerous, but it seems quite plausible that both Griffis and Chamberlain were correct.

INTRODUCING WESTERN SCIENCE

William Elliot Griffis was instrumental in promoting the growth of western science in Fukui, although it would be going too far to claim any seminal or national influence for his efforts.[62] Nakamura Takeshi describes how, in the decades preceding the Meiji Restoration, the Dutch "taught navigation, the theory and practice of shipbuilding, artillery and other military crafts, as well as astronomy, land surveying and mathematics."[63] Frances Helbig suggests that Fukui was not alone in encouraging instruction in western science as "all of the stronger and more enlighted han were moving swiftly in this direction" and, indeed, "three other provincial chemical laboratories [were] functioning about the same time. . . . presided over by the Germans."[64]

This having been said, it is important to point out that Griffis' role within Fukui was a significant one. His Japanese hosts saw Griffis as having a great deal to teach them. Why else would he be greeted with such respect and enthusiasm, given a one-third increase in salary before arriving in Fukui and treated with deference and consideration during his sojourn in Matsudaira's realm?

Settling down to his work, Griffis was pleased to find that "I have a good interpreters and the officers have provided me with a good blacksmith, tinsman and joiner to make my apparatus." Not worried about the limits to their talents, Griffis would simply "send to America for what I cannot get here."[65] A careful search through the shops of Yokohama, however, yielded "a few glass tubes, some utensils and materials" which enabled Griffis to begin his classes.[66] Despite the skill of Japanese artisans and his own "Yankee ingenuity," Griffis soon found that he had to order certain items from America and England. He had high praise for "the Japanese skill, fineness of work and ability to 'catch on' to the foreigner's ideas. . . . The great trouble was that without models for copying and both chemical facts and nomenclature not being then familiar either to the educated or to the plain folk, progress at times was slow."[67]

Griffis was constantly chafing over the long time lag between the placement of his order and the arrival of the materials, and he continually reminded Maggie, who acted as his agent, to be sure to account for every cent that he sent her for supplies. He was very sensitive that he was an expensive "item to the government" with his high salary, expensive laboratory and housing costs not to mention his interpreter's salary, etc.[68] For example, on March 28, 1781, he cautioned his sister to

Tell Mr. McAllister to make out a bill, naming each article shipped, its cost, etc. The amount of packing, insurance, etc. should be included in a separate bill and sent to me, *the letters* to *Yokohama,* the *freight* to *Kobe.* Tell him to write me, the first week after the receipt of the order, telling me what things I must wait for, what can be sent immediately, the rate of insurance, and the amount of the entire order, in money etc.[69]

Both his patience and ingenuity were however, severely taxed when only three days after he arrived in Fukui, he was asked "to teach the men in the war departments . . . of Echizen how to blow up a man of war with submarine mines!"[70] In another place he revealed that "when I tried to show in the course of years an iron spike would not only rust, but 'eat' away the timber in which it was once tightly pounded, the school officials wondered what that had to do with science."[71]

According to his diary, among the topics that Griffis covered in his chemistry classes were water, air, voltaic batteries, sulphur, hydrogen, carbon dioxide, iodine, mercury, silver, air pumps, magnetism, and arsenic, and his students' response to his teaching appears to have been a positive one. For example, he confided to his diary on March 23 that he experimented with oxygen in his class with " 70 spectators in my room," which he found "exciting work to teach."[72]

The large and airy hall in which Griffis delivered his lectures was located in Matsudaira's castle. Helbig describes it as "about thirty-five feet by twenty feet with the southwest side of the room almost entirely of glass," and topped by a large skylight.[73] Shortly after Griffis' arrival, the Prince began to build a new laboratory for him in a garden adjoining the lecture hall.[74] Three months later the laboratory was not quite completed, but Griffis was pleased that it was "already roofed and ceiled, and when finished, will be as fine as any laboratory in the U. S. except of course the great Sheffield and Lawrence laboratories of Yale [and] Harvard."[75] His anticipation was justified, for upon its completion in early September, 1871, he wrote to Margaret that "I wish you could fly over to Japan some day, and see my lecture room and laboratory. All in fine order and arranged in best American college style."[76] The only major problem was that "*no apparatus* has arrived in Fukui, though several boxes have been in Yokohama since July 28th."[77]

Despite the lack of materials, Griffis was able to proceed using a few utensils that he had purchased in Yokohama and with what could be made from local materials. Fortunately the hospital in Fukui provided his classes with a minimum of chemicals needed for simple experiments until the overseas orders were filled.[78] At about this time, Griffis informed his sister that "I teach about 4 hours each day except Sunday, and will soon have my hands full of all sorts of teaching and work for them, all of which will be entirely voluntary outside of school hours."[79]

Griffis devoted one of his earliest projects to "organizing a staff of scholarly interpreters who put into the vernacular many of the traditional terms as well as the newly coined and more exact scientific terminology."[80]

For another project, Griffis planned a chemistry textbook in the vernacular that would be relevant to Japan. Writing in a slightly different context, Robert Schwantes credited Griffis with being one of the "few American teachers [who] have tried to devise materials specially adapted to Japanese needs."[81] Griffis recognized that "all our books are adapted to our style of life and civilization," so "my aim is to search all good English and American textbooks, and with my own notes, arrangement and illustrations, to produce a book for the Japanese and translate it into Japanese."[82] He made preliminary arrangements with Hatakeyama Yoshinari, a young Japanese who had been a student at Rutgers, was converted to Christianity, and who had briefly attended the Second Reformed Church of Philadelphia with Griffis, to translate the proposed text into Japanese.[83]

Although no evidence has yet been found indicating that this book was ever, in fact, completed, the fact of his intention to write such a volume, is in itself, revealing. During his entire life, Griffis perceived himself as a conscious bridge between Japan and America, an interpreter of the Japanese, if you will, to his fellow countrymen. This textbook project had much of the same flavor, except, in this case, Griffis was to act as an interpreter of the best western scientific knowledge to the Japanese to whom the book would be directed. Much of his informal social contact with the Japanese during his three-and-one-half years in Japan also had this character and will be discussed in more detail later.

Several months later, Griffis was still at work on the book and described to Margaret how he had "visited the [Fukui] hospital dispensary gleaning much curious information concerning Chinese and Japanese medicines" in order that the textbook would be as "thoroughly Japanese" as possible, including descriptions of "the natural productions of Japan, the province whence each comes, etc."[84]

While waiting for his own book to be completed, Griffis used such works as *School Laboratory of Physical Science* (author unknown), *The Young Mechanic* (author unknown), Eliot and Storer's *Inorganic Chemistry*, and Roscoe's *Chemistry*.[85]

Perhaps some of Griffis' most rewarding teaching occurred outside of school, and a substantial amount of it dealt with modern science. He wrote Maggie, "Three or four evenings in the week I hold evening classes in my own house. On Mondays I lecture on Physiology, on which evening my hearers, about 16 in number, are from the Medical School and hospital."[86] Another typical evening was spent "with several of the scholars, who had come from the school and about a half dozen or more principal men of the village, who had come to hear the foreigner tell of all the wonderful things in his country, to answer questions in science, manufactures, etc."[87]

Griffis' audiences included not only schoolboys and older men from town, but also the highest figures in local government. He described how "the two chief officers of the Prince came to witness chemical experiments, and were highly pleased."[88] On at least one occasion the Prince attended one of Griffis' lectures and "expressed himself delighted," after he had "listened and questioned very attentively" during a Saturday morning lecture lasting ninety minutes.[89]

Griffis looked back at his first eight months in Fukui with evident satisfaction:

We have nearly 125 promising pupils in chemistry and physics, and with two good interpreters, apparatus from America, a printing press, and earnest young men to help in translating and applying the knowledge gained in school, we hope to make the "Fukui Scientific School" one of the centers whence shall radiate the new civilization.[90]

GRIFFIS THE PEDAGOGUE

Griffis' methods of teaching were not uncommon for the age in which he lived, but it would perhaps be helpful to discuss briefly a few of the fundamental assumptions that he brought with him to the classroom. The single most pervasive characteristic that runs as a leitmotif through all of his teaching, preaching, and writing was a didactic one. The teacher, Griffis, was the instructor of others and at the center of each learning or teaching situation; *he* was the disseminator of knowledge and his students or audience were the receptacles.

He criticized the Japanese teachers of Tokugawa Japan whose major qualification was their personal knowledge of the Chinese classics, and as Griffis saw it, their "chief duty was to stuff and cram the minds of . . . pupils. To expand or develop the mental powers of a boy, to enlarge his mental visions, to teach him to think for himself, would have been doing precisely what it was the teacher's business to prevent."[91] What Griffis opposed, however, was neither the centrality of the teacher to the learning process nor his propensity "to stuff and cram the minds of his pupils." Instead, he argued that "the native teacher of the future must depend less on traditional authority, and more on the resources of a *richly furnished* mind."[92] He suggested that while the "old teacher was a drill master; the new one must be that and more. The old one stifled questioning; the new one must encourage it."[93] Griffis' concern, then, was primarily modifying the traditional lecture method in ways would make it more effective. He was a reformer, not a radical.

He explained how in his own teaching he "introduced largely, the blackboard system of instruction" in which "all the teaching has been by experiments and lectures verbally translated."[94] Thus, most of his formal teaching consisted of his either lecturing or demonstrating an experiment, and using the blackboard for listing formulae or illustrating various points. His interpreters translated the abstract ideas he presented into the vernacular as best they could given the state of the Japanese language at the time. Since Griffis' knowledge of Japanese was never fluent, he required translation assistance for all but the most rudimentary communication with his students.[95] One wonders how much was lost in the translation.

As a man or as a teacher, Griffis was very serious in everything that he did. He always stressed the importance of securing a sound knowledge of fundamentals before attempting to master any field of knowledge. He consistently emphasized the importance "of a thorough *elementary* training," the lack of which could "never be fully made up."[96] He wrote approvingly, for example, that the Rutgers Grammar School "aims first to lay the sure foundations of a good English education, by continual drilling and practice."[97] In advising his sister Margaret on the education of one of his relatives, Griffis urged that he learn "the Greek alphabet, the structure of Greek and Latin prefixes, affixes, changes of verb roots, sentences, etc." and stressed the necessity of being "drilled thoroughly in the formation of scientific knowledge and terms of science."[98]

Griffis' solution to teaching large classes of students containing a wide variety of ability levels was a very conventional one. Given what has been said so far about his educational views, one is not surprised that he did what he could to control carefully the selection of students and worked in special classes with the bright. With satisfaction he reported that

> I do not have large classes as I had at first, but that it because the novelty is over and as chemistry means work, I have weeded out the lazy ones, and have about $\frac{1}{2}$ the former number, but all earnest, patient students. My class of 15 boys in French are doing well, so are the seven older German scholars, and the 15 small boys in German, under Masaki, my best pupil.[99]

Another technique to cope with large classes that he used was the so-called Lancasterian System in which one teacher instructed a number of older pupils who in turn, taught younger ones carefully prescribed lessons. Griffis wrote, "In school I have organized new classes, setting the assistants to work at teaching, give private lessons to the smartest and best students in German & French—in my house and set them to teaching in the schools."[100]

Of his students he wrote,

> All were bare-headed, with the top-knot, cue and shaven midscalp, most of them with bare feet on their clogs and with characteristic dress, swagger, fierce looks, bare skin exposed at the scalp, neck, arms, calves, and feet, with their murderous swords in their belts, they impressed upon my memory a picture of feudalism I shall never forget. As I walked, I wondered how long it would require to civilize such "barbarians." Here were nearly a thousand young samurai. What was one teacher among so many? Could it be possible that these could be trained and disciplined students? . . . A few months later, and I had won their confidence and love. I found they were quite able to instruct me in many things. I need fear to lose neither politeness nor sense of honor among these earnest youths. In pride and dignity of character, in diligence, courage, gentlemanly conduct, refinement and affection, truth and honesty, good morals, in so far as I knew or could see, they were my peers.[101]

In another place he described the "average Japanese student" as "bright, quick, eager, earnest and faithful." A Japanese student, Griffis recorded, "delights his teacher's heart by his docility, his industry, his obedience, his reverence, his politeness. In the course of five years, the writer can remember no instance of rudeness, no case of slander, no uncanny trick, no impudent reply from any of his many pupils."[102]

Griffis took many of them into his home, and by the end of October, 1871, he had seven young students living with him. In that active house Griffis spent much time informally instructing them in the virtues of the American constitution and in the wisdom of the western world. As was perhaps inevitable, Griffis had his favorites especially one lad named Kasawara whom Griffis described as "a pretty boy of lovely disposition and very bright."[103]

In return for Griffis' attention to them, either as part of their school assignments or as goodwill gestures to their host, these students provided Griffis with a great deal of firsthand information on Japanese life that eventually found its way into print in his articles and books. The Griffis Collection at Rutgers contains several score of essays written by Griffis' young students. The numerous topics covered the students' native cities and towns, the geography of their provinces, games played by Japanese children, Japanese money, signs and theaters, burial customs, their first impressions of foreigners, etc. One does not have to read very far into Griffis' extensive writings to recognize the source of much of his information.

ENTHUSIASM VS. AMBIVALENCE

We know that Griffis' scholarly reputation was strong enough to attract four young men from Higo (today's Kumamoto) who were "cousins of one of my old pupils in America [Numagawa whom he had taught at Rutgers] who came 600 miles to study with me although they have a foreigner in Higo."[104] Upon their arrival in Fukui, the four students gave Griffis a basket of eggs and arranged an "entertainment in my honor," which convinced him that "the Japanese are by no means an ungrateful race."[105]

The people of Fukui, from *daimyō* to commoner, clearly appreciated Griffis' efforts to help them achieve progress, and they plied him with gifts and kind sentiments. He later wrote that during his months in Fukui "unceasing kindnesses were showered upon me . . . I have nothing to record but respect, consideration, sympathy and kindness. My eyes were opened. I needed no revolver, nor were guards necessary . . . and among the happiest memories are those of Fukui."[106] Despite these mutual feelings of warmth, affection, and satisfaction with his work, Griffis was troubled by his role in Japan's modernization efforts. Often during late-night walks beneath the stars, he felt an occasional tinge of doubt.

> I had come hither to be a builder of knowledge to help bring the new civilization that must destroy the old. Yet it was hard to be an iconoclast. I often asked myself the question—Why not leave these people alone? They seem to be happy enough; and he that increaseth knowledge increaseth sorrow.[107]

Reflecting upon living in an ancient Japanese home, he worried that the "sacredness of human belief and reverence had consecrated even the old shrine, and other hands than mine must remove the stones of the deserted fane, the vulgarity to make a dining room of the family oratory, where the ancestral tablets once stood, and sacred lights and incense burned."[108]

Despite misgiving of this sort, Griffis was an articulate advocate of Japanese modernization. In many ways he saw the United States as the model that Japan "ought" to emulate. He was convinced, for example, that one of the primary reasons for America's rapid development lay in her people's willingness to roll up their sleeves and dirty their hands. He therefore argued that "Japan can never be a great country while it is a disgrace to labor with [one's] hands."[109] On those occasions when he was invited to dine with the Prince, usually with Lucy, he pushed this point very hard.

> Mr. Lucy and I . . . were invited to meet with the Prince in his summer mansion, about 2 miles from the college. We rode out and met him there, with four of his head officers, and found a gorgeous dinner spread out, cooked by our trained cook, served by the pages and in thorough style. And eaten properly, chairs, tables, plates, knives and forks were of the best. The course numbered 10, the wine and beer of course were there; and finding the officers and Prince Matsudaira in good humor, I told him of our glorious country with its free schools, free institutions, where labor with the hands was not in disgrace, where our chief magistrate came from the people, where we educate our women as highly as ourselves. We told them that Japan could never be a great country until they honored labor, trade, the privileged classes work, educated their women, and elevated and cared for the common people. Think of it! [sic] in a despotic country, and in a *Daimio*'s presence, promulgating such revolutionary ideas.[110]

DOMESTIC LIFE

Although Griffis' domestic life in Fukui was materially comfortable and quite varied, he often complained to his sister about his gnawing sense of loneliness and his unhappiness over his diet. As early as March 23, 1871, he wrote, "I don't grieve over beefsteak. . . . I have always found that a temperate diet enabled me to do about twice the work of ordinary students and kept me in fair health. I do not propose to change being mainly satisfied with rice and fish."[111] In the same letter he revealed that "I use the chop sticks splendidly, [and] the 'nerve-fluids' flow most exuberantly, and my liver is in good state."[112]

A month later, however, he suggested that "I am indeed at the ends of the earth," but "I am beginning to enter into, and understand Japanese life quite well."[113] After describing his activities to Margaret, Griffis explained that "I fear lest you think that I have fallen into satisfied exile content to be stranded out here at the ends of the earth caring scarcely for those at home."[114] He reassured her that this was emphatically not the case and concluded, "I cannot put my heart on paper, I cannot write what I feel. . . . "[115]

One of the most interesting sources of material about the details of Griffis' sojourn in Fukui is his "Fukui Scrapbook" in which he assiduously compiled a vivid record of his daily life during most of 1871.[116] In it we find that a "typical" day looked something like this:

7 A.M.	Rise and make toilet (bathing twice per week and shaving three times per week) followed by breakfast.
7:30–8 A.M.	Reading Greek and devotion
8–10 A.M.	Study (usually Japanese, Physics or Chemistry)
10–12 NOON	Teaching
12–1 P.M.	Lunch and Reading
1–3 P.M.	Teaching
3–6 P.M.	Walk
6–6:30 P.M.	Supper
6:30–8 P.M.	Japanese
8–11 P.M.	Writing

Further detail can be garnered from a typical daily menu, contained in a latter to Margaret, in which his breakfast consisted of fried potatoes, "some sort of omelette and batter cake combined," plus rice and coffee. Lunch was very simple, a cup of rice or an orange and tea. The evening meal was more substantial: "a full dinner of soup, fish or fowl, rice, coffee, etc.—the etc. not being in great variety."[117] This particular meal was a special treat since his servant had "killed a cow" and as a result "about 50 dogs have been sniffing and prowling about all morning."[118] Griffis supplemented his regular diet with vegetables he and Lucy had planted in their own garden. These consisted mostly of lettuce and radishes. Griffis and Lucy envisioned a greater variety eventually gracing their table.[119]

By the end of May he had, however, settled into a comfortable domestic life which he described as "quite perfect" with a "pull bell for door and servant, regular meals in good civilized style, good furniture, mosquito netting that makes my bed room an object of delight and wonder to the Japs."[120]

In this apparently blissful life, he was still able to become worked up over an "exciting event" when a party of four Europeans passed through Fukui. After entertaining them and escorting them on their way, Griffis proudly recounted how they had been "completely and agreeably surprised to see how comfortably we were situated."[121]

With the departure of Lucy in July, 1871, Griffis' one contact with his western heritage was lost to him. He fell into increasingly lonely moods. At about the same time, his interpreter and companion, Iwabuchi, married "a blushing damsel of 15." But, Griffis prudentially added, "it must be remembered that the Japanese girls develop at least two years sooner than American or European girls."[122] This marriage, as noted earlier, took Iwabuchi away from his "close connection with me, [and] leaves me more lonely than ever."[123]

By the middle of August, his spirits were lifted by the completion of a new house which the Prince had ordered built for Griffis. However, this meant new expenses for him, and he informed Margaret on August 17, 1871 that he "must take on a new servant and be under other expenses." She was a "girl of about 17, who will wait on the table, and take care of my room specially."[124]

It is not surprising that this new situation proved to be more than young Griffis was able to handle. As early as March 28, 1871, he recognized the temptations facing a Christian man in Japan and confided to his sister Maggie that he was having doubts as to the wisdom of trying to find a position for his younger brother. Indeed, he wrote, it is "little less than madness to bring even a brother to this land of fearful temptations and no restraints."[125] Three months later, he informed Maggie that "my saddest and sorest need is for something to love, something to caress or at least some congenial soul and presence. The temptations to a lonely man here are fearful. I dare not have an idle moment."[126]

In light of these feelings, it is not surprising that young Griffis experienced a moral crisis when his acute loneliness, an attractive young woman in his house, and his sexual mores intersected during late August and early September, 1871. His ambivalence and inner turmoil can be seen in the following passage of a letter written to Margaret on September 9:

In my own household, I have made another change. The young girl . . . whom I took for a servant to wait specifically on me proved to be very faithful, diligent and pleasant in every way, anticipated my every want, and made my house almost as comfortable as a home; I liked her very much. All of which to a sometimes weary and home-sick young man must necessarily be be a strong temptation in his lonely hours. I found after two weeks, that she made too much comfort for me, and was too attractive herself. After having her [for] 11 days, I sent her away, before temptation turned into sin. . . . and now, though with less comfort and a more lonely house, I can let all my inner life be known to you without shame.[127]

Evidently he had written to Guido Verbeck in Tokyo to seek support during his difficult time, for in a letter to Griffis dated September 30, Verbeck reacted as a minister of the Dutch Reformed Church.

Do not think of *temptations!* If your religion does not hold you up, think of your parents [and] sisters, of your *future* wife. *Put* it *out of the question* . . . . Nonsense! Don't frighten a man with such mean trash! *Name, influence, respect, future, happiness, present peace, all* would be irretrievably gone: Be a true man [and] Christian. Friends far [and] near are watching you—[and] so is God—No, no, you only meant to stir me up [and] you have done it. [128]

This experience seems to have served two useful purposes for Griffis. He reminded Margaret in a letter dated December 3, that "out of weakness, make strong," and he was sure that this was the ultimate effect on his own person.[129] Finally, this incident appears to have made him determined to keep his younger brother away from Japan. He wrote, "I am sure you see now the madness, the folly of sending anyone here, but one clothed in the whole armor. . . . So, let this subject pass forever."[130]

His personal sex life was only one of the problems facing Griffis in Fukui. Financial considerations were part of his reasons for coming to Fukui, and the shortage of money plagued him throughout his sojourn in Japan. Griffis received a handsome salary in Fukui, "expressed in currency [it] is about $4,140.00 per year," he wrote Maggie, and counting a ten-percent premium since he was paid in gold, he estimated that he was making close to $4,500.00 per year.[131] This was in addition to his house, a horse, and transportation expenses from his home to Japan.[132]

Another characteristic of Griffis that now stands out in bold relief is his deep dislike of being in debt. He had borrowed money—from friends and his church—when he left America for Japan, and he longed for the day when that burden could be removed from his shoulders. The accomplishment of this goal was complicated by the very shaky financial situation of his family in Philadelphia. Willie contributed a significant portion to their support. Soon after his arrival in Japan, Griffis promised them

. . . I shall do all that I can. I shall not be stingy with my money, but I do not expect in three years to save much of it, family and home expenses, life insurance policies, debts and living here, will cost me much, and besides that I intend to [re]pay every cent of the money given me for my education, amounting in all to $2,100. No one suggested it, but I wish to be free of every bond, even those of gratitude.[133]

His correspondence with Margaret is replete with economic disagreements. She, in her letters, asking for more money and he, explaining why he could not oblige her. Beneath every explanation is his firm intention "to let nothing stand between me, and the discharging of my obligations."[134] Griffis constantly reminded his family that he understood their financial situation,

. . . but here I live on rice, fish and milk—my constant and unvarying diet, rarely giving entertainment to company, much as I desire it, for it *costs money*. . . . so I live far closer than I ever did at College, because I am determined not to wear even the fetters of gratitude.[135]

Although one can sympathize with Griffis' plight—an attractive salary, but a family with an insatiable appetite for money—there seems little doubt that he exaggerated his frugal life style, though perhaps for good reasons. His letters indicate that he spent a fair amount of money on subscriptions to newspapers and magazines, as well as receiving a substantial number of new books. In addition, he periodically ordered expensive canned meat and fruits from Yokohama and paid for his servants. Finally, he did entertain the Prince and other local officials on occasion and he seems usually to have had a number of students living with him. There is nothing to indicate that he received any room or board from these boys although that was possible.

To complicate the home situation further, young Griffis' father lost his meager job. The elder Griffis had finally obtained a position in the jewelry firm of Willie's former employer, John Carrow. After being on the job for only a short time, Carrow had to let him go. In a letter to young Griffis, Carrow assured him that "we would not send him off without cause. . . . but there was no other course left us. The risk was too great."[136]

In order to supplement the family income, Griffis tried subtly to encourage Japanese students going to Philadelphia to stay as paying boarders at his home. In describing one such conversation, Griffis informed his sister Margaret of how delicately the subject had to be approached:

I told Kinamura to do just as he found it best. I urged nothing on him. I had to talk to him through my interpreter, and I would have cut my hand off almost before I would let anyone here know that I wanted anyone to go to my house as a boarder. The Japanese have not the slightest idea of what a private boarding house or anything approaching it is. All my reputation

and influence and the great respect shown me here arises mainly from the
fact that the people and the Gov[ernment] regard me as a teacher who came
to instruct the Japanese for the love of it, and utterly aside from the money
. . . . anything pertaining to the calculation of the merchant or money-
seeker would grieve them . . . [and] injure my prestige.[137]

Although a few Japanese students did find their way to Philadelphia
and to his household, Griffis was not entirely successful in this venture.
Margaret complained to her brother about the "sponging propensities"
of the Japanese boarders, and Griffis promised to contact the boys and
to "talk pretty plainly to them."[138] He urged Margaret to "leave all this
to me, and show all kindness, give all welcome, and be all patient for
their people have been kind and grateful to your brother."[139] Gently
scolding his sister, he wrote

In kindly criticism and perfect fair play let me remark that in dealing with
those Japs, my sisters so generally gifted with race tact, showed little of it,
in allowing the Japs to get the idea that *boarders* were wanted in my home
. . . . I can't write it down point blank to my loved ones at home, but if it
were anyone else I should ask, "tell me truly, didn't it serve you right when
the Japs didn't come to board, even when invited? At any rate, did you act
very polite?[140]

Exactly what occurred after this is difficult to assess for no further
reference to the Japanese boarders are found in the available correspondence between Griffis and his elder sister. However, it is apparent from
the above that Griffis was extremely sensitive to the opinions the Japanese
held of him and his family.

GRIFFIS AS MISSIONARY

In his excellent monograph, *Christian Converts and Social Protest in Meiji
Japan,* Irwin Scheiner defines the dual tasks facing western missionaries
as "proselytizing" and acting as "both the conscious and unconscious
carriers of the American cultural, political and social traditions."[141] He
goes on to argue that "most American missionaries . . . agreed that
proselytizing must be accompanied, if not preceded, by education, and for
many this also meant the introduction of American social institutions and
political ideas."[142] He suggests that "Secular and religious aspects of the
West were so indivisible to them that Christianization assumed the
character of Westernization, and Westernization implied the necessity of
conversion to Christianity. . . . They linked Western science to Western
norms, which were directly attributable to Christianity," and they "believed that they could use Western knowledge to expose traditions to ridi-
cule at the same time as they led the students of Westernism to the logical

conclusion that Protestant Christianity stood at the base of Western development."[143]

Griffis' words in *The Mikado's Empire* support Scheiner's thesis:

Can an Asiatic despotism, based on paganism, and propped on a fiction, regenerate itself? Can Japan go on in the race she has begun? Will the mighty reforms now attempted be completed and made permanent? Can a nation appropriate the fruits of Christian civilization without its roots? I believe not. I cannot but think that unless the modern enlightened ideas of government, law, society, and the rights of the individual be adapted to a far greater extent than they have been, the people be so thoroughly educated, and a mightier spiritual force replace Shintō and Buddhism, little will be gained but a glittering veneer of material civilization. . . .

Gently, but relentlessly, Christianity is leavening the nation . . . With those forces that centre in pure Christianity, and under that almighty Providence who raises up one nation and casts down another, I cherish the firm hope that Japan will in time take and hold her equal place among the foremost nations of the world. . . .[144]

Although Griffis was not a missionary in the proselytizing sense of that word, the Board of Education of the Reformed Church of America "felt when you [Griffis] were selected for Japan that although it was not directly a licensed ordained minister's work, such Prudential guidance secured to direct it, that duty called you there [and it was] your purpose to still live [and] labor for His kingdom."[145] Although his contract with the government explicitly forbade his preaching, Griffis wrote that it "is my fervent prayer and ardent hope" that all Japanese "may be children of God, and their lives consecrated to Our Master."[146] He was especially anxious for his students to become Christians for, as he often suggested, "in a patriarchial government like Japan, the country if Christianized will be by the *rulers* [and] educated men."[147]

Griffis went about this in his usual fashion, and soon his Fukui home "became a sort of club where his students could discuss such subjects as Christian education, Christianity and Shintoism."[148] Despite this, however, prudence dictated that he not push Christianity too hard or too openly. In addition to contractual constraints, there were a substantial number of "traditionalists" who would not hesitate to cut down a Christian "barbarian" on the slightest pretext. In fact, almost a decade *after* Griffis had left Fukui in 1881, two theological students who had spent their summer preaching in Fukui received threats from a Shinto fanatic who signed himself as "Nobuakira, the Keeper of the Holy Empire." He warned them to "repent" as "we have weapons to destroy what is harmful to the country."[149]

EDWARD WARREN CLARK

Edward Clark was a Rutgers classmate of Griffis, both graduating in the
same class in 1869. Clark had gone to Europe for theological training in
Geneva, and as we have seen earlier (see page 16), Griffis and his sister
Maggie had traveled with Clark during their summer European holiday in
1869.

While at Rutgers both of these young men nourished an interest in
Japan—a country "which so lit up our imaginations . . . [and] caused our
dreams to run wild in fairy land, [and] our poetic fancies to soar to marvel-
lous heights."[150] Once Griffis arrived in Japan, he began to keep an eye
peeled for a suitable position for Clark. Clark continually reminded both
Willie and the Griffis family that he was still anxious to go to Japan. On
June 21 Griffis' mother wrote, "Mr. Clark longs to be employed in Japan
[and] he is preparing . . . for the work and says that you are leading
him."[151] A few weeks later, Willie acknowledged that "Clarkie has been
studying to go to Japan for several months past and I am afraid he will be
greatly disappointed if he don't [sic] get to Japan."[152]

Despite Griffis' pessimism over Clark being offered a position, prospects
brightened when on July 25, 1871, a messenger from Suruga arrived in
Fukui "asking for a foreign teacher from America."[153] Soon afterward,
Griffis sent Clark an offer to teach in Suruga "with a salary of $3600 per
year . . . mainly chemistry and Natural Philosophy."[154] Although
Griffis' published writings on Fukui offer a positive analysis, he wrote
to Margaret that "had I my choice seven months ago, *knowing all I do now*,
I should have gone to Suruga."[155]

In the meantime Clark had left for Japan before Griffis' offer could
reach him. Upon arriving in Yokohama, Clark informed Griffis that he
"rejoiced in the prospects that are before me." Even though "a few months
ago I anticipated going to Higo" since receiving "your letter asking me to
go to Surunga [sic], I considered [and] do consider as definite [and] decisive
. . . inasmuch as I had not previously *bound* myself to Higo or any other
place, I am expecting now to fulfill the contract which you have made for
me with Surunga [sic], [and] I am only waiting to hear from you as to when
I shall go there."[156]

Although Clark knew of the arrangements that his good friend had
made for him, few other people were informed. On October 29, Verbeck
reprimanded Griffis for his carelessness.

Mr. Clark is here; your arrangements about his going to Suruga, or rather,
their precise nature [and] conditions are not very clear [and] tangible to me,
nor to any one else I know, Mr. Clark not excepted. . . . the Minister of
Foreign Affairs says that so far no application has been made to his Depart-

ment, as by law must be done first, in regard to a foreigner's going to that province. . . . The Fukui officers say they know nothing of it. If worst comes to worst, I can keep him here. In the meantime, let us please know how matters stand, [and] forward any papers about Mr. C.'s being *entitled* to a position in Suruga.[157]

An officer from Suruga visited Griffis on November 6 to work out the contractual details of Clark's employment. It seems unlikely that Verbeck's letter had arrived in Griffis' hands before this meeting, but if it had, there is nothing in Griffis' diary or correspondence to indicate it. In a letter to his sister, written the same day, Griffis revealed that the proposed contract contained "a clause saying that [Clark] must teach nothing concerning religion—a clause I was not surprised to see, yet it disgusted me very much, and I was about to demand its rejection, but a moment's reflection showed me that if I did; the officer would immediately suspect him to be a missionary and break off all further negotiations." He rationalized this action further by writing that "if Clarkie did not go there, some indifferent or libertine would most probably get there, and Our Master's cause suffer harm."[158]

He explained that the Japanese did not want missionaries because "They look on Christianity with the same feelings that we look on heathenism; and it is only by the gradual introduction of our Christian civilization, that we can hope to introduce the religion that have made the barbarian Anglo-Saxons what they are now."[159]

Clark's reaction to the article forbidding the teaching of religion and to Griffis' tacit support of it was both negative and swift. With tongue in cheek, but yet not allowing it to mask his serious disagreement with Griffis, he twitted his long-time friend when he wrote,

Is it possible that *Wm. E. Griffis* (strong in his faith [and] Christian enthusiasm [and] firm in doing *right* notwithstanding the consequences,) could yet so far forget himself as to give me the advice that he did in that note? Is it possible, that *he* could advise a Christian man to bind himself to go for *three years* among a heathen people, [and] yet to hold his tongue on the Christian religion! I know that this can hardly be what you intended to say; [and] yet I must say it seems difficult to put any other construction on your words. You politely [and] kindly try to *smooth over* the passage in the contract, on which you think . . . that might possibily stumble . . . on the old principle of "Do evil that good may come," you lead me to think that I had better not make a fuss under the circumstances with "Imperial Law."[160]

To the surprise of Griffis and many of the Americans in Tokyo, the Japanese authorities conceded to Clark's point. The Japanese asked Clark to rewrite the contract to suit him and it was "just after I had written the last English copy of the contract . . . and just after all official business was finished, that your letter came, telling me not to make a fuss. *Oh, my poor boy*!!!"[161] However, Clark's scolding was tempered by a hint that Griffis might be destined for a post in Tokyo. "I find," Clark confided, "there is some little thought of getting a gentleman to the Kaiseijo [a school for the study of western sciences] by the name of Wm. E. Griffis. (!) Please don't tell anybody. . . . They say it might now be done, if Mr. Griffis is willing; I don't know but that it might be well for all parties concerned. However, so far it is only *talk*."[162]

How much effect this news had on Griffis is difficult to prove, but it can be shown that his letters and diary entries increasingly reflect his desire to leave Fukui for the capital.

THE END OF FEUDALISM IN FUKUI

Jacob Burckhardt, writing in another context, once observed that "The historical process is suddenly accelerated in terrifying fashion. Developments which otherwise take centuries seem to flit by like phantoms in months or weeks, and are fulfilled."[163] Certainly, the period that William Elliot Griffis lived in Fukui fits this description nicely. Griffis was proud to have "lived at Fukui in the far interior, within what, in 1871, was still the pulsing body of feudalism, with its ideals and century-old routine of daily custom, virtually unchanged."[164] He was, indeed, an eyewitness to the end of Japan's feudal institutions and the beginners of her transformation to modernity. One source referred to him, in 1888, as "the only American living that has made the interior of Japan his residence and has seen the feudal system there in operation."[165]

With the accession of the Emperor Meiji to the throne in 1868, one of the major problems facing the new government was the replacement of the old Tokugawa feudal structure with a centralized government that could meet the challenges of the new era. This revolutionary transformation, however, was one that had to be approached with caution, and so the rulers moved slowly and in several stages. Wisely, they made use of the talents of a large number of men who had exercised power under the old regime.

One of the first major steps occurred in 1869 when the feudal lords of Satsuma, Chōshū, Hizen, and Tosa voluntarily returned their domains to the authority of the new emperor. In the same year, class-based restrictions on professional employment were removed, and a year later commoners were, for the first time, permitted to acquire family names.

Griffis' descriptions of feudal life are fascinating. He was one of the handful of westerners who experienced it at firsthand and one of the still fewer observers who recorded it for posterity.

Of medievalism and feudalism, in their picturesque quaintness and their repulsive horrors, I saw much. At the frontier of each fief, or province, were the barrier gates and guard houses kept by armed men. Long before coming to one of them, we could see the three long handled black iron hooks used to keep fighting men further than sword distance. The rank and the ball of barbed hooks were especially effective against drunken fellows in flowing garments, together with the iron yoke to pin, by the neck, to the earth. Often in a single day of travel, on passing from one fief to another, I had to show my passport and change my paper money from three to five times, and prove authorization before being allowed to pass these dividing lines of feudalism. On my first entrance-journey, each one of my porters, some forty or so, engaged to transport the American teacher's luggage and belongings . . . carried at his girdle the wooden ticket or kitte, branded with his name and place of abode. The mysterious power, the government . . . was supposed to be able to tell where every man or woman in the empire had been during the previous twenty-four hours.[166]

While Griffis busied himself with his everyday duties and his home problems, vast national changes were in process throughout Japan. Although even his earliest diary entries and correspondence indicated that he sensed at least some of the drama of a nation in flux, even he seemed not to have understood the magnitude and meaning of those changes. In *The Mikado's Empire* he recounted that the Prince's return from Tokyo on July 11, 1871 suggested that "something more is in the political wind . . . What can it be? Some event is casting its shadow before."[167] A careful examination of the manuscript of his diary, however, uncovers nothing remotely resembling this prescience. The diary entry for July 11, referring only to his daily duties at school and his personal activities, varies little from any other entry.[168] His diary entry for July 18, one week later, and his account of the events of that date in *The Mikado's Empire,* however, are relatively parallel. His diary records the decision of the Imperial Government "dispensing with officers and reducing incomes—excitement among thousands of families all over Japan . . . [and] in the school."[169] Looking back on the day in *The Mikado's Empire,* he wrote with much more detail and a great deal more dramatic effect:

The thunder-bolt has fallen! The political earthquake has shaken Japan to its centre. . . . Intense excitement reigns in the homes of the samurai of the city to-day. I hear that some of them are threatening to kill Mitsuoka, who receives income for meritorious service in 1868, and who has long been the exponent of reform and national progress in Fukui.

At ten o'clock this morning, a messenger from Tokio arrived at the *hancho* [han headquarters]. Suddenly there was a commotion in the school. All the native teachers and officials were summoned to the directors' room. I saw them a few minutes afterward. Pale faces and excited nerves were in the majority. The manner in which some of them strode to the door, thrust their swords into their belts, stepped into their clogs, and set off with flowing garments and silk coat-tails flapping to the leeward, was quite theatrical, and just like the pictures in Japanese books.[170]

Strangely enough, in a letter to his confidant Margaret which he began on July 12 and finished on July 22, he makes absolutely no mention of the events which he recounts in his book. All the more puzzling then, are his comments in *The Mikado's Empire* which describe his pleasure at the reduction of Fukui officers from 500 to a mere 70 and the drastic reduction of his own school and personal staffs.

> The change affects me for the better. Hitherto the school directorate consisted of fourteen officers. "With too many sailors, the boat runs up a hill." There are now only *four*. An official from the *han-chō* waited upon me to announce that my four guards and eight gate-keepers are dismissed from office. I shall henceforth have but two gate-keepers. . . . Japan's greatest curse for ages have been an excess of officials and lazy rice-eaters who do not work. Sinbad has shaken off the Old Man of the Sea. Hurra [sic] for the New Japan![171]

The same kind of discrepancies are found between Griffis' official diary entries and the revised entries found in *The Mikado's Empire* for a number of dates.

Soon after these events, Tokyo decreed the end of the *han* and the movement of the old feudal lords from their domains to the capital. This decision shattered the gains that had been made in Fukui and accelerated the process of driving the best young minds from the provinces.[172]

In any event, the exodus of students from Fukui to overseas or to the capital, which had begun to increase in the spring of 1871, turned into a torrent after the abolition of feudalism. In May of 1871 Griffis was asked to appoint two Fukui students to study in the West after an initial course of study in the capital. This incident is important in another way for it illustrated Griffis' sense of fairness and the importance of abiding by decisions already made. The individual "most fitted" for such an appointment was Griffis' assistant, Nakano, "a bright young fellow of 19, [who] had been looking for such an appointment." Griffis did not nominate him, however, because he had promised Griffis, a few weeks earlier, "to give up the idea, if I would take him for my assistant."[173] Griffis finally found two young men qualified for the responsibility, and they accepted the opportunity.

Gradually, more and more of Griffis' students began to leave Fukui on their own account for Tokyo. In mid-July, for example, he complained to Maggie that "Kinoshita, one of my best scholars, leaves Fukuwi to go to Yokohama . . . to remain several years and perhaps permanently. He will learn some trade or business there."[174] By the middle of September, "No less than six students left the school this week," but Griffis could not bring himself to blame them too much. "I do not wonder," he informed Maggie, "at anyone leaving their dull provincial city for the gay capital or the new and lively Yokohama."[175] What bothered him about this exodus of students was that "the grown-up men are liable . . . to break off study and go [into] business." Griffis therefore wrote, "I care more for, and place my hopes on the smaller boys, many of them bright and quick."[176]

On October 28, Griffis complained, "There seems to be a perpetual exodus to Yedo" and even several of the civil servants "have been called to Yedo."[177] A month later, he wrote Margaret, "At least *700 men* have made exodus from Fukui alone, since March, the retired prince, all the former chief officers and scores of the most talented young men have gone. . . ."[178] This was not a completely negative trend, for he wrote,

> Of course I have lost some good scholars, but in the main, have improved and condensed rather than suffered loss, besides, in the developments of the future, it is better . . . to have my chief friends, and those I most influenced . . . go to the Imperial Government, as high officers, instead of their being petty local dignitaries.[179]

Despite this, Griffis was not happy with the situation. He described his last meeting with the Prince in a letter to his sister,

> The Prince leaves for Tokio, early tomorrow morning [October 2]. He will never again, most probably return to Fukuwi. . . . It is a new era for Japan, destined to be the grandest of her history. . . . Yet there is always sadness, even though I am here for the very purpose of laying, or helping to lay the foundation of modern civilization on the ruins of the old past.[180]

Prior to leaving Fukui for the last time, the Prince was bid farewell in an impressive ceremony which Griffis recorded in *The Mikado's Empire*.

> I went over to the main hall at nine o'clock. I shall never forget the impressive scene . . . Arranged in order or rank, each in his starched robes of ceremony, with shaven-crown, and gunhammer top-knot, with hands clasped on the hilt of his sword resting upright before him as he sat on his knees, were the three thousand samurai of the Fukui clan . . . . It was more than a farewell to their feudal lord. It was the solemn burial of the institutions under which their fathers had lived for seven hundred years.[181]

Griffis was the only foreigner to witness this event, and he was later honored by the Prince with a thirty-minute visit to his home to bid him farewell. Griffis confessed that "I am feeling more than usually lonely today."[182]

The loneliness that Griffis felt was both real and understandable. While his first few months in Fukui had been exciting and had opened up to him an exotic world which his fellow Americans at home were anxious to hear about, the vast changes which were sweeping Japan had, in a very real sense, made Fukui obsolete. The abolition of the *han* accelerated the already significant "brain drain" to Yokohama and Tokyo. In addition, the loss of Mr. Lucy several months earlier had robbed Griffis of western companionship, and the departure of the Prince for Tokyo led him to conclude that "the glory of Fukuwi as well as many another province has departed."[183]

In order to follow this "glory," Griffis began to set in motion the events that would lead to his appointment in Tokyo. It is important to remember, however, that the foundation of Griffis' success as a popular interpreter of Japan to American audiences was based more on his brief tenure in Fukui than on his longer term in the capital. As one of the very few westerners who had experienced the remnants of Japanese feudalism firsthand, Griffis promoted this aspect of his life with great skill. When Fukui's mine of raw materials began to thin, Griffis characteristically opted for others that held more promise.

NOTES

1. WEG to Miss Bella Swan, February 26, 1924, GCRUL.
2. Griffis, *The Mikado's Empire*, p. 423.
3. Pat Barr, *The Deer Cry Pavilion: The Story of Westerners in Japan, 1868–1905* (New York: Harcourt, Brace & World, 1968), p. 50. In a letter dated April 2, 1871, Griffis told his sister Maggie that Fukui's population was between 85,000 and 100,000 people. Yazaki Takeo, in his useful study, *Social Change and the City in Japan* (San Francisco: Japan Publications, 1968), estimated Fukui's population at 27,000 in 1878, and 43,000 in 1897. It appears, therefore, that Griffis' figure of 85,000–100,000 is probably inflated and the actual population of Fukui in 1871 was somewhere between Barr's 12,000 and Yazaki's 27,000.
4. WEG to MCG, April 2, 1871, GCRUL.
5. Griffis, *The Mikado's Empire*, p. 430.
6. Griffis, *The Mikado's Empire*, p. 430.
7. Griffis, *The Mikado's Empire*, p. 430.
8. Griffis, "In the Heart of Japan," n. p.
9. Griffis, "Japan at the Time of Townsend Harris," p. 14.
10. George M. Wilson, "The Bakumatsu Intellectual in Action: Hashimoto Sanai in the Political Crisis of 1858," in Albert Craig and Donald Shively, *Personality in Japanese History* (Berkeley and Los Angeles: University of California Press, 1970), p. 241; hereafter cited as Wilson, "The Bakumatsu Intellectual."
11. Sansom, *The Western World and Japan*, p. 303.
12. Jansen, *Sakamoto Ryōma*, p. 408.

13. William Elliot Griffis, *The Mikado: Institution and Person; A Study of the Internal Political Forces of Japan* (Princeton, N.J.: Princeton University Press, 1915), p. 68; hereafter cited as Griffis, *The Mikado, Institution and Person.*

14. Sansom, *The Western World and Japan*, pp. 266–267.

15. Ronald P. Dore, *Education in Tokugawa Japan* (Berkeley and Los Angeles: University of California Press, 1965), p. 265.

16. Kanai Madoka, "Fukui, the Domain of a Tokugawa Collateral *Daimyō:* Its Tradition and Transition" (paper presented at the Rutgers-Japan Conference, Rutgers, the State University, April, 1967), n. p. I am indebted to Dr. Shiro Amioka, Professor of Philosophy of Education, University of Hawaii, and former State of Hawaii Superintendent of Education, for providing me with access to this paper.

17. Wilson, "The Bakumatsu Intellectual," p. 237.

18. Griffis, *The Mikado: Institution and Person*, p. 69.

19. Quoted in Motoyama Yukihiko, "The Education Policy of Fukui Han and William Elliot Griffis" (paper presented at the Rutgers-Japan Conference, Rutgers, the State University, April, 1967). I am also indebted to Dr. Shiro Amioka for access to this reference.

20. Motoyama, "The Education Policy of Fukui Han and William Elliot Griffis."

21. Motoyama, "The Education Policy of Fukui Han and William Elliot Griffis."

22. Griffis, *The Mikado's Empire*, p. 424.

23. WEG to MCG, April 2, 1871, GCRUL.

24. WEG to MCG, March 9, 1871, GCRUL.

25. WEG to MCG, March 9, 1871, GCRUL.

26. WEG to MCG, March 9, 1871, GCRUL.

27. WEG to MCG, March 9, 1871, GCRUL.

28. Griffis, "Diary," March 4, 1871, GCRUL.

29. Griffis, *The Mikado's Empire*, p. 428.

30. WEG to MCG, April 9, 1871, GCRUL.

31. Griffis, *The Mikado's Empire*, p. 431.

32. William Elliot Griffis, "The New World of Books in Japan," *Critic* (August, 1905): 128–133.

33. Griffis, *The Mikado's Empire*, pp. 433–434.

34. Griffis, "Diary," March 7, 1871, GCRUL.

35. WEG to MCG, March 23, 1871, GCRUL.

36. WEG to MCG, July 22, 1871, GCRUL.

37. Griffis, *The Mikado's Empire*, p. 401.

38. Bush, 77 *Samurai*, pp. 184–185.

39. Griffis, *The Mikado's Empire*, p. 401.

40. Griffis, *The Mikado's Empire*, p. 401.

41. Griffis, *The Mikado's Empire*, pp. 401–402.

42. WEG to MCG, August 13, 1871, GCRUL.

43. WEG to MCG, March 9, 1781, GCRUL.

44. WEG to MCG, March 9, 1871, GCRUL.

45. WEG to MCG, March 9, 1871, GCRUL.

46. WEG to MCG, March 12, 1871, GCRUL.

47. WEG to MCG, March 26, 1871, GCRUL.

48. WEG to MCG, March 26, 1871, GCRUL.

49. WEG to MCG, July 15, 1871, GCRUL.

50.   WEG to MCG, March 26, 1871, GCRUL.
51.   WEG to MCG, March 12, 1871, GCRUL. The use of the word "Jap" in the
        nineteenth century had none of the racial connotations that its use has today;
        it was simply a descriptive term.
52.   WEG to MCG, July 5, 1871, GCRUL.
53.   WEG to MCG, May 12, 1871, GCRUL.
54.   WEG to MCG, June 5, 1871, GCRUL.
55.   WEG to MCG, July 5, 1871, GCRUL.
56.   John Black, *Young Japan: Yokohama and Yedo; A Narrative of the Settlement
        and the City from the Signing of the Treaties in 1858, to the Closing of the Year
        1879, with a Glance at the Progress of Japan during a Period of Twenty-one
        Years,* 2 vols. (Yokohama: Kelly & Co., 1883), 2: 425.
57.   WEG to the Editor of *Scientific American,* July 18, 1872, quoted in Helbig,
        "William Elliot Griffis: Entrepreneur," pp. 57–58.
58.   Hazel Jones, "The Meiji Government and Foreign Employees, 1868–1900"
        (Ph.D. dissertation, University of Michigan, 1967).
59.   Hazel Jones, "The Griffis Thesis and Meiji Policy Toward Employment of
        Foreigners" (paper presented at the Rutgers-Japan Conference, Rutgers, the
        State University, April, 1967), pp. 4–5; hereafter cited as Jones, "The Griffis
        Thesis."
60.   Jones, "The Griffis Thesis," pp. 3–4.
61.   Jones, "The Griffis Thesis," pp. 40–41.
62.   Nakamura Takeshi, "The Contribution of Foreigners," *Journal of World
        History* 9, no. 2 (1965); 295–305.
63.   Nakamura, "The Contribution of Foreigners," p. 294.
64.   Helbig, "William Elliot Griffis: Entrepreneur," p. 56.
65.   WEG to MCG, March 9, 1871, GCRUL.
66.   William Elliot Griffis, "Introduction of Chemistry into Japan: An Apprecia-
        tion of the Service of Charles William Eliot as a Chemist," *Chemical Age,*
        April 17, 1924, n. p.; hereafter cited as Griffis, "Introduction of Chemistry."
67.   Griffis, "Introduction of Chemistry."
68.   WEG to MCG, April 2, 1871, GCRUL
69.   WEG to MCG, March 28, 1871, GCRUL.
70.   WEG to *New York Tribune,* September 4, 1904.
71.   William Elliot Griffis, "Pioneering in Chemistry in Japan," *Industrial and
        Engineering Chemistry* 16, no. 11 (1924): 1165, quoted in Helbig, "William
        Elliot Griffis: Entrepreneur," p. 63.
72.   Griffis, "Diary," March 23, 1871, GCRUL.
73.   Helbig, "William Elliot Griffis: Entrepreneur," p. 58.
74.   "William Elliot Griffis: Entrepreneur," p. 59.
75.   WEG to MCG, June 5, 1871, GCRUL.
76.   WEG to MCG, September 3, 1871, GCRUL.
77.   WEG to MCG, September 3, 1871, GCRUL.
78.   Griffis, "Introduction of Chemistry," n. p., quoted in Helbig, "William Elliot
        Griffis: Entrepreneur," p. 62.
79   WEG to MCG, March 9, 1871, GCRUL.
80.   Griffis, "Introduction of Chemistry," n. p.
81.   Schwantes, *Japanese and Americans,* p. 188.
82.   WEG to MCG, March 12, 1871, GCRUL.

83.   Edward W. Clark to WEG, October 17, 1871, GCRUL, quoted in Clark, *Life and Adventure in Japan*, p. 139.
84.   WEG to MCG, August 17, 1871, GCRUL.
85.   WEG to MCG, August 7, 1871, GCRUL.
86.   WEG to MCG, April 28, 1871, GCRUL.
87.   WEG to MCG, April 10, 1871, GCRUL.
88.   WEG to MCG, June 18, 1871, GCRUL.
89.   WEG to MCG, September 17, 1871, GCRUL.
90.   Helbig, "William Elliot Griffis: Entrepreneur," p. 64.
91.   William Elliot Griffis, "Education in Japan," *The College Courant*, May 16, 1874, n. p.
92.   Griffis, "Education in Japan."
93.   Griffis, "Education in Japan."
94.   WEG to MCG, September 9, 1871 and December 3, 1871, GCRUL.
95.   Helbig, "William Elliot Griffis: Entrepreneur," p. 63.
96.   William Elliot Griffis, "Primary School and Elementary Teaching," in Griffis, "Scrapbook," p. 64, GCRUL.
97.   Griffis, "Primary School and Elementary Teaching."
98.   WEG to MCG, July 5, 1871, GCRUL.
99.   WEG to MCG, July 5, 1871, GCRUL.
100. WEG to MCG, September 9, 1871, GCRUL.
101. Griffis, *The Mikado's Empire*, p. 434.
102. Griffis, "Education in Japan."
103. WEG to MCG, November 1, 1871, GCRUL.
104. WEG to MCG, March 23, 1871, GCRUL.
105. WEG to MCG, March 23, 1871, GCRUL.
106. Griffis, *The Mikado's Empire*, p. 429.
107. Griffis, *The Mikado's Empire* pp. 439–440.
108. Griffis, *The Mikado's Empire*, pp. 439–440.
109. Griffis, "Diary," March 15, 1871, GCRUL.
110. WEG to MCG, April 2, 1871, GCRUL.
111. WEG to MCG, March 23, 1871, GCRUL.
112. WEG to MCG, March 23, 1871, GCRUL.
113. WEG to MCG, April 28, 1871, GCRUL.
114. WEG to MCG, May 12, 1871, GCRUL.
115. WEG to MCG, May 12, 1871, GCRUL.
116. Griffis, "Fukui Scrapbook," p. 16.
117. WEG to MCG, December 3, 1871, GCRUL.
118. WEG to MCG, December 3, 1871, GCRUL.
119. WEG to MCG, June 10, 1871, GCRUL.
120. WEG to MCG, May 28, 1871, GCRUL.
121. WEG to MCG, April 28, 1871, GCRUL.
122. WEG to MCG, August 17, 1871, GCRUL.
123. WEG to MCG, August 18, 1871, GCRUL.
124. WEG to MCG, August 17, 1871, GCRUL.
125. WEG to MCG, March 28, 1871, GCRUL.
126. WEG to MCG, June 25, 1871, GCRUL.
127. WEG to MCG, September 9, 1871, GCRUL.
128. Guido Verbeck to WEG, September 30, 1871, GCRUL.

129. WEG to MCG, December 3, 1871, GCRUL.
130. WEG to MCG, December 3, 1871, GCRUL.
131. WEG to MCG, November 19, 1871, GCRUL.
132. Schwantes, *Japanese and Americans*, p. 188.
133. WEG to MCG, March 26, 1871, GCRUL.
134. WEG to MCG, July 5, 1871, GCRUL.
135. WEG to MCG, July 5, 1871, GCRUL.
136. W. E. Carrow to WEG, November 11, 1871, GCRUL.
137. WEG to MCG, October 28, 1871, GCRUL.
138. WEG to MCG, October 28, 1871, GCRUL.
139. WEG to MCG, October 28, 1871, GCRUL.
140. WEG to MCG, October 28, 1871, GCRUL.
141. (Berkeley and Los Angeles: University of California Press, 1970), p. 13; hereafter cited as Scheiner, *Christian Converts*.
142. Scheiner, *Christian Converts*, p. 14.
143. Scheiner, *Christian Converts*, p. 14.
144. Griffis, *The Mikado's Empire*, p. 578.
145. John S. Lee to WEG, October 31, 1871, GCRUL.
146. WEG to MCG, April 28, 1871, GCRUL.
147. WEG to MCG, May 28, 1871, GCRUL.
148. Yamamoto Masaya, "Image Makers of Japan: A Case Study in the Impact of the American Protestant Foreign Missionary Movement, 1859–1905" (Ph.D. dissertation, Ohio State University, 1967), p. 127.
149. Otis Carey, *A History of Christianity in Japan*, 2 vols. (New York: Fleming L. Revell, 1909), 1: 155.
150. Edward W. Clark to WEG, October 17, 1871, GCRUL.
151. Anna Marie Griffis to WEG, June 21, 1871, GCRUL.
152. WEG to MCG, July 5, 1871, GCRUL.
153. Griffis, "Diary," July 25, 1871, GCRUL.
154. WEG to Edward W. Clark, August 4, 1871, GCRUL.
155. WEG to MCG, August 20, 1871, GCRUL.
156. Edward W. Clark to WEG, October 26, 1871, GCRUL.
157. Guido Verbeck to WEG, October 29, 1871, GCRUL.
158. WEG to MCG, November 6, 1871, GCRUL.
159. WEG to MCG, November 6, 1871, GCRUL.
160. Edward W. Clark to WEG, November 24, 1871, GCRUL.
161. Edward W. Clark to WEG, November 24, 1871, GCRUL.
162. Edward W. Clark to WEG, November 24, 1871, GCRUL.
163. Quoted in Kenneth B. Pyle, *The New Generation in Meiji Japan: Problems of Cultural Identity, 1885–1895* (Stanford, Calif.: Stanford University Press, 1969), p. 1.
164. William Elliot Griffis, *Some of Japan's Contributions to Civilization, Direct and Indirect* (New York: Japan Society Pamphlet, 1928), p. 39.
165. "William Elliot Griffis," *Appleton's Cyclopaedia of American Biography*, 1st ed., 7: 765.
166. William Elliot Griffis, *Townsend Harris, First American Envoy to Japan* (Boston: Houghton, Mifflin & Company, 1895), p. 162.
167. Griffis, *The Mikado's Empire*, p. 525.
168. Griffis, "Diary," July 11, 1871, GCRUL.
169. Griffis, "Diary," July 18, 1871, GCRUL.

170.   Griffis, *The Mikado's Empire*, p. 526.
171.   Griffis, *The Mikado's Empire*, p. 526.
172.   Schwantes, *Japanese and Americans*, p. 156.
173.   WEG to MCG, May 17, 1871, GCRUL.
174.   WEG to MCG, July 15, 1871, GCRUL.
175.   WEG to MCG, September 9, 1871, GCRUL.
176.   WEG to MCG, September 9, 1871, GCRUL.
177.   WEG to MCG, September 9, 1871, GCRUL.
178.   WEG to MCG, November 26, 1871, GCRUL
179.   WEG to MCG, November 26, 1871, GCRUL.
180.   WEG to MCG, October 1, 1871, GCRUL.
181.   P. 534.
182.   WEG to MCG, October 1, 1871, GCRUL.
183.   WEG to MCG, November 26, 1871, GCRUL.

Chapter 4

Griffis In Tokyo, 1872–1874

FINAL DAYS IN FUKUI

Years after the fact Griffis wrote, "On the breaking up of the feudal system, I was called by the Department of Education to organize a polytechnic school in Tokio."[1] Griffis understandably neglected to reveal the extent to which he lobbied from Fukui to gain a position in the increasingly cosmopolitan capital. His yearnings for an assignment in Tokyo multiplied as more and more of his students fled the interior and journeyed to Tokyo to seek their futures. This phenomenon sharpened his own sense of loneliness, and on October 1, 1871, Griffis wrote to Maggie describing the last dinner he shared with the Prince before that ruler's final departure to the capital and confessed that "I shall be more lonely than ever" with Matsudaira gone to Tokyo.[2] Griffis clearly perceived the significance of this ultimate shift of power from the feudal fiefs to the central government in Tokyo when he informed Maggie,

> It is a new era for Japan, destined to be the grandest of her history . . . hereafter Japan will live and act as a unit, and will realize the truth of the old maxim, in union there is strength. Yet there is always sadness, even though I am here for the very purpose of laying, or helping to lay the foundations of modern civilization on the ruins of the old past.[3]

Griffis knew beyond a shadow of a doubt that this shift of power to Tokyo negated the advantages that living and working in feudal Fukui had given him in terms of future materials for his writing. The "action" was now in the capital, and Griffis realized that Tokyo's importance would continue to increase as centralization became greater. With this vision of the future, the allure of Tokyo was more than Griffis could resist.

It appears that soon after Matsudaira's departure from Fukui, Griffis "addressed a communication to the Minister of Public Instruction in Tokio, urging the establishment of a polytechnic school."[4] In a letter dated November 26, Griffis' old college friend, Edward Warren Clark, hinted that Reverend Guido Verbeck was seriously considering bringing Griffis to Tokyo.[5] Although Griffis did not mention to Maggie his proposal for the establishment of a technical school in Tokyo, he did tell her that he had written to one or two high officers" in the capital "relative to a National system of education providing for the first and greatest educational need of Japan—good teachers. I have suggested that six or eight National *Normal* Schools be established."[6] In making these overtures, Griffis insisted that "my contract is binding on the Gov[ernment] here," but he seems to have overlooked the other side of the coin—that is, his contract was also "binding" on him.[7] Despite this reality, he suggested to Maggie, "a higher position [in Tokyo] may be in store for me."[8] To further confuse the issue, Griffis revealed,

> I know I am highly appreciated by the men of Fukuwi, and am more than willing to stay here, patiently and laboriously training the young men of Fukuwi. In a few weeks I shall choose out ten of the brightest of my advanced class, given them special lessons in chem[istry] with practical experimenting by each one, and thus in time send forth ten . . . good teachers.[9]

As he waited for a response from Tokyo answering his queries and suggestions, Griffis continued his busy Fukui schedule in addition to beginning a serious study of the Japanese language. Admitting that "since I came to Japan, I had done almost nothing at [sic] the language," because of a busy schedule and several extremely competent and congenial translators, he wrote, "I have resolved to go manfully at the language [and] have trained my ears to distinguish [and] my brain to think in Japanese, so . . . that my progress is fairly good."[10] The evidence available indicates that Griffis was able to secure a fairly good working knowledge of spoken Japanese, but his reading ability was minimal. Griffis recounted a story, in his biography of the American missionary James Hepburn, of how he and Hepburn were visiting a Japanese temple one day, and Hepburn "tried several times to get from a group of soldiers standing, nearby, an explanation of something . . . which he wished to know about." Since the soldiers did not understand Hepburn's polite level of usage, they were unable to understand the request, so Griffis "put the question to the soldiers in a dialect most familiar to me and to them, and received so prompt an explanation that both [Griffis and Verbeck] had a good laugh together."[11]

Keeping busy offered small consolation, however, and Griffis continued
to long for a change. Many of his letters home reflected this theme, and he
often referred to his students' seemingly "perpetual exodus to Yedo."[12]
It was at this point that he hit upon an alternative plan of relieving his
own sense of isolation. He informed Maggie, "female education is being
eagerly discussed in Yedo," and "I learn that 3 ladies have been appointed
to teach Jap girls," and a job for her *might* "loom up in the distance."[13]
Starting with this letter, he constantly urged his sister to be ready to come
to Japan upon short notice. Several months later Griffis brought her to
Japan to seek employment.

Griffis kept busy. But meaning drained from his work. Events seemed to
be passing him by as long as he remained in Fukui. In late November
1871, he complained,

> Japan is rapidly changing. . . . With the destruction of the Provincial
> Governments, the abdication of all the princes, the consequent centraliza-
> tion of all the talent and energy of the people on the great cities . . . the
> glory of Fukuwi as well as of many another province has departed.[14]

A few days later he reiterated these points, and added, "no man can as yet
forsee [sic] the consequences of these changes. I believe [that] after a while
however, the Imperial Government will establish a National System of
education for all classes."[15] Some of the first fruits of centralization were
already becoming apparent; Griffis, for example, realized that his "salary
is not paid by Fukuwi Han, which no longer exists, but is actually paid by
the Imperial Government."[16] To further confirm this shift, Griffis wrote
with approval to Maggie that "A messenger from [Tokyo] arrived last
week bearing a decree that all the local military schools and organizations
were disbanded and hereafter all officers were to be appointed from Yedo
and everything centre there. It is very hard for you to understand or me to
describe the state of things, but you may safely imagine all the results
flowing from the entire dissolution of a collection of feudal principalities,
and the establishment of a strong central imperialism. I hope and believe
it will be for the lasting benefit of Japan."[17]

The approaching Christmas season, however, turned Griffis' thoughts
to other things. His students and Japanese friends, it appears, were fasci-
nated by this Christian holiday, and were "seized with a sudden Christmas
infection."[18] Griffis spent his first Christmas in Japan explaining the
holiday to the Japanese. In a letter written on Christmas Eve, 1871, Griffis
recounted how he told the young Japanese boys about hanging up their
stockings the night before Christmas, and after they went to bed, Griffis
"armed with lump sugar, lozenges, raisins, currants, writing paper,
pencils, pens, small jars of jams, toys, small pieces of money . . . filled

[their stockings] to oversticking [*sic*] out."[19] On Christmas morning Griffis taught until 10:30 A.M. and gave the boys the remainder of the day as a holiday. He invited all of his students, colleagues and school officials to visit him and upwards of seventy showed up.

> Everybody seemed happy and merry. I had unlimited quantities of chocolate and coffee made, a large box of soda biscuit, plenty of Japanese cake, etc. Most of them had never before tasted either drink, so they tried both, and I kept their cups full. . . . The American flag . . . was out in full glory and attracted much attention. Several strangers dropped in to see what was going on, and they were also seized, dragged in, coffeed, caked and Happy Christmased. It was really curious to have the name of Jesus blasphemed and outlawed on the Gov[ernment] Kosats [*Kosatsu*—"edict boards"], and a festival in his honor held in the same city. Of course, they inquired what the observance was for, and probably it was a new idea for many to know that any good thing came out of the *Yasou* [Jesus].[20]

With the end of the holiday season, Griffis began to worry once more about his own future. Finally, on January 10, 1872, several long awaited letters from the capital arrived, and he happily informed Maggie,

> Letters came from Yedo to-day, deciding a matter which had been in abeyance for several weeks of which I had said nothing in my letters to you, waiting until some definite decision had been made. That decision is, by invitation of the Minister of Education and at the urgent desire of Mr. Verbeck, I shall go to Yedo. Let me explain. A few months ago, I wrote to the Department of Education, urging them to adopt a National System of Education, and the establishment of several Polytechnic or Scientific schools in various parts of the country. Clarkie hinted in a letter Nov. 26 that Mr. Verbeck wanted me in Yedo. On the same day, I was called to the Gov't. office and informed that the Dept. of Education in Yedo had sent to Fukuwi, ordering them to transfer me to Fukuwi [*sic*, Yedo], but the Echizen officers had so earnestly remonstrated and wished to keep me, that all that was needed to keep the Fukuwi school in prosperity was my cordial assent to remain in Fukuwi. I told them I should consult with my best friend in Japan, and leave the decision to him. I wrote to Mr. Verbeck, stating the whole matter, and telling him, that if the call were repeated, I should gladly come to Yedo.[21]

While the question of his leaving Fukui for the capital was an abstraction, Griffis could claim on October 1, "I know I am highly appreciated by the men of Fukuwi, and *am more than willing to stay here*, patiently and laboriously training the young men of Fukuwi."[22] When the question became a concrete choice for Griffis to make, however, he seems to have forgotten his rhetoric only three months old. This contradiction evidently bothered him since he ostensibly declined to make the final decision himself, leaving it to Verbeck whom one suspects Griffis expected to reissue the original offer. In any event he related to Maggie,

> To-day the letter came, one from Mitsōka [Mitsuoka; later mayor of Tokyo] informing me that the first Polytechnic School would be established in Yedo very soon, and the Department wished me in Tokio to consult, in reference to the plans suggested in my letter. Mr. Verbeck's letter contained a request from the Minister of Education that I should come to Yedo, to fill the Professorship of Chem[istry] and Nat[ural] Phil[osophy] in the new Polytechnic School in Yedo, salary the same as in Fukui. Mr. Verbeck urging me to come soon, by all means.[23]

The Fukui officials, however, were not about to let their foreign teacher exit so easily. Murata Ujihisa, the chief school officer in Fukui whom Griffis described as "determined and strong-willed,"[24] refused to acquiesce to Griffis' departure. The reason for this, Griffis was convinced, was based on "the very fact that I had worked hard day and night, and the laboratory and classes here are in such good condition and progress."[25]

Griffis, on the other hand, was just as determined to leave for the capital. Both his isolation from "civilization" and his feeling that he was far removed from the important events of the day led him to complain,

> For over six months I have not seen one of my own race. The tax on the nervous system of being isolated, looked at as a stranger and a curiosity, made the target of so many eyes, and the constant friction and chafing of one Caucasian against a multitude of sharp angles of an Asiatic civilization, as represented by servants, petty officials, and ignorant people, and the more delicate work of polite fencing with intellectual rapiers against cultured men educated under other systems of morals and ideas; the ruin of temper and principle which such a lonely life threatens, are more than I wish to attempt to bear, when duty as well as pleasure invite me to the capital.[26]

Griffis was adamant in the face of Murata's determined opposition to his leaving Fukui for Tokyo. He submitted a request to the provincial authorities for twenty-five days' leave so that he could visit Yokohama and Tokyo during February "though it is not laid down in the contract, and I of course wanted them to pay all expenses & my salary during the holiday."[27] He rationalized this request by pointing out that twelve of the thirteen days would fall during the Japanese New Year holiday. "They refused," Griffis wrote, "to let me go at the time I specified . . . but said if I would wait one month (Just too late to receive any appointment in Yedo) I could go [and] take *40* days, all expenses paid."[28] Angered by their refusal, Griffis "sent back word *that I must go* on my expected [and] promised visit, starting from Fukuwi *Jan. 14th* and should go even if *I went alone & on foot* in the snow, whether in disgrace or honor."[29]

GRIFFIS IN TOKYO   75

One of the most interesting aspects of this dispute with the Japanese
was Griffis' sensitivity to the cultural context in which he had to conduct
his case. He wrote that he had two, two-hour-long interviews with Murata
in the government office, and Murata "used all his keen mind to frame
unnumbered arguments to deter me from my purpose, & to keep me in
Fukuwi till all danger of appointment in Yedo was over."[30] This is apparently a reference to Murata's offer of forty days' leave rather than
twenty-five which would have, in effect, served that purpose. Griffis,
however, did not fall into that trap and countered by moving his departure
date forward by fifteen days. He recognized that both "skill and patience"
were required "to overcome these polished Japanese officers."[31] Any other
approach, he suggested, was self-defeating. "Although intense feelings may
scald the veins and jar the heart, even though life and death may hang in
the scales, all is done with perfect and polished etiquette. Any angry or
loud tones or hasty speech—and the case is lost."[32] Either before, or as a
result of the two meetings with Murata, Griffis wrote him a draft of a
letter. There is no decisive evidence that Griffis ever sent the letter, but the
draft version reflects his anxiety and frustration over the situation. In
addition, it would not have been out of character for Griffis to have done
so.[33] Griffis began by offering his regrets that his leaving would cause
hardship on the Fukui school, and he suggested that his departure was not
as sudden as it seemed. "Months ago," he claimed, "I wrote and told
friends in America, Yokohama, Yedo and . . . Shidzoka [Shizuoka] that
I should be in Yokohama"[34] in early February, "and now I must fulfill
that promise and attend to urgent business in Yokohama." He requested
permission for his departure, but made it clear that, permission or not, he
would leave.[35] Furthermore, somewhat disingenuously, Griffis argued that
"I have known for months past and so have my friends that I shall leave
at this time, therefore, it is hard for me to understand it, when you say I
leave in a hurry."[36] While it is true that Griffis wanted to leave months
earlier, he did not know that a Tokyo assignment was in the offing until
Clark's letter to him, dated November 26, and it was not until a month
later that the official invitation arrived. To argue that he knew that he was
to leave at this time does not seem completely truthful. Even had he known
this, still it does not explain why Murata and the other officials were not
notified until the last minute.

As though he sensed the above arguments were not compelling enough,
Griffis promised that "if I am dismissed with honor, I shall strenuously
endeavor to get the Tokio officers to continue the school here. If you wish,
I shall be most happy to write a letter now to the Mom Bu Sho [Ministry
of Education] urging them to continue the school with a good teacher."[37]
Griffis was at best naive in using this argument for it was clear to most

yatoi that their influence with the Japanese authorities did not extend beyond the day-to-day details of their own particular sphere of expertise.

Finally, in what can only be described as a bald-faced lie, Griffis claimed, "I left a good position in America, with a salary nearly equal to what I receive now."[38] No part-time teacher at the Rutgers' Preparatory School was making anywhere near $3,600 per year in addition to having a house, horse, and servants furnished.

These arguments advanced by Griffis illustrate his desperation in wanting to leave Fukui for the capital. He ended his letter by pleading with Murata.

> Please do not let me go away alone and in disgrace to Yokohama. If I were a drunkard or whoremaster you would be glad to be rid of me. Please treat me as well as you would a servant. I wish to go to Tokio and ask them to keep up the Fukuwi school, I don't want to see my work scattered. . . . but in honor or disgrace, alone or attended I must leave Fukuwi on the 14th day of this month and whether I come back to Fukuwi or not, whether I am lost in the snow, come good, come harm, I have a clear conscience in doing what I have looked forward to for many months. . . . Please be kind to me, and grant my request. Do not treat me harshly but as a father.[39]

Whether Murata ever saw this letter, Griffis finally succeeded. As Griffis conceded, "By the contract . . . they were right; and they had the full power to deny my request."[40] On the other hand, what did they have to gain by refusing this adamant young man their permission to leave? It appears he had persuaded them that he was not bluffing, and that he would leave, preferably with permission, but in any event, he would leave on him terms. As he later wrote, "they could let me go alone, pay me only up to the day of leaving Fukui and brand me a contract-breaker according to the letter."[41] However, as he informed his sister Maggie,

> . . . they missed their man if they thought they could force me into any rough word, hasty speech or loud voice. The battle was with rapiers, not with bludgeons, and I knew it. I was firm as a rock, was fully resolved to set out alone, if necessary, in spite of snow, mountains, speechlessness or robbers. I answered every argument, and by one happy stroke, which Iwaboochi translated splendidly, I got them laughing, upset their dignity, and finally *won.* They gave me an officer as an escort, pay my expenses, continue my salary till a new contract is made, gave a grand final merry-making at the chief eating house & saloon here.[42]

Despite his tone of self-righteousness, Griffis did have pangs of conscience over his insistence on leaving Fukui. In reaching an accomodation between his actions and their effect on Fukui, Griffis listed several "unanswerable reasons" to justify his leaving.[43]

1st, Fukuwi is changed, it is no longer a province dependent on itself, but is merged into all Japan, and the Imperial Gov't. who now pays my salary have a right to take me. 2nd, Mr. Verbeck first sent me here [and] he now urgently calls me away. . . . 3rd, All my best students are continually leaving Fukuwi for Yedo thus spoiling my plans. 4th, At least 15 of my best students are in raptures of my going, because they will follow me. . . . To say nothing of an *exiles* personal reasons, my duty to Dai Nippon, would call me away.[44]

A closer analysis of these reasons seems to indicate that the first is the only one which may have had a degree of validity. The fact remains, however, that Fukui originally hired Griffis, not the central government, and it was only later that the central government began to assume his salary and expenses. The second, third, and fourth reasons listed seem to all be of a self-serving nature, having nothing to do with the terms of the contract which he agreed to abide by with his signature. It seems obvious to me that Griffis' fundamental reasons for leaving Fukui are contained in his phrase "an *exiles* personal reasons."[45] If one examines the question of *who* would benefit by Griffis' departure from Fukui before the end of his contract, one can only conclude that it would be Griffis himself.

Both Griffis and his Japanese hosts put a good face on the situation, and the townspeople and officials graciously feted him prior to his departure on January 22. Writing to Maggie just before leaving that morning, Griffis noted that it had been snowing for five days, and the snow was piled up to three feet deep. Despite this harsh weather, he wrote, "about 50 of my pupils and citizens will accompany me three miles then bid me good-bye. The chief officer [Murata] of the school & about 12 others will go 12 miles with me."[46]

All day yesterday, my house was filled by my pupils, officers, citizens, and everybody generally, who came to bid me farewell. All bring presents in money, lacquer ware, confectionary, curios, etc. My tables are filled with all kinds of things, the smallest a present of 2 *shu* (13 cents) and the greatest, a handsome inlaid Jap table, (small and low) from Muratta, the chief officer, and an ancient silver-mounted flute (very peculiar) and 1 pair very handsome gilt and gorgeous screens, a Jap sword, etc.[47]

In light of this send-off, it is interesting to note that Griffis forgot whatever pangs of conscience he may have had over the circumstances of his departure. His letters and diary are silent on this question, but he did make it a point to tell Maggie that "I go away in honor and regretted by all. Many students have already made ready to follow me, but all but 5 have been hindered by the gov[ernment] until I am fairly settled in Yedo."[48]

The journey across the mountains was difficult and dangerous. A few miles out of Fukui the snow was so heavy that the road became "nothing but a foot-path . . . and we could only find the path by punching through

the snow, as we floundered on."[49] It took five full days to negotiate the
fifty miles across the mountains to reach the Tōkaidō as "the rough wind
pelted our faces with barbed arrows of snow, and every step was a great
exertion. . . . In many cases we had to hire eight mountain guides to go
ahead in snowshoes, find the road by punching for the hard bed, and then
tramp it down for us to follow."[50] Finally reaching the Tōkaidō, the Griffis party started toward Shizuoka where he had arranged to spend a brief
period with Edward Clark. Ten miles from that objective, the two met and
and rode to Clark's home for a joyous reunion before Griffis left the next
afternoon to continue his journey to the capital.

The next portion of the trip was easier, and at 2:30 on the afternoon of
February 2, they arrived at Yokohama. Griffis wrote, "I immediately
called on the tailor, ordered clothes, etc. as I am about as shabby as one
would be after a year in the wilderness."[51] After two days' rest at Reverend
James Ballagh's home, Griffis took a steamer from Yokohama to Tokyo
"finishing a journey of 329 miles, blistered, weary & sore and faint from
loss of rest, sleep & the effects of a Japanese 13 days diet."[52] Although he
had been in the interior for only a year, Griffis was surprised by what he
found.

Tōkiō is so modernized that I scarcely recognize it. No beggars, no guard-
houses, no sentinels at Tsukiji, or the castle gates; city ward-barriers gone;
no swords worn; hundreds of yashikis disappeared; new decencies and pro-
prieties observed; less cuticle visible; more clothes. The age of pantaloon has
come. Thousands wearing hat, boots, coats; carriages numerous; jin-rika-
shas countless. Shops full of foreign wares and notions. Soldiers all uni-
formed, armed with Chassepot rifles. New bridges span the canals. Police in
uniform. Hospitals· schools, and colleges; girls seminaries numerous. Railway nearly finished. Embassy rode in steam-cars to Yokohama. Gold and
silver coin in circulation. Almshouses established . . . . An air of bustle,
energy and activity prevails . . . . Old Yedo has passed away forever.
Tōkiō, the national capital is a cosmopolis.[53]

LIFE IN THE CAPITAL

Upon arriving in Tokyo, Griffis made his way to the home of his old friend
Guido Verbeck with whom he stayed until his assigned house was ready
for occupancy. In a letter to his sister Maggie, written after he was en-
sconced in the Verbeck home, Griffis admitted that "I have done nothing
but rest since I came here."[54] Soon however, he was anxious to begin his
teaching and chose his "new lecture room in the Polytechnic School,
which is to be in the old yashiki of the Shidzoka's Daimio."[55]

Not having had the opportunity to attend regular religious services in
Fukui, Griffis was anxious to recharge his spiritual batteries. Less than a

week after arriving in the city that was to be his home for the next two-and-one-half years, Griffis journeyed to Yokohama for a weekend where he "had the pleasure of worshipping God with a congregation, for the first time since last February."[56] This visit also provided him with his first real opportunity to mingle in polite society for a long time, and he made the most of it. A glimpse of Griffis' future calling can be seen in the following passage written to Maggie: In the foreign settlement "a *social* Christian element has been developed & a church—a union church organized. Rev. Dr. Brown is pastor of it, but as he teaches 6 hours daily Sunday excepted the task of preaching is a severe one, and therefore as a Christian brother, I ought to help him."[57] In order that he be prepared to do so, Griffis asked Maggie to "send me *all* my sermons."[58]

Griffis was not a man to sit idle with time on his hands. During the period between his arrival in Tokyo and the beginning of his teaching duties, he kept occupied with a myriad of activities. He threw himself into these activities in a manner which seems to suggest that he was afraid to let himself be idle for fear that he would suffer the same sense of loneliness and isolation that he had left Fukui to escape. Always the opportunist, Griffis took advantage of the Japanese interest in the education of women as a vehicle for bringing his sister Maggie to Japan as a companion. He described how the Japanese government was planning to open a school for girls the following week, and the wife of a missionary had been hired to teach for $1,200 per year. He wrote,

> I do not know how far this movement will extend but I have no doubt, that there will be need . . . for more. Now I must ask you honestly, what do you, or either Mary or Martha think of it? Suppose I could get one of you out? I want you here myself, but cannot yet afford to bring you out. Of course all must depend on the condition of dear mother's health, but I simply write you this to let you know what is in the future. Now, since I am in Yedo, since there is some society here, and plenty in Yokohama, good physicians, almost all the comforts of home, there need be no fear of coming to Japan. Do not mention this matter to anyone, but be ready for circumstances, and know how to decide.[59]

As he mentioned to Maggie, the stumbling block in bringing out at least one of his sisters was his mother's health. He did not know when he wrote these words that his mother had passed away on January 17.

Ever since his arrival in Japan, young Griffis had dutifully sent money home for rent, food, and various other necessities. Despite this filial responsibility that he undertook to fulfill, his family constantly bombarded him with requests for more money. As recounted earlier, he often had to scold Maggie for her constant requests for money. The common thread that runs through much of his correspondence with Maggie is Griffis' disillusionment and frustration over the lackluster financial performance of his father and his brothers. The former had not held a steady job in years, and had brought disgrace on the family when he was dismissed from the same jewelry firm for which Willie had worked, presumably for theft. His brothers, on the basis of Griffis' pointed comments in his letters and diary, appear to have been ne'er-do-wells who drained more than they contributed to the family income. In exasperation, Willie pleaded with Maggie,

> For the sake of my peace of mind, if nothing else, I beg of you not to mention Pop or Clarence in your letters, unless in brief paragraphs. You would be surprised to see your own letters so filled as they are with what I know and feel, but *cannot help*. I find no fault nor upbraid you because our home needs money. I promised $300 per year as rent for the house. I have paid it, and will pay it. I must confess I did not think my offer of $200 per year for Pop would be availed of for at least a year to come, nevertheless, I shall pay it, and pay it only into the hands of those who keep home . . . . Tell me all that may be hopeful and redeeming in *our men*, and don't think me unpractical, or lacking in sympathy. If you could do me or yourself any good by exposing their faults, I would not mind.[60]

It is apparent that Griffis was not able to escape all his problems by relocating himself the 330 miles from Fukui to Tokyo. It is equally apparent, however, that Tokyo contained many more entertainments and distractions, which enabled him to push his cares into the background. One of the first that he enjoyed took place during February 12–13, 1872, when he received his first scrutiny of the Imperial Government. On February 12, in company with Guido Verbeck, Griffis called on Oki Takato, chief minister of the newly created Ministry of Education, for an official interview. Although Griffis nowhere mentions the content of their discussions, it is likely that they discussed the terms of his new contract and his new duties.[61]

The following afternoon, again with Verbeck, Griffis made his way to the Emperor's palace through a storm which had already left four inches of snow on the ground. Once there, they joined other foreign teachers "at the Mom Bu Sho's finest chamber, near the Mikado's throne room" for an official reception.[62] Griffis later described the scene:

> The Japanese officers wore their ancient native caps and gowns, the Americans and Europeans black dress suits, though the German Surgeons, Müller and Hoffman, had donned their uniforms of black and gold, holding their spiked helmets in their hands by the *pickel-haube*. The French and Prussians were not as yet very cordial to each other, for their war was just over. The Minister of Education sat at the head of the long table.[63]

Even though the new polytechnic school was not yet open, Griffis did much reading on educational questions and planning for his own teaching. In one of his first letters home following his arrival in the capital, he urged Maggie to send him "Anything in the way of school literature," in addition to "2 or 3 copies of the Report of the Comptroller of the Public Schools of Phila[delphia]."[64] In the same letter, the conscientious young pedagogue also asked for two copies of George Baker's chemistry textbook which he had used with good results in Fukui.

Whereas in Fukui interpreters were necessary because his own Japanese was inadequate, especially at the outset, and because few of the students understood English well enough to follow the lectures with any degree of comprehension, the situation in Tokyo was somewhat different. The language of instruction in classes taught by foreign professors was English, and the students were required to have at least an elementary knowledge of that language in order to attend. In an important sense, the complaint of the post-World War II American teacher in Japan applies to the early Meiji period.

No matter what he teaches in the United States, the chief function of any American teacher in Japan will be to teach English. . . . The students who take his courses will be there primarily because they are given in English. . . .[65]

As a result of this phenomenon, Griffis was not in as dire a need of a good interpreter as he had been in the interior. On February 26 Griffis noted that Iwabuchi had been "left behind in Fukui," but that he would have the services of another young man from Osaka.[66] There is evidence that this young man, Ichikawa, never actually worked with Griffis, for in addition to classes being conducted in English, Griffis' Japanese had improved a great deal since his arrival in Japan. For example, while visiting Edward Clark in Shizuoka he "conversed in Japanese first rate, greatly to [Clark's] astonishment."[67]

Three months later Iwabuchi turned up in Tokyo to see Griffis. He had obtained a position in Yokohama teaching at the Light House School. Before leaving Tokyo, he made Griffis a gift of his sword. Griffis quoted him as telling him, "I have worn this from childhood, and it has been like a soul to me. I beg you to accept it both as a token of personal friendship and as a historic memorial that the samurai of Japan have laid their swords aside forever." Griffis was very pleased with this thoughtful and prestigious gift as the "blade was a fine one, with black lacquered scabbard, ribbed and feruled with oxidized silver carved into waves on which floats the emperors [sic] crest. . . . The handle was of white sharkskin wrapped with brown silk sennet."[68] He especially appreciated this gift because Iwabuchi "has been a kind, faithful friend and helper."[69]

"Let Maggie Come to Japan"

As we have seen, Griffis strove unsuccessfully to secure positions in Japan for various members of his family from the time of his arrival during the winter of 1870–1871. He hoped to have his siblings near so that he could enjoy a semblance of family life. While in Fukui, however, he clearly recognized that this goal was not a realistic one, and he contented himself with keeping his eyes and ears open for possibilities for his brothers in in Yokohama and Tokyo.

We have also seen that he renewed his interest in bringing one or more of his sisters to Japan in his last days in Fukui and especially upon his arrival in the capital. He had apparently mentioned this possibility to Edward Clark during his brief visit to that college friend in late January of 1872. Clark was fond of Maggie and had shared their travels in Europe during the summer of 1869, and thus, was also anxious for Maggie to come to Japan. Less than a week after Griffis left his Shizuoka home for Tokyo, Clark appealed to Maggie to come to Japan.

> . . . Next to seeing "Willie" himself in Japan, I want to see his sister Maggie here! Never was there a more promising field for you. You could never be more urgently needed than just *here*. Never could you do greater good, & never could you labor with More love for the work, & more joy in its results . . . . Now that your "Darling Willie" is in Yedo, come & be with him. Now that Japan & its seekers after truth want you, come, come![70]

It seems that Griffis began to work quietly to find a position for Maggie. He visited the new school for girls and reported that the new teacher "is doing very well in the girl's school."[71] On March 22 he asked Maggie point blank: "Let me know what you think of coming to Japan."[72] It is likely that his need for female companionship, when added to the grief he experienced with his mother's death, his frustration with his father and brothers, and his financial problems, convinced him of the desirability of action. He suggested to Martha that Maggie come to Japan.

> I am very glad that you and Maggie gave me the full particulars of Dear Mother's death and burial and that her departure was . . . calm and radiant and that she was buried in honor. All the bills of the Doctor . . . I shall cheerfully assume and pay. Yet it is the last ounce on the camel's back. Our home is now broken up. I have ever tried to do my duty, but after being in Japan sixteen months I find myself without a dollar to spare, and with unpaid debts, policy fees, etc. that forestall my salary for five months to come. Now I ask is it fair that I should be called on as before? I am henceforth unable to do so. I therefore advise the following plan. Let Maggie come to Japan, I am sure I can get her a position here and I must have company. I can't stand it alone. I have one year and seven months to stay yet. It will rob you of Mag but it will benefit me and herself. . . .[73]

He went on to make suggestions as to how the remainder of the family might look after themselves. He clearly felt that he was unable to continue to carry the financial burden and informed Martha, "I henceforth withdraw the $300 rent, I formerly paid. Even when I do that, every cent of my salary *is spent* for 5 months to come."[74] He urged them "to consult about it and agree what to do, if indeed you have not already done so. I know it is a bitter thing for you three sisters to separate, yet think of my lonely life for so long, and remember that Mag's coming here may be the best for all of us. Her coming here will make it more likely that I shall come back when my time is up."[75] This was one of the most prophetic sentences he wrote while in Japan.

Griffis assumed his sisters would agree to these arrangements, for on April 21, less than a week after he had dispatched his request, he confided to Maggie, "I want you to come to Japan as soon as possible." His mental state was "sad and lonely," as the death of his mother "has laid its burden on me, the cross seems too heavy to bear."[76] Driven by his grief, he placed a high priority on Maggie's coming to Japan even though the job situation was cloudy. "I am not certain of getting you a position, but I want you with me, and even by a private school, with my influence, I can make it pay well."[77]

It appears that the thought of having Maggie by his side was not enough to comfort Griffis. He also wrote to Ellen Johnson, the young woman with whom he had broken several weeks before his departure for Japan. After swearing Maggie to secrecy, he informed Maggie that he had asked Ellen "to come to me." Recognizing that the "chances are one in a million," he admitted that his actions "show you what a fool I am."[78] The odds that Griffis quoted proved to be accurate for his second attempt to win Ellen proved fruitless. In writing to Martha and Mary months later, Maggie concluded that his bitter experience with Ellen was a "great disappointment [which] has influenced his whole life I am sure."[79]

In any event, Maggie agreed to come out to Japan. After making the necessary arrangements, she left for San Francisco to claim the ticket that her brother had arranged for her to pick up at a friend's store. After missing her first ship, she finally left on the steamer *China* which arrived in Yokohama on Saturday, August 10, 1872, at 6 o'clock in the morning.

Maggie's initial reactions to Japan were favorable. Just two days after arriving, she accompanied Willie and a small party to Hakone for a short visit. She confided to her sisters that "of all the strange sights and sounds I ever experienced . . . the strangest [was] coolies who do all the work in the Eastern countries that we give to animals, go about almost entirely naked."[80] Despite this initial shock, she conceded, "I was never in a lovelier land and the people are kind, gentle, simple & perfect[ly] innocent, different from the common run in other countries."[81]

The arrival of Maggie had at least two effects on Griffis' lifestyle. With her supervising the household and providing him with the companionship he had so badly needed, he was able to enjoy the domestic life he had missed. In addition, he no longer felt it necessary for him to write long and descriptive letters home; now Maggie took over that responsibility, and more of Willie's time could be devoted to writing articles for both Japanese and American newspapers and periodicals.

THE POLYTECHNIC SCHOOL FAILS TO OPEN

Griffis' primary professional motivation in coming to Tokyo was to help lay the foundation of technical education in the empire. After resting in Tokyo, visiting friends, and in general, adjusting himself to society after eleven months in the interior, he prepared for teaching and exchanged his temporary quarters for a new house.[82]

> It is a poor affair compared with my Fukuwi mansion. It is new, however, and one of a row of four. It has four rooms & a kitchen, servants [sic] room, bath-house, etc. I shall give all down-stairs to my Fukuwi scholars, who follow me to Yedo, and keep the upstairs for myself. I have had to buy furniture for my study room, bedding, etc. and for my bedroom, have sent to San Francisco.[83]

His expectation of beginning teaching in early March was frustrated when necessary "alterations" prevented the school from opening on time.[84] He was not disturbed over this development as it gave him time to pursue his study of Japanese, to become more deeply involved in the work of the new Union Church of Yokohama, and to become acquainted with members of the American Scientific Commission in Japan whose members included its head, General Horace Capron, former United States Commissioner of Agriculture in the Grant administration.[85] Griffis was particularly enthusiastic over Yokohama's Union Church to which he subscribed $100 soon after arriving from Fukui. He described his attendance at services on Sunday, March 7.

> They worship now in the Theatre building, a very nice one, and about 200 were present. In the afternoon, I attend[ed] Mr. Ballagh's Bible Class in the little Missionary Chapel; about 50, all Japanese were present, taught in their own language. To-day, about 8 of them will be baptized . . . . All this is done openly, with no hindrance.[86]

Further delays in opening the polytechnic school prompted Griffis to remark, "I find it the best philosophy to wait patiently and improve my leisure time for myself, although I am sorry that the Japs have to pay me for doing nothing."[87] However, he evidently did do some teaching although not at the proposed technical school. The new government had established in February 1870, the so-called Daigaku Nankō (a school for western studies) at which Mr. E. H. House taught. He was an American who later became editor of the *Tokyo Times*. Griffis' diary entry for February 24 contains a reference to House being confined to his home with a case of gout in his foot.[88] Further entries in this diary, as late as March 1, indicate that Griffis taught House's classes while he was ill.[89]

During this period Griffis became acquainted with a certain Mr. Chipman, the representative of H. H. Bancroft Publishers of San Francisco. After a few preliminary social meetings, Chipman and Griffis "had a long talk . . . relative to the publication of a series of educational works for Japan, primers, readers, science, etc."[90] Chipman had in mind "a complete series of school and college textbooks to be prepared by the best teachers in Japan."[91] Griffis was delighted that he had been asked to produce a primer, a speller, two readers, "all filled with original matter suited specially for the Japanese," in addition to textbooks in geography, chemistry and physics.[92] Griffis anticipated taking at least a year to complete them, and was to receive "5 percent of the cost of the book, or about 35 percent of the profits" as his share of the financial rewards.[93] He was so excited over the prospects, however, that he exclaimed,, the "work is such a real labor of love that, had I time, I should be willing almost to do it for nothing."[94]

While the anticipatory glow of this project still warmed him, Griffis received further bad news about his expected teaching duties. The polytechnic school would not be opening, and he was to take on new duties.

> The Polytechnic school failed. It never opened because the scholars were too few for the Prof. of Law and Astronomy, while for me, although they were plenty (20 or so) the students were really of a grade of education & ability inferior to those in the College. I was then offered a position with the Department of Public Works, to instruct the young Japanese engineers in an outline of Chemistry, or the post of Prof. of Chem. at the Yedo College [Daigaku Nankō]. I chose the latter.[95]

His agreement to switch from the proposed polytechnic school to Daigaku Nankō was the cause of his eventual dispute with the Monbushō, and indirectly at least, a major cause for his leaving Japan in the summer of 1874. However, he was pleased at the time of the switch because "I occupy a position second only to Mr. Verbeck the President."[96] His responsibilities consisted of teaching "Chemistry, Physiology, and Comparative Philology. . . . I teach in the three higher classes [and] all my pupils are bright, eager, and industrious. They range from 16 to 21, and they will, in the future be the leading men in Japan. It is my highest joy— my work."[97]

PROFESSOR GRIFFIS AT DAIGAKU NANKŌ

The institution to which Griffis had been assigned, Daigaku Nankō, was established in 1870 but its origins could be traced to 1684. At that time the shogunate established the Temmon Kata (Astronomy Office) devoted to Dutch studies. As the Japanese scholar Nagai Michio has pointed out, Daigaku Nankō was really "the end product of a series of mutations in which the Temmon-kata became successively the Bansho Wakai Goyō (Office for the Interpretation of Barbarian Books), the Yōgakusho (Institute for Western Studies), the Bansho Shirabesho (Institute for the Investigation of Barbarian Books), and the Yōsho Shirabesho (Institute for the Investigation of Western Books)."[98]

In early 1872 when Griffis began to teach, Daigaku Nankō was really "a replica of an American grammar school."[99] The schools' English division included about 500 students,[100] and these students were "of every age, and from every quarter of the empire."[101] Griffis left us a colorful description of conditions in the school upon his first arrival in January 1871, and it is doubtful if the picture had changed drastically by the time of his return a year later.

> The middle-aged and old men, who wished to learn merely to read and translate, and not to speak, a foreign language, were mostly in the "meaning school." The younger, though some were over thirty, learned the alphabet, spelling, conversations, writing, and, in the higher classes, geography, arithmetic, and simple history. The buildings were rows of sheds with glass windows, deal desks and seats, and unpainted wood partitions.[102]

If the students were unlike those in western institutions, the teachers were even more unusual. As one student of the period has declared, "It is an unalloyed truth to say that the majority of the 'Professors' in the schools of . . . [Tokyo] were graduates of the dry-goods counter, the forecastle, the camp, and the shambles, or belonged to that vast array of unclassified humanity that floats like waifs in every seaport."[103] Warming to his task, he accused these teachers of "Coming directly from the bar-room, the brothel, the gambling saloon, or the resort of boon companions, they brought the graces, the language and the manners of those places into the school room."[104]

The quality of teachers in Daigaku Nankō had improved substantially by the late winter of 1872. Perhaps the Japanese had grown more selective in hiring foreigners to teach, and certainly, the supply of qualified men outstripped the relatively limited demand. For example, when Griffis first considered having Maggie come to Japan, he had no doubt that he could find her a position without difficulty. Within a short time after her arrival in Japan, both Willie and she agreed that finding a teaching position would be a long, difficult process. By the fall opening of school, Griffis was besieged with requests from people in America who were seeking positions, but as Maggie wrote home, "there is nothing for them here. The government has enough foreigners on hand."[105] The days when almost any foreigner could land a position, despite his qualifications, were at an end. Japan was anxious to hire as few foreigners as possible and to phase out, as soon as possible, as many of those already employed. As many developing nations are learning today, expatriate teachers may possess badly needed skills, but there comes a time when their value reaches a point of diminishing returns. Hazel Jones aptly described the Japanese policy:

> Recognizing the use of foreign employees as a stop-gap measure, Japanese officials began to stress education of Japanese to replace foreigners as qucikly as possible. Of all the means open to the Japanese to modernize, the employment of foreign specialists may be seen as one wing but the other was the education of Japanese at home and abroad. [The Meiji oligarchs were] clear that the primary purpose of foreign employees was to educate the Japanese to replace them.[106]

In terms of cost alone, Nagai Michio points out that in 1873 the Japanese government was devoting 14 percent of the total education budget for the salaries of foreign teachers. Some of these men "were paid up to ¥600 per month. This sum exceeded the salary of the president of Tokyo Daigaku, who received only ¥400 per month when the school was founded four years later."[107]

The teachers already hired at Daigaku Nankō came from a wide variety of backgrounds and countries. The faculty apparently was divided into English, French, and German departments and was composed of at least 11 foreigner teachers.[108] In a letter home written prior to Maggie's arrival, Griffis described how "I enjoy fully the presence and contact of kindred souls" during meals in "the mess." This was "an assemblage of the four German, one English, one Dane, and three American teachers."[109] This organization, which appears to have been an eating club, cost each of its members $25 per week and provided good fellowship in addition to food. Mr. House, he wrote,

> is my kindred intellectual soul. I love him. Mr. Scott is a splendid and genial young man a Kentuckian but for several years, principal of the San Francisco High School. The others are all pleasant men, especially, Mr. Rosenstand, lecturer on Law & Prof. Wagner a fine German technical scholar from Berlin. Mr. Holz, another German is at home on English, German, Italian & French.[110]

Griffis soon grew weary of this arrangment and confided that "I

should rather live with a family," but that the families he preferred—
Verbeck and Wilson—"naturally prefer to be alone," while Reverend
Veeder, "though a good and pleasant man in many respects, has not sufficient magnetism to draw me within his reach."[111] It is at this point that
Griffis began to show some of the arrogance that Maggie was soon to
complain about to her sisters. He resigned himself to continuing his dining
arrangements, but "Unfortunately my prestige and position here, is second only to Mr. Verbeck, and to keep rivalry within proper bounds and
not to chafe a man who has more affection than intellectual ability, it is
best to be on terms of polite deference, rather than familiarity. So I am
left alone at the club."[112] Shortly after her arrival in Japan, Maggie observed that Willie "is a little changed by his great disappointment, he
is more irritable and don't [sic] care whether people like him or not or
what anyone thinks of him, he cares nothing for the world."[113] She struck
the same theme when she complained,

> He is not what he used to be I can tell you, he is a little *cynical*, severe. I sup-
> pose his disappointment [break with Ellen Johnson] has caused it, but I
> seldom say anything. I think he needs to get married to soften him. I tell
> [you] he is a little uncivilized . . . . he is pressed for money and annoyed at
> trifles more than I ever knew him to be before. He sets people down and is as
> independent of everybody's opinion as possible. . . . He isn't at all jolly
> like he used to be, and smiles but seldom.[114]

It appears that Maggie was correct in laying at least part of the blame
for Willie's irritability on his break with Ellen Johnson. His strong desire
to have Maggie join him in Japan was obviously part and parcel of his
desire for female companionhip. After his experience in Fukui with his
teenage girl servant, Willie seemed unsure of how well he could handle a
similar temptation in the future. Maggie would not only provide him with
companionship, but would also be an insurance policy against temptation. Maggie knew her brother quite well and was on target when she
commented only a week after joining him, "Willie wants to get a wife,
and he needs one."[115]

The arrival of Maggie, and Ellen Johnson's confirmation that she
would not be coming to Griffis seem to have cleared the air and enabled
Willie to be less irritable. In a letter to "Dear Mr. Griffis," dated October
19, Ellen Johnson assured him that

> I have obeyed your request, and destroyed every letter you ever sent me,
> except three, written since you left America, and which are merely friendly
> letters. These also I will destroy, if you wish it, but if you do not seriously
> object, I would like to keep them, in memory of our friendship.[116]

She continued, "It has been a sad task to burn these letters, but I acknowledge its expediency, and beg you in return to destroy mine." In concluding what was probably the last letter exchanged between them, Ellen wrote,

Oh, Mr. Griffis, deeply as I regret ever having caused you the slightest pain I cannot be sorry that I have known you. I do not believe there is another man on this Earth who would have shown the same unselfish forbearance, and I honor you for it more than words can tell . . . . Now let us seal forever these pages in our lives, and begin afresh in truest friendship.[117]

Even before Griffis could have received Ellen's letter, Maggie noticed a change for the better. When she first reached Japan, she "found him rather harsh, cynical, even cross . . . he was our old Willie at all." Recently however,

I have seen a great change in him, he has grown quite gay, and is just as loving and kind as anyone could possibly be, he sings about the house, is not irritable, is not severe & sharp in his conversation, [is] more patient with people he does not like. I felt at first that he was growing into a severe man, feeling himself superior to all who were not up to his level of thought, etc. but I think that there is a great change and that I came just in time to soften, to influence and bless his life.[118]

Griffis' letters and diary speak very little of his teaching in Daigaku Nankō, and Maggie's letters say even less about this phase of their life in Japan. We do know, however, that soon after Willie's arrival from Fukui, he asked that two copies of George Baker's chemistry textbook be sent to him as soon as possible, and it is likely that this was the book he relied on most for his chemistry teaching. The major reason for the lack of information regarding Griffis' teaching experience was Maggie's assumption of the letter-writing duties upon her arrival. She naturally wrote to her sisters in Philadelphia about the things which interested her most, and Willie's teaching seldom met this criterion.

One of the most interesting things about Griffis' teaching in Tokyo was his characteristic trait of taking on many more responsibilities than he could legally be expected to assume. Although he was contracted to teach chemistry and physics to the students at Daigaku Nankō, he also taught geography, physiology, literature and later, law. Probably as a result of the tight financial situation in which he found himself, Griffis attempted to secure a salary increase based on this extra teaching. In September 1872, he addressed a letter to the minister of education in which he presented his case.

I have been teaching in Nan Ko, now seven months. You remember that I was called here from Fukuwi, to be Professor of Chemistry and Physics in the Shem Mon Gaku [Senmon Gakkō—"technical school"]. It was with that distinct understanding, that I came. But I was exceedingly sorry to hear that after I had been kept idle for two months, that the Shem Mon Gaku could not be opened. This was a great disappointment to me, more than I can tell. However, I volunteered to teach in Nanko, and have tried to be a faithful teacher. A Professor of Chemistry and Physics however does not expect to teach over two hours a day, because he must prepare many drugs, and get ready and keep in order his instruments. I told Mr. Verbeck I would teach other studies for a few months, as I expected the Shem Mon Gaku to open soon again. However, I do not know when the Shem Mon Gaku will open, and at present my time is fully occupied both in school, and often after school hours, because I teach many studies, and have to explain and teach more than other teachers, because there are no textbooks that are easy enough for the pupils. I have also often to prepare drugs and apparatus, which takes a long time.

Please remember that my contract binds me to teach Chemistry and Physics only, and from the 1st day of the eighth month, please excuse me from teaching Geography, Physiology & Literature. If however my salary is increased to $350 [from $300] per month, I shall continue as before, and will pay the salary of an assistant myself. I do not need any other help.

If my salary is increased to $350 per month, I shall continue to teach 27 hours per week, as before, in accordance with your wishes.[119]

There is no indication whether this request was granted, although Griffis' diary for July 10, 1873—eleven months later—contains an entry which indicates that he was to receive a $30 per month raise effective that date.[120]

GRIFFIS AS SENSEI[121]

If we accept the thesis, upon which I shall build a succeeding chapter, that publication is a legitimate form of teaching, we must consider Griffis' rather prolific writing in any evaluation of his teaching. While in Japan, particularly during his sojourn in the capital, Griffis contributed numerous articles dealing with both historical and current Japanese topics to such newspapers and periodicals in both Japan and America as *Nature*, *Lippincott's Magazine*, *Transactions of the Asiatic Society of Japan*, *American Educational Monthly*, *Japan Weekly Mail*, *Appleton's Journal*, and *Overland Monthly*. In addition, Griffis was active in church circles and preached the Sunday sermon on a number of occasions. Finally, one cannot omit mention of the Japanese readers and primer that he contributed to H. H. Bancroft's publishing enterprise in Japan.

Since his teaching in Fukui had been mainly through lecturing and demonstrating various experiments, there is no reason to believe that he handled his chemistry and physics classes in the capital any differently. The one major difference, as we have seen earlier, was that he no longer had to rely on an interpreter or on his own knowledge of Japanese. Presumably, this meant that he was able to cover more material more efficiently than in Fukui.

Virtually nothing is known about his methods of teaching his other classes in geography, literature, etc. Since his educational theory placed the teacher at the center of the learning process and the students as the receivers of his knowledge, it seems reasonable to assume that he lectured a great deal. We do know that he introduced some sort of a "Game of Authors" to his literature class, but this was less than two months before he returned to America which casts some doubt on how "innovative" his teaching was during this period.[122]

The educational interest of the Emperor Meiji throughout Griffis' residence in the capital is quite clear. The Emperor often received foreign teachers in a formal ceremony and even visited the schools in Tokyo not only as a political gesture, but also because of his serious interest in what was taking place in these institutions. One of his visits to Griffis' school took place on May 7, 1872.

> . . . the mikado visited the school to-day arriving at nine A.M. and remaining till 12:30. He witnessed a number of experiments in physics and chemistry, and listened to the students read, answer questions in English, French and German. Several of his cabinet ministers were present, and about twenty of his courtiers in court costume. His Majesty was dressed in a wide long robe of heavy white silk with bloomer-like trousers of red silk. His hair was cut round to his head, on which rested a cap of shining black material with a plain ornament of fluted gold with an upright projection several inches high. According to prescribed etiquette his countenance was passive, lacking expression, except occasionally when his interest was excited sufficiently to show a firm and manly, but not handsome face. As I stood for nearly and hour within six feet of him, I studied his face carefully. So far as I could judge, there was neither profound wisdom nor deep-set purpose in his countenance. It was that of an intelligent, earnest Japanese. The exercise having been finished, those present remainded respectfully seated. The mikado and courtiers proceeded to the reception room, His Majesty advancing first, along the passage. As I turned I came within three feet of a collision with the august personage. I sheered off backward to a side recess, hiding my diminished head until [the Emperor] had passed by. The emperor returned his thanks to his foreign servants by a letter and banquet.[123]

Griffis was not the type of teacher who put in his several hours of classroom time each day and spent the rest of his time pursuing his own interests. From the time he moved into his own house in the European quarter of Tokyo, he had several young Japanese students living under his roof. Their numbers fluctuated from time to time, but they were always present in significant numbers. During Christmas 1872, for example,

Griffis informed his sisters at home that in order to celebrate Christmas properly, "I shall have my five Japanese boys in my house hang up their stockings on Xmas eve, and on Xmas day we shall have a children's party."[124] It was not until January 1874, when Ed Clark received a post in Tokyo, that the young students left Griffis' house to enable Clark to move in with Willie and Maggie.

Not long after settling in Tokyo, Griffis received word from a correspondent in America that Birdsey G. Northrop, State Superintendent of Schools in Connecticut, was scheduled to journey to Japan and to serve as an advisor to the Monbushō. This was ironic because, in the words of Professor Stewart Fraser, Northrop had "launched a remarkable campaign in 1873 against what he considered were some of the evils of 'foreign education.' He deplored the growing practice of sending American youth abroad for their precollegiate as well as their undergraduate studies."[125] Although he ultimately did not go to Japan, he did not reject the Japanese offer until the last minute. Presumably, he was not unwilling to inject a "foreign" element into the Japanese educational context but saw that element as destructive in an American context.

For several months Griffis repeatedly received word that Northrop was coming, but a firm date had not yet been set. In January 1873, however, Samuel Lockwood wrote to Griffis that to the surprise of almost everyone, David Murray, a Rutgers mathematics professor would be going to Japan in Northrop's stead.

> We were all surprised last week by the intelligence that Prof. David Murray had received not only the appointment, but also his commission, as Superintendent of education in Japan. If I understand it, this is indeed an important trust, as it involves the oversight and direction of every department of public instruction, both collegiate & common, or academic. We all feel that the appointment is one conferring high honor, and as for myself, my own judgment is that this honor has fallen on very worthy shoulders.[126]

By this time Griffis had been corresponding with his old Rutgers professor for several months. In mid-August of the preceding year, Murray had told Griffis that he was greatly impressed with the Japanese who had come to the United States seeking advice for the future of their educational systems. These men, Murray wrote, "are certainly of great intelligence and have a perfectly clear insight into the wants of their country and the difficulties to be encountered in regard to them."[127] In retrospect, Murray's own insight into these problems is remarkable. He was in full agreement with the outlines of Griffis' ideas on the future of Japanese education. He felt that Griffis' views, which agreed with his own, were particularly valuable since Griffis "must have caught, what I think no one from an outside

position can get, something of the national spirit of the Japanese people.
. . . [that is] their national aspirations, and in what directions their
efforts at advancement are likely to be successful."[128] Without Griffis'
advantage of being on the scene, Murray still was perceptive enough to
realize

> The work of inaugurating a country must be slow, and must be accomp-
> lished by agencies working from within and not from without. They must
> work on their own inauguration. Foreigners can do very little to help
> them . . . . Their own laws, forms, institutions must be the basis on which
> any new superstructure is to be built.[129]

Griffis fully agreed with the idea that in the final analysis, the future of
Japan depended upon the Japanese themselves and, particularly, on the
young Japanese who were energetically studying the knowledge of the
West. Being in Tokyo rather than in Fukui gave Griffis access to the very
best of these young students. The Meiji government encouraged students
to come to Tokyo as a method of securing and strengthening its control,
and Nankō became a center for these students.

In later years, Griffis was to claim, "I know personally every one of
the fifty-five men who made up the new [Meiji] government."[130] This,
indeed, may have been true since we know that through his connections
with Dr. Verbeck and by virtue of his position in Tokyo, Griffis moved in
the same social circle as the Japanese leaders. We also know that Griffis
was a member of the so-called Meirokusha ("Meiji Six Society"), "a literary society for the encouragement of western studies,"[131] which was
composed of "the leading students of the West and the most progressive
thinkers of the day."[132] Among the original founders of this society were
Mori Arinori, Fukuzawa Yukichi, Nishi Amane, Nishimura Shigeki,
Nakura Masano, Katō Hiroyuki, Tsuda Masamichi, and Mitsukuri
Rinshō or, in Donald Shively's phrase, "the private scholars and officials
best informed about the West."[133] Many of these scholars were also
prominent members of the government at various times during the period.
Griffis' participation in this context is important not only because it
brought him into direct contact with some of the best minds of Meiji
Japan and informed his voluminous writing about Japan, but also because
it gave his ideas an entrée into influential Japanese minds. The measure of
his influence eludes our calipers. But since the Meirokusha was "for
several years perhaps the most important channel for the introduction of
information and ideas from the West," we can be assured his ideas moved
in Japan's highest circles.[134]

We also know that Griffis was proud of his contacts with influential
Japanese government figures and powerful Americans who interacted with

the Japanese government. On at least three occasions Griffis dined with
Iwakura Tomomi (whose son he had taught at Rutgers) whom E. Papinot
described as "Until his death . . . the most conspicuous politician in
Japan."[135]

Whatever influence Griffis had on individual Japanese was probably
most forcefully exerted on his students in Tokyo. Perhaps the most
prominent of them was Komura Jūtarō whom Griffis described as "my
star pupil in the University of Tokio from 1872 to 1874" to whom he
taught law and "often discussed American ideas and policy."[136] Upon
completing his studies at Tokyo, Komura was sent to Harvard Law
School on a government scholarship. Upon returning to Japan, he began
his career as a judge before taking a minor position in the Ministry of
Foreign Affairs. In 1893 however, he was posted to Peking as First Secretary in the Japanese Legation. After two years he was transferred to
Seoul and in 1896, became Vice-Minister of Foreign Affairs. In 1898 he
was in succession appointed Japanese Minister to Washington and to
Russia. After the Boxer Rebellion, he was sent back to Peking to repre-
sent Japanese interests in the international conference which followed that
unfortunate event. As a reward for his services, Komura was named
Minister of Foreign Affairs in the first Katsura cabinet in 1901. He played
a major role in the 1902 Anglo-Japanese Alliance. The high point of his
career came in 1905 when he was named Japanese plenipotentiary to the
Portsmouth Peace Conference, which concluded the Russo-Japanese
War. In 1908 he became Foreign Minister for a second time and played
an important role in the annexation of Korea.[137]

Another of Griffis' students in Tokyo was Viscount Kuroda, and there
is evidence of Griffis' influence on his future. In a letter to Griffis, dated
April 12, 1915, he wrote,

> I often say that without your help I could never have been successful in ac-
> complishing my course of study at the University and . . . I could never
> get my present position with the Imperial Household.[138]

Takahashi Korekiyo was another recipient of Griffis' hospitality. In
an unpublished manuscript Griffis credited Takahashi with reading to him
a "good deal of native Japanese literature."[139] Takahashi later became
president of the Bank of Japan, twice his nation's Prime Minister, and the
Finance Minister who stabilized the yen in the early 1930s, but was
assassinated by army fanatics in the February 26 (1936) Incident because
of his opposition to its actions in China.

Not all of Griffis' students were influential or prominent. A number of
them were merely successful in the various endeavors which they chose to
devote themselves. A certain Nishimura, a student in Fukui, edited a

journal, *Gakusei (Student)*, devoted to young people. In a letter to Griffis, dated March 5, 1915, the young editor asked his former teacher for a short contribution to his journal, and his assistance in tracking down a copy of a book Nishimura had written, *A History of Japanese Vessels in the United States*, that had been published in America.[140] Another of his students who falls into this category was also from Fukui, Karl Kasahara (this might be his favorite "Karl" who lived with him in both Fukui and later Tokyo), who became the manager of the Kobe Pier Co., Ltd.[141]

We would be remiss if we did not mention two of Griffis' many students from Rutgers who have become at least footnotes to history. The first, Kusakabe Tarō, was a brilliant student at Rutgers and unfortunately, died of tuberculosis just prior to his graduation in 1870. It was Griffis' sad duty to present Kusakabe's Phi Beta Kappa key to his grief stricken parents when he arrived in Japan, a few months later.

Another of his Rutgers "boys" was Hatakeyama Yoshinari. Although he did not graduate, he returned to Japan and served as an interpreter with the Iwakura Embassy before serving as an administrator in Tokyo University soon after its founding and later in the Ministries of Education, Home, and Foreign Affairs. He also died in his early thirties of tuberculosis.

If a teacher, is, indeed, known by the students he has taught, William Elliot Griffis was a success in that calling.

THE CALM BEFORE THE STORM

As we have seen, the arrival of Maggie had a salutary effect on Griffis' mind, and he gradually became more like the "Willie" his sister had known before he left for Japan. Living together in a large comfortable house in the middle of the European quarter with several of Griffis' students, Maggie quickly adjusted to life in this precursor to the "golden ghetto"—the westerner's answer to the discomforts of living in a foreign country. Maggie described it in a letter to her sisters at home.

> In Yedo there are about 150 foreigners, [and] in the place we live called a Compound there are about 30 persons including children, also many servants, carriages & horses. If you look in the map of Yedo, just in the centre is the Mikado's palace, and a large moat around it of seven miles, we live on this side.[142]

Maggie was pleased with the elevation in status and lifestyle which provided more comforts than she ever had in Philadelphia.

> We live in . . . a large, one story house with 8 rooms, but the rooms are as long as our old house—as long as one whole floor. I like it very much . . . .
> I have a man-cook and a woman for the house work, we keep a carriage and

have two coolies to pull it. We have a large garden, plenty of society and as
Willie only teaches until 12 o'clock, he takes me out all over Yedo every
afternoon.[143]

After experiencing her new life for less than a month, Maggie described
its joys to her sisters. It was not an unmitigated success, however, since
her cook, although "an excellent one . . . cannot make any dessert but
rice pudding."[144]

> . . . I will describe our breakfast, coffee—tea—toast, omelette, fried sau-
> sage, (these are put up in cans), fried potatoes and then rice-batter cakes
> with syrup. For dinner we have soup (always) then fish & potatoes, then meat
> and vegetables, then boiled rice and curry, then dessert. Four courses every
> day. Everybody lives in this manner and some as high as seven courses. My
> girl has lived in a foreign family in Yokohama and does excellently. No
> trouble with servants here. We give the cook a certain sum every night, then
> give orders for the meals next day, and he goes out to buy everything and
> our care is ended.[145]

The fall of 1872 was Maggie's high point while in Japan. Her health was
good, she was enthusiastic about seeing more of Japan, and she had a
cook, servants, and few serious financial worries. In addition, as we shall
see, her social life far outstripped what she had known in America. Although she had not been able to secure a position in the new girl's school,
she did manage to find a pupil who came for an hour a day and this earned
her four dollars a month.[146] It is no surprise that she informed those at
home that "I feel pretty well at home in Japan."[147] In the full flush of her
good times, she revealed that Willie was thinking of returning to America
for a visit the following year. "He wants a wife . . . [and] has given Ellen
up entirely & I believe if there were any one out here suitable, he would
marry very soon."[148] In a comment that must have surprised, and even
distressed those at home, she suggested, "I am almost sure that Willie
will always live here. I have good ground for thinking so."[149]

A few weeks later, she reaffirmed her happiness in Japan, and wrote
that if her sisters were with her and she were employed, "I could live here
for years happily."[150] An active social life certainly encouraged her feeling.

> The English seem to rule society here and have all their stiff rules & regula-
> tions and although at first I could not bear Yedo yet now I am so glad I live
> here, for there is more fuss & style and rules in Yokohama than I believe in
> Washington . . . I couldn't begin to tell you a hundredth part of the life &
> gossip here, but nevertheless I like it. It is a new world to me and therefore
> rather interesting, to be a looker-on.[151]

With his sister enjoying herself so thoroughly, it is little wonder that

Willie was also in good spirits. Although it was not apparent at the time, the future of the Griffis "family" in Japan began to cloud. By November 2, Maggie was concerned that each "steamer brings new arrivals and most persons want to teach so that the papers are full of advertisements" from potential teachers looking for pupils.[152] A short time later, she complained to her sisters, "the longer I live here the less I see any prospect of you ever coming. There are people here ready to *snap up* anything that offers and sending to America [for teachers] is given up." Things were getting so bad that the Japanese were "reducing teacher's salaries," and "four gentlemen in the College who teach the lower classes, get but $150 a month where they formerly got $200."[153]

In the meantime Willie remained busy writing his primers, readers, and spelling books for H. H. Bancroft Company, but would not see any profits (assuming there would be profits) for at least a year because "they are not yet perfect enough to sell."[154] Maggie wrote,

> He does not see the proofs to correct them, so a small number are printed & sent back from San Francisco (full of errors in printing) to be corrected, then sent to America to be reprinted.[155]

This was not an efficient way to prepare textbooks, but Griffis had no control over the situation. By this time, November 1872, four of the books were either printed or in press—[t]he First & Second Primer, the Spelling Book, the First Reader and we have just finished another Reader for advanced pupils that is getting ready for the Press. I say we because, I select and write, and correct with Willie and it keeps me busy."[156]

An important pedagogical aspect of this book-writing enterprise was that Griffis was one of the "few American teachers [to] have tried to devise materials specially adapted to Japanese needs."[157] He attempted to take into account the peculiar needs of the students who would be using these books which were "graded in difficulty but not juvenile in content."[158] This last principle, "graded in difficulty but not juvenile in content," was one which Griffis followed throughout his life in much of his prolific literary output. He always put the interest of the reader and an easy writing style above pretentiousness. If nothing else, his writing was geared toward describing and explaining Japan and Japanese events to the masses of the American people.

At about this time Maggie began to complain of physical discomforts. "I have not," she informed her sisters, "been in clover since I came [to Japan] . . . . First my heart, then indigestion and then lacquer poison."[159] It seems that Willie had brought a freshly lacquered piece of furniture into their dining room, and the effect on Maggie was severe.

> I must have touched it and at least smelled it, for I was too sick to keep

any food in my stomach for two days, my eyes swelled and inflamed until I was sure I had erysiphelas [sic], I could scarcely see and the inflammation extended down nearly to my mouth, then my ears gathered and are still aching terribly, until I was a picture of distress.[160]

Soon thereafter, she complained that "I have not been well since I came," and "I have spent nights of pain with a gathered ear."[161] These problems came on the heels of a "severe palpitation of the heart," and an "enlargement of the liver."[162] Maggie worried a great deal about her health, once commenting that she knew she suffered from "an incurable disease,"[163] and that she was "losing" her health.[164]

Despite being happy otherwise, her health continued to deteriorate. In early December she confided that "I am still feeling very badly," and "I am getting so very thin."[165] Such comments are found in many of her letters home, and it is reasonable to assume that they were no stranger to Willie's ear.

Although plagued by Maggie's ill health since her arrival, the Griffis household in Tokyo was doing quite well in the months following Maggie's arrival. Slowly however, the pendulum seems to have swung in the opposite direction. The prospect of a teaching position for Maggie dimmed considerably in the fall of 1872, and Willie's financial situation further soured as unanticipated expenses cropped up and his book-writing project failed to produce the expected profits. These events led Griffis to inform Maggie that during 1873 he would continue to do a great deal of writing for both newspapers and magazines. "All of this writing is only helping me to stake out the ground for the book [The Mikado's Empire] and for lectures on Japan—when and by whom, I shall at some time tell you. These are plans only, as yet; but I wish this year to keep intact all the cash I can save, as to be penniless here, is dangerous, and at least our passage money ought to be ready at hand always."[166] This is the first real hint that Griffis was considering returning in the near future, and six months later, a crisis occurred which may have led to the nonrenewal of Griffis' contract.

As we have seen, Griffis was very much interested in the establishment of the principle of female education in Japan. Although it is easy to recognize that part of his motivation for this enterprise was to create a position for his sister, there is another side to this picture. Throughout his long life, both in Japan and in America, Griffis was an outspoken advocate of the education of women, probably because he placed so much emphasis on the importance of education in the first few years of a child's life in which "our first teachers are our mothers."[167] There is also evidence to suggest that he advocated higher education for women at Rutgers long before it had become a popular position to take.[168]

In any event, Griffis could not help but be pleased when Maggie finally secured a teaching position early in 1873. Despite this, his diary entry for February 18 included this good news almost as an afterthought. The only other reference that either Maggie's or Willie's available papers make to this event is Willie's diary entry of March 3, which simply recorded the fact that Maggie "began teaching in girl's school."[169] Years later, however, Griffis proudly wrote that the first government school for Japanese girls was established in 1873 "of which Mrs. Veeder and Miss M. C. Griffis were the first instructors." He went on to describe how his sister worked as a teacher in the Jogakkō ("girls' school"), out of which "grew the Peeresses' School in which taught Miss Alice Bacon."[170]

Thus, in the summer of 1873, both of the Griffis teachers were employed and, despite Maggie's ill health, enjoying Tokyo's social life. Willie's writing was progressing well, and he was even able to secure a commitment from the *New York Evening Post* to pay him anywhere from $7.50 to $10.00 for each column of his material they printed.[171]

GRIFFIS' CLASH WITH JAPANESE BUREAUCRACY

As we shall see, the major bone of contention between Griffis and the Monbushō was over the interpretation of Griffis' contract in Tokyo, and especially his situation resulting from the failure of the polytechnic school to open in the late winter of 1872. The event that appears to have triggered this whole affair, however, grew out of the American teachers' celebration of their July 4th, Independence Day holiday, in 1873. These teachers, living in the European's compound, were determined to celebrate their national holiday with the traditional fireworks in spite of the Japanese officials' prohibition of such a display just a day earlier.[172] The Japanese authorities were justifiably concerned over the fire hazard that the American celebration would pose to the flimsy wooden structures which made up the bulk of the capital's structures. The Americans, on the other hand, felt that the concept of "extraterritoriality" prevented the Japanese from interfering. In any event, the fireworks display took place on the night of July 4, with Griffis watching it from his friend Marion Scott's residence.[173] The following day, Griffis' diary records that a Mr. Wilson, presumably one of the teachers suspected of complicity in this affair, was "questioned" etc. by police and school authorities.[174]

One must keep in mind that the Japanese were extremely jealous of their sovereignty and were looking for ways in which to have the unequal treaties with the western powers abrogated. The American defiance of Japanese regulations undoubtedly was irksome to the governmental officials. It appears that the Japanese, stung by this turn of events, looked for a vehicle with which they could reassert their authority. The result was the "Sunday Question."

Soon thereafter, the school officials announced that they were shifting the

the teacher's Sunday holiday to conform to Japanese holidays. As Griffis summed up the situation in a letter home,

> The educational authorities are determined to enforce the observation of the Japanese holidays, and to require all foreign teachers to disregard Sunday. The Japanese holidays are the 1st, 6th, 11th, 16th, 21st, 26th of each month. Such a rule would give us more holidays, but we should have to teach on Sundays. It was given out that in all new contracts, the anti-Sunday clause would be inserted. A few weeks ago, a request from the Mombusho was sent us asking us to teach on Sunday. We replied, "*no*, not for $10,000 per month."[175]

In his 1900 biography of Guido Verbeck, *Verbeck of Japan*, Griffis devoted several pages to this event. His interpretation of events. a quarter of a century later, was no softer than it was at the time of their occurrence.

> Evidently it seemed to politicians in charge and to the men of the Department of Education who were behind them, that they could arbitrarily break faith in order to carry out their plans. As there were more Japanese holidays than Sundays in each month, it was doubtless expected by them that the foreigners would yield. In this they reckoned without their quest. At least one man was determined not to stand such treachery.[176]

Griffis, secure in his knowledge that righteousness was on his side, immediately began to rally his compatriots in opposition to this decision. He wrote, "I went to see the English-speaking teachers, both British and American. All agreed to protest against the changing of rest days from Sunday to [the Japanese system]."[177] The Japanese authorities, according to Griffis' account of the incident (there seems to be no reason not to accept his version here), did not take kindly to his activities.

> This action on the part of the American in Japan, though done with all courtesy . . . immediately aroused the wrath of the gentleman [Minister of Education Tanaka Fujiro] then in control who stands in memory as the typical Japanese politician and spoilsman, about as closely resembling the American "boss" as any creature ever met with.[178]

Much to his surprise, Griffis received notice on July 15 that his contract was not to be renewed. This communication not only shocked him but must have angered him also. He was a hard-working, conscientious professor, well-liked by his students, with the best interests of Japan at heart. He had led Maggie to believe that he might stay in Japan for a long time and in addition, he saw himself doing God's work in opposing the shift of rest days from Sunday to the Japanese system. His initial response to this unwelcomed news was to fight back. He took the 2 P.M. train to Yokohama where he sought out both American Minister to Japan DeLong and Reverend Brown who had been in Japan for years. Unfortunately for

Griffis, Guido Verbeck had left Japan on July 10 to return to Europe on leave. It is not certain whether he was able to see Brown, and DeLong was out when Griffis called. However, he left a message and the following day received a note from DeLong apologizing for not being home to receive him but promising to do what he could. The American diplomat cautioned him, somewhat cryptically, that "my position now is that of a crippled man. I am about going out of office under a cloud, which fact these authorities know and some now are taking advantage of."[179]

Griffis welcomed any help that DeLong could offer, but he was not one to place all of his eggs in one basket. He wrote a private letter to the *Japan Mail* complaining about the situation and received a reply from the editor.

I have said a few words this week upon the Sunday question, which I hope may do some good. But I know the Japanese are in a very uncomplying mood . . . [and] have a class of men in office who delight to answer a foreign ministers [sic] remonstrance on such a subject with a snub. For a long time they were servile when their seat was yet insecure. Now they are insolent —like all ill-bred grooms as half of them are—or little better.[180]

In addition, he began to contact influential political figures in the Japanese government to protest what he considered unfair treatment at the hands of "a petty underling."[181] In 1900 he wrote that solving the problem was a simple matter; "I dropped a note to Mr. Iwakura [Tomomi], the junior prime minister, simply stating the case. The matter was very quickly settled to my satisfaction. Another position of equal honor and emolument for three years was offered me, which I declined with thanks."[182] As in much that Griffis wrote, there is truth in this interpretation, but he selectively omitted much which would cast his actions in a different, even unfavorable, light. In the first place, Griffis' diary and correspondence indicate that, in addition to seeking the intercession of Iwakura, he also contacted Mori Arinori, Matsudaira Shungaku, Judge Horace Bingham, the new American Minister to the Japanese government, and others.

In late July he informed his sisters in Philadelphia,

This, will most probably finish my career in Japan, and I am not sorry that I have so good a reason for leaving the Japanese civil service. I am a little sorry, as I should like to have remained six months longer at least. After near three years service in a foreign land, I have in bank now, *just enough to take me home.* For the future however, I have no sort of fear, and though I never expect, nor care to be a rich man, not making wealth an object, I expect to win a name and place in my native land. The tide in the affairs of Japan may turn, but at present, it is most decidedly anti-Christian and reactionary.[183]

Although there is no indication of such an offer being made to him in any of his other correspondence or published writings, Griffis informed his sisters, "I am proud to say that I could stay at an advanced salary of over $4,000, were I [to] consent to give up my Sundays."[184] His students' opposition to the decision of the authorities and their promise to "petition the Department of Education that I be retained" also cheered him.[185]

An examination of the available correspondence between Griffis and Minister of Education Tanaka indicates that their differences clearly revolved around the interpretation of Griffis' contract more than on the burning question of whether foreign teachers should teach on the western sabbath. It seems that Griffis felt very strongly that he was brought to Tokyo to fill a specific position in the proposed polytechnical institution which, for various reasons, failed to open at the scheduled time. On the other hand, Griffis had been "willing to volunteer . . . to teach the 1st class students at old Nankō (now Kaisei Gakkō), until that special school was opened." With the school now opened in the Kaisei Gakkō, Tanaka pointed out, "you have . . . been appointed, as promised, as the professor of the same, that is to say, Law and Physics,"[186] so the contract is fulfilled. Moreover, the government had even added thirty yen per month to his salary "so that our contract to engage you as professor at the special school was wholly and satisfactorily fulfilled."[187]

Upon receiving this letter, Griffis felt compelled to reply "because silence on my part would be misunderstood."[188] The major thrust of Griffis' disagreement with Tanaka revolved around three aspects of the contract. First, Griffis reiterated his stand that he was hired for a specific position, that is in the technical school, and when that school failed to open, he "could have waited, had I so chosen, doing nothing, until the Educational authorities were ready to carry out their contract with me."[189] He claimed to have "volunteered" for Nankō in order to be useful, and "on the condition that I should have my proper position as Professor of Chemistry and Physics, for the term contracted for, i.e., two years."[190] Griffis seemed especially agitated over the education minister's interpretation of the reason for paying Griffis thirty yen per month extra. Griffis contended, with apparent justification, that the extra thirty yen per month was due to *extra* chores that he had voluntarily taken on, above and beyond his normal contractual duties. "I never asked for any increase of salary," Griffis told Tanaka, "nor do I want any, except as honest payment for honest extra work, done outside my contract." He concluded by informing his antagonist that if he persisted in his interpretation of this matter, "I do not wish, nor will I receive, the extra 30 yen per month, recently added."[191]

Griffis evidently took steps to reduce his workload and perhaps to exert pressure on his adversary in anticipation of Tanaka's continued insistence on his interpretation in the matter of the extra thirty yen. Griffis' students did not look with favor on Tanaka's view. Between August 20–22, they wrote four letters of support to Griffis, and perhaps to Tanaka also, although there is no evidence of the latter. The self-interest of the students is in the forefront of their letters, but there is also a strain of opposition to Tanaka's attitude and of real, if muted, affection for their *sensei*. One class requested his "mercy to continue in teaching us as you have done during a year and a half, that is to teach us on the other branches besides Chemistry. Indeed . . . it would be beyond your proper duty to the school. But we shall be very happy if you grant this request."[192] His students in the First Legal Class appealed to his pedagogical pride, telling him that no matter how "greatly learned teachers we may have in the future, it is quite certain that we shall not get the teacher like you who has great skill in teaching according to the character and ability of each scholar."[193] Perhaps the most poignant appeal came from his "affectionate scholars of the 2nd Legal Class."

> In this school, many teachers are of different classes of men, some are soldiers, some are sailors and others are mere drinkers or bad men, though there are a few educated teachers who are very kind, such as you and two other gentlemen. There is a great difference between the lower classes of men whose only objects are to make money and the educated teachers whose purpose are to help the Japanese in advancing in civilization. But if the officer think all to be the same object, he is quite mistaken. Of course, we honor you as our dear teacher and distinguish you from lower classes of men.[194]

The appeal of his second scientific class was much more broadly based than those of his other classes. These boys also asked him to continue teaching them the subjects outside of his contract, but they concluded by telling him, in their struggling English, that "we have occasioned to have [a] thousand anxious [anxieties] about your returning to your mother country during the year. If it be the case, we will be like a boy left out in the middle of the African desert. At least we hope you will stay three years more in the school as the eyes of the world appoint you our teacher."[195]

This support from his students must have buoyed Griffis' spirits considerably in his battle with the Monbushō. Be that as it may, the fact remained that Griffis' contract had not been renewed, and he had an extremely small financial cushion to fall back on in the event of a real emergency. He undoubtedly had this in mind when he wrote to Iwakura Tomomi again on September 11.[196] There is no record of the contents of this letter, but a reply to it was written by the busy official's son on September 19, 1873. Young Iwakura acknowledged Griffis' letter and apologized that his father was unable to see him at that time due to his "exceedingly busy" schedule, which his son complained, left him "no time to talk

even to us."[197] Lest this be interpreted as a lack of interest on the foreign
minister's part, it should be pointed out that the summer and autumn of
1873 saw the eruption of Japan's "Korean Crisis."[198] These events kept
him constantly involved with weighty matters of state, and a foreign teacher's contractual problems had to take second place. Griffis had been the
Rutgers teacher of Iwakura's son and thus, Iwakura undoubtedly did what
he could under the circumstances.

There is, at least, circumstantial evidence that Griffis placed much of
his hopes in Iwakura's hands. In a letter to Griffis, his close friend Ed Clark
reminded him, "If Iwakura's return [from Europe] produces any marked
effect 'for better or for worse' please let me know. Or if W. E. G. [Griffis]
contemplates any bold strategical 'dash' in any direction, do let us have
it."[199] This would seem to indicate that Griffis had corresponded about his
problems and probably laid out for his friend the outline of his strategy.

By October 10, it appears that there was some movement in the negotiations between Griffis and Tanaka. In a letter of that date, Tanaka reaffirmed his basic position that Griffis had "no reason . . . of any dissatisfaction on your part," but added the significant phrase, "if you have
anything to be proposed, please give it in detail to the Director of the
Kaiseigakko, and whether your service after the expiration of your term is
left to the convenience of the school. . . . " In this letter Tanaka appears
to be backtracking somewhat from his previous hard line. We cannot be
sure, but it was possible that between Griffis' last letter of September 11
and Tanaka's letter of October 10, Iwakura had contacted Tanaka in an
attempt to work out some sort of face-saving compromise.

If this was, indeed, what had occurred, Griffis' response to this letter
takes on new meaning and despite some strong language, illustrates
Griffis' willingness to accept a compromise solution. On October 13 he
wrote a long response which is worth quoting at some length. Griffis
argued that when he came to Tokyo "I was made Professor of Chemistry
and Physics *only*. I did not teach English in Fukui, but science only."[201]
Once more this is true, yet it does not reflect the situation accurately.
Griffis did teach English in Fukui on an informal, after hours, basis. One
of the inherent functions of English-speaking teachers in Meiji Japan was
the teaching of their native tongue. Griffis continued,

> I did not come out from America to teach the elementary branches. I came
> to Japan to teach science, and I am not satisfied that the Mombusho do not
> seem to make the proper distinction between Professors of special studies
> and teachers of elementary branches; and between regularly trained profes-
> sional Gentlemen from Colleges in America, and the men who are picked up
> in Yokohama, and are not real teachers. So far, it seems to me that the
> Mombusho officers suppose that I ought to be satisfied if I receive my salary

regularly. But I am not satisfied with money only. I want my proper position. . . .

I told Mr. Verbeck that I would teach in Nan Ko, *provided that when the Polytechnic school should be opened, I should have my proper position as Prof. of Chem. and Physics for the time of my contract, i.e., two years.* I should not have gone into Nan Ko if I had thought that the Polytechnic School would not open for a year and a half afterwards, and then receive my proper [*sic*] position for six months only. I could hardly believe my own ears, when . . . informed me that my services would not be required after Jan. 5, 1874 when my present contract would have expired, if I had been two years in the Polytechnic School, but I have thus far, been in the Polytechnic School three months, and by Jan. 5, it will have been only six months. . . .

This, then, is the chief subject of my dissatisfaction. I contracted to be a professor of special branches in the Polytechnic School for two years. I have been waiting one year and a half to get my proper position and justice and solemn contract guarantees me that position for two years.[202]

Griffis thus reaffirmed his original position with great vigor and asserted that he did not want to be unreasonable in his claims. In the next breath, he suggested that "I do not wish to force myself on the Japanese officers," and if the Monbushō "cannot carry out your contract with me, I shall return to my own country, and tell everyone that a contract with the Mombusho is worth nothing."[203] After detailing the problems of teaching in Japan without sufficient apparatus and without colleagues who could help by teaching the other branches of chemistry, Griffis presented an acceptable compromise.

I am willing to endeavor to do what will be for the "convenience of the school." I know you have many foreign gentlemen, whose claims are to be attended to, and I do not wish to give you any trouble. I cannot understand, however, how *justice* is done to me, if I am sent away in Jan. 1874. According to strict contract, and my agreement with Mr. Verbeck, I ought to hold my position as Prof. of Chem. and Phys. in the Polytechnic School from July 10th 1873 to July 10th 1875, but I do not want to stay in Japan so long as that. I only wish to stay nine months after Jan. 1st 1873, i.e., until Oct. 1st 1874.[204]

The conditions which had led Maggie to tell her sisters that she had reason to believe that Willie would stay in Japan for a long time no longer held. It is clear that as of the autumn of 1873, Griffis had pretty well decided that he would leave Japan within the next year. Not only did he tell Tanaka that he would not stay in Japan beyond October 1, 1874, but he also refused an offer of a position as a teacher of chemistry in Kyoto.[205] This was not the only job offer that Griffis received while living in Tokyo. In September 1872, he had "a very tempting offer made to me, it was—to become the editor of the *Japan Mail*—a very influential and able newspaper in Yokohama. It is proposed to make it American. It would give me the opportunity of making money out of the job-printing which is always done by a newspaper paper press."[206] Despite the advantages this position offered, Griffis did not take it because he felt he "must be assured of $4,000 per year . . . . I am nicely situated here, that I prefer to finish out my time here," and if the paper is started, "I will become a paid contributor."[207] When Griffis refused the offer of the editorship, the newspaper's owners secured the services of Captain Frank Brinkley, who at one time had been scheduled to serve as a military instructor in Fukui during Griffis' tenure in that city but was retained at the last minute by Imperial Government in Tokyo. Brinkley, as editor of the *Japan Mail*, soon established an enviable reputation during his long sojourn as an English-language journalist in Japan. As we shall see later, in order to return to America with Maggie, Griffis also refused an offer to accompany General Horace Capron on his journey to Hokkaido in May 1874.

While awaiting the decision of the government as to the future of his contract, Griffis spent his time teaching, writing, and visiting both people and institutions in Tokyo and Yokohama. He made numerous trips to Yokohama and paid calls on many of his missionary friends as well as other prominent members of the foreign community. The Japanese authorities accepted his offer to prepare a chemistry course of study for future implementation, and he forwarded it to the Kaisei Gakkō authorities on November 24, 1872.[208]

Meanwhile his own future was never far from his thoughts, and in early December 1873, he composed a letter "for Mr. Verbeck to send to the Mombusho."[209] A short time later, Verbeck returned the draft to Griffis and apologized that he had been too busy to finish editing it but promised that he would do so within a couple of days. In addition, Verbeck felt, "from conscientious scruples, I have to alter more in the letter than at first seemed to me necessary; yet I hope it will satisfy you in its altered form."[210] We do not have Verbeck's edited version of Griffis' letter, so it is not possible precisely to gauge what differences existed between the two documents. We do know, however, that Griffis' original draft was stronger and more detailed in several ways than the arguments he had been putting forth for the past several months. The major differences in substance and/or emphasis that concern us here are as follows:

2nd Not wishing to remain idle [after the failure of the technical school], he was requested and agreed to teach in the Nan Ko, provided that he should receive his proper position according to the contract, viz. to be Prof. of Chem. and Physics in Shem Mon Gakko as for the space of two years. At the same time, he distinctly gave me notice that he should ask for an increase of salary for doing extra work, within a few months. He believed at that time, as I told him, that the Shem Mon Gakko would be opened in five or six months.

3rd At the end of that time, he applied as he had given notice, for an increase in salary. As this was objected to, Mr. Griffis promised . . . that if his position was fully defined to him, that he would withdraw his claim for extra salary.

4th Mr. Yagimoto [Monbushō official] brought to him a paper . . . written in Chinese, which being translated verbally to Mr. Griffis, appeared to satisfy him, because as he understood the translation, it seemed to be what he had desired.

. . . .

7th If the Mom Bu Sho cannot agree [that Mr. Griffis' contract should legally run from July 10, 1873 to July 10, 1875], they are indebted to Mr. Griffis for teaching extra studies and working extra hours from the beginning of his work with Nan Ko, until July 10, 1873, a period of fifteen months.

7th [sic] When Mr. Griffis made his contract, it was agreed that he was to be a professor, and not a tutor only, and was to be employed but two hours per day in teaching, and was requested by Mr. Morris [identity unknown] and myself not to alter the printed matter of the contract. I pledged my honor to maintain him in this. Since that time however, he has taught from five to three hours a day, (27 to 21 hours per week).[211]

This document informs us for the first time that Griffis had, in the winter of 1872–1873 "distinctly" given notice that he would soon ask for an increase in his salary to cover the extra work involved in his position, that he was given a "fully defined" position description in lieu of his salary increase, that he agreed to a verbal translation of a document "written in Chinese" clearly implying dishonesty on the part of the Monbushō, that at a minimum, the Monbushō owed him back pay for fifteen months for the extra work he had done without compensation, and that Verbeck personally asked Griffis to accept the contract as written, without alteration, and he would personally guarantee that Griffis' understanding of it would prevail in any dispute. None of these claims are found in any of the available letters that Griffis wrote to Tanaka.

Griffis' seemingly hopeless battle with the authorities took a turn in his favor on December 19, 1873. On that day, as Griffis jubilantly recorded in his diary, Hatakeyama Yoshinari, the former Sugiwara Kōzō, a friend of Griffis from his student days at Rutgers was "appointed Chief Director of Kai Sei Gakko today."[212] Griffis shared lunch with Hatakeyama the same day and offered his congratulations upon his appointment to his new position.[213] On December 22, just three days later, Griffis learned that his contract would expire on February 16, 1874, rather than on January 5, 1874.[214] During this breathing space afforded to Griffis by the contract's extension, an agreement was worked out which enabled Griffis to remain as Professor of Chemistry for an extra six months. It seems reasonable to conclude that Hatakeyama probably played a role in this turn of events.

Looking at this struggle in retrospect, it is not surprising that Griffis was able to prevail, at least in the short term. What is puzzling is that Griffis was forced into a relatively unfavorable compromise. After all, he did have a strong personal tie to Iwakura Tomomi, whose son he had taught at Rutgers. In a Japanese context Griffis was more than the English word "teacher" implies; he was the *sensei* of young Iwakura. In a sense, it is surprising that this did not count for more in this situation. In addition, his allies included Guido Verbeck (although there is some evidence to indicate that his support was qualified), who was held in very high respect by the Japanese, the American Minister to Japan DeLong, and his old Rutgers student Hatakeyama. Of all these men, it appears that the one finally to act in Griffis' behalf was Hatakeyama almost as soon as he assumed the executive authority at Kaisei Gakkō. Yet we find that Griffis had won only a partial victory of a six-month extension to July 1874, rather than his proposed compromise date of October 1874.

This episode ended with David Murray's letter to Griffis on January 24, 1874:

> Allow me also to express the pleasure I feel, in seeing the matters at issue are settled in an honorable and satisfactory manner, and on which must be regarded as highly complimentary to you, and I must add creditable to the Japanese officials.[215]

FINAL DAYS IN JAPAN

Before the decision was made to extend Griffis' contract from its original January 5 expiration date to February 16, the Japanese authorities searched for a replacement for Griffis on the earlier date. Ironically, the man invited to Tokyo to replace Griffis was none other than his old college friend, Edward Clark, who had been teaching in Shizuoka.[216] This was, however, an unexpected windfall for Griffis for when Clark arrived in Tokyo, the authorities "had no suitable house for him," so he moved in with Willie and Maggie.[217] This meant that the Japanese boys who had been living with Griffis had to leave so that there would be enough room. "We were glad indeed to have him & so he had taken the dining room which is very large."[218]

This arrangement worked out very well for all parties; Willie had the companionship of Clark as well as of Maggie, but he could discuss many things—particularly both men's dislike of the Japanese bureaucracy—more comfortably with Clark than with his sister. Both young men had often talked about going home to America via India and Africa and during this period Griffis seriously considered following that route.

One of the last major social events that Griffis and Maggie attended in Japan occurred during the Christmas season in Yokohama. After describing the home of their host and hostess, a Mr. and Mrs. Baker, in great detail, Maggie enthused that "I was never at such a splendid affair in my life."[219] In a very real sense, this final big party symbolized the Griffis' stay in Japan. As Maggie wrote, "Here I move among laces & jewels . . . . Dresses that cost fortunes [are] all around me and I [am dressed] extremely plain, fortunately black excuses all."[220] Maggie was anxious to return home to her loved ones, but there is no doubt that she was not anxious to leave her new life behind her.

> I am feeling all the time as if I were soon going home, and the delight of being with you again draws me, but I do confess that it will be very hard to go back to the old life after two years here of perfect independence and perfect equality in society, and even superiority to many. For if we had only had means we have education to go in the very best society there is. This I have found out since I have been here, for the most high flung people are my especial friends, and the idea of hunting a situation and all that is not very pleasant to think of . . . . yet although I dread the old life, yet I know we can have very comfortable times together and I long to get back to you once more.[221]

These social pretensions made it very difficult for Maggie to accept their new cook. She noted scornfully, "In disquiet at Japanese cooks we have hired an American black man and turned over the house into his hands paying him so much a month & he furnishes everything. So we board with a nigger . . . . We will try it for a month."[222] One suspects that the black cook was probably Willie's idea. Although he exhibited many of the typical nineteenth-century racial attitudes of most Americans, his views were relatively mild. For example, while visiting in Yokohama in September 1872, he recounted that he was "scraped and clipped and combed into proper proportions," by a "black barber who employs white assistants."[223] The absence of other comments is revealing.

In the meantime Willie worked devotedly on his literary projects. He was still contributing several articles to newspapers and magazines, both in Japan and America, in addition to working on several commercial tourist works. These included *The Tokio Guide, The Yokohama Guide,* and a *Map of Tokio* which was published in July 1874 (shortly before his departure for America).[224] Griffis also put in a considerable amount of work on *The Kamakura Guide* which was never published as far as can be ascertained.[225]

During this period Griffis began work on his magnum opus, *The Mikado's Empire*, and he made a sustained effort to collect as much material as possible to use in this book. For example, in April he paid a visit to the Tokyo Prison and used the results of that visit for *The Mikado's Empire*, magazine articles and public lectures upon his return to the United States.

He was an interested spectator during these last months to the political fallout of the abortive "Korean Crisis" of 1873 and the struggle for power in the government between the progressives and the conservatives.[226] These topics undoubtedly served as lightning rods for debate during the informal social gatherings of his students at his home[227] as well as at the prestigious Meirokusha meetings that he attended.[228]

By this time, Griffis had reconciled himself to going home, and even began to look forward to the prospect.

> I have made up my mind . . . to go home, and shall only remain until August or Sept. 20 at farthest. I want to spend a few weeks in China before I leave the orient. Clarkie wants me to go around the world with him, but time is precious to me, and autumn is the true beginning of the year to me. I hope to come home with my book on Japan finished and ready for the press, so as to be out by Christmas, so I *must* come home in the summer or early fall.[229]

Six weeks later, however, Maggie spoke of going home around the world. This would be, she continued, the culmination of a "life-long dream" that "I cannot give up now when the *chance* is here."[230] She described how it could be done in the following words:

> It will as I told you cost only a few hundreds, as Willie & I know how to travel cheaply and can get letters of introduction to missionary families where we can stay much cheaper than hotels. I shall work these six months for that object and expect to accomplish it.[231]

In an apparent attempt to make the departure less painful, the siblings talked a great deal of "coming back here as missionaries in a few years."[232] It is always less difficult to leave a pleasant location if one can convince himself that the time away will be temporary and short. In a very profound sense, Griffis was leaving Japan physically, but not in spirit. He planned to maintain his knowledge of Japan and to continue his literary ways. "I understand the ways of authorship now," he wrote, "literary wares can always find buyers, if the article is good, and more than one customer is tried."[233] Soon after writing this, he made arrangements through his sister Martha to have his name and expertise advertised through the American Literary Bureau.[234] This was a wise move for, soon after arriving home, he became a popular lecture-circuit speaker on things Japanese.

As we have seen, there was an ever-changing difference of opinion between brother and sister during the last few months as to when and by what route to return to their homeland. It is clear, as has been pointed out, that they were ambivalent about leaving Japan, but had more or less committed themselves to this course of action. Maggie's health resolved their indecision in short order. In early May 1874, Maggie complained to her sisters, "I am in very bad condition . . . [and] cannot stand up two minutes, nor walk at all and I have severe dragging pains."[235] Initially uneasy about being intimately examined by a male doctor, she was able to arrange for an examination to be conducted by a talented young English lady, Matilda C. Ayrton, who was recommended to her as "a person of ability."[236] Maggie's discomfort was great, and she worried that "this falling of the womb is a very painful thing and may make me an invalid for life."[237] Her condition, which may have been a form of cancer, led her to give up the idea of returning home through India and Europe.

Willie, on the other hand, was still anxious to make a visit of several weeks to China before returning to America. Due to this, Maggie was certain that they would not "get away from Japan before the middle of October," even though she would be free of her school obligations on July 15.[238]

> I shall wait for his [Willie's] trip to China and then we hope to come back together. I often beg him to come home in August, but he still clings to the hope of going around the world, so all is uncertain as to time.[239]

Maggie was not a bashful woman in advancing her claims, and she started a campaign to persuade Willie to leave Japan for America as soon as it was practicable. Her success is reflected in her letter of May 15, to the Griffis sisters in Philadelphia.

> . . . I have at last succeeded in coaxing this blessed brother of ours to give up his trip to China and to come home *this summer*. Today he promised me, *I and he*, should leave Japan *before* Sep lst. Isn't that glorious? I can't realize it. I don't dare to rejoice over it for fear something should happen.[240]

Of course, Maggie interpreted her brother's decision to be in his own self-interest and not as a sacrifice for her health. "*It is too hot* to go to China before October," she wrote, "and I urge that Willie should be home early in the Fall, if he wants to do any work or begin a career."[241]

The day before Maggie's letter, May 14, General Horace Capron, the former Commissioner of Agriculture in President Grant's administration and advisor to the Imperial Government for the settlement of Hokkaido, offered Griffis a position "as private secretary" at "$2,000 per annum" on the eve of Capron's move to Hokkaido.[242] It is not known exactly how much Griffis told his sister about the offer, but she wrote home that Capron had made Willie an offer, but it was to accompany him to Hokkaido and "to stay until Fall."²⁴³ She did concede, however, that Willie declined this offer "although he would very much like to go."²⁴⁴

Griffis spent the last few weeks in Japan teaching, buying numerous gifts and mementoes from the various shops of Tokyo and Yokohama, putting the finishing touches on his guidebooks and maps, paying farewell calls on friends and acquaintances, and packing in preparation for his return home. He attended his duties at the school for the last time on Friday, July 17, at which time the authorities presented him with a cabinet and the new director of the school, his former Rutgers friend Hatakeyama, testified on his good and faithful service. Unfortunately, this testimonial is not available in Griffis' papers at Rutgers so we cannot know what Hatakeyama said.²⁴⁵ We do have, however, a letter of commendation written by David Murray for this occasion.

> As you are about to leave the service of the Japanese government, and return to the United States, I desire to testify to you in the most emphatic manner of the high estimation in which I hold your services. For more than three years you have been a professor of Chemistry in the . . . National University at this place. The faithfulness with which you have performed your duties, and the success which has [characterized] your instruction must be your commendation.²⁴⁶

Griffis left for home on the following day, July 18, 1874, 1,297 days after his arrival. He did not, however, put Japan completely behind him. A statement that he made many years after leaving Japan is perhaps the best way to summarize his return to America. He wrote, "I returned to my native country to have a hand in its making and resolved to be the interpreter of Japan to America, to make the man of the Orient and the man of the Occident understand each other better."²⁴⁷

NOTES

1.   Griffis, *Verbeck of Japan*, p. 252.
2.   WEG to MCG, October 1, 1871, GCRUL.
3.   WEG to MCG, October 1, 1871, GCRUL.
4.   *The Mikado's Empire*, p. 538.
5.   WEG to MCG, October 1, 1871, GCRUL.
6.   WEG to MCG, October 1, 1871, GCRUL
7.   WEG to MCG, October 1, 1871, GCRUL.
8.   WEG to MCG, October 1, 1871, GCRUL.
9.   WEG to MCG, October 1, 1871, GCRUL.
10.   WEG to MCG, October 28, 1871, GCRUL.
11.   William Elliot Griffis, *Hepburn of Japan and His Wife and Helpmates: A Life Story of Toil for Christ* (Philadelphia, Penna.: The Westminster Press, 1913), p. 95.

12. WEG to MCG, October 28, 1871, GCRUL.
13. WEG to MCG, October 28, 1871, GCRUL.
14. WEG to MCG, November 26, 1871, GCRUL.
15. WEG to MCG, December 31, 1871, GCRUL.
16. WEG to MCG, December 31, 1871, GCRUL.
17. WEG to MCG, December 3, 1871, GCRUL.
18. WEG to MCG, December 24, 1871, GCRUL.
19. WEG to MCG, December 24, 1871, GCRUL.
20. WEG to MCG, December 25, 1871, GCRUL.
21. WEG to MCG, January 10, 1872, GCRUL.
22. WEG to MCG, January 10, 1872, GCRUL.
23. WEG to MCG, January 10, 1872, GCRUL. I have been unable to find Mitsuoka's letter, but the full text of Verbeck's letter, dated December 21, 1871, to Griffis follows:

"We are about to begin, besides but connected with the present school, a polytechnic school, and as we should like to begin as soon as possible, his [Excellency], the Minister of Education would like to have you come here as one of the Professors of Nat[ural] Phil[osophy] and Chemistry. This now depends altogether on the question whether you would accept the proposition or not. Your terms would of course be the same here as there (with the exception of the hourse, & would be the same as Dr. Veeder's. We have a good collection of instruments, & are expecting more ere long. This school will be in another compound from the present one, but your residence will be where the other professors live."

"How do you like it? Do you ask my advice?—I say, come by all means."

"The difficulty of finding a substitute for you has been overcome, as far as the languages are concerned & much more they will not want for some time to come. I know you will feel like sending home for a substitute, but that would amount to a refusal, for if we can wait for that, we can send ourselves as well, & need not disturb you now."

"Please let me know your mind by extra post, so that we may know if we had better engage some one else here or not, & much oblige [sic]."

24. WEG to MCG, January 20, 1872, GCRUL.
25. WEG to MCG, January 20, 1872, GCRUL.
26. Griffis, *The Mikado's Empire*, p. 539.
27. WEG to MCG, January 29, 1872, GCRUL.
28. WEG to MCG, January 29, 1872, GCRUL.
29. WEG to MCG, January 29, 1872, GCRUL.
30. WEG to MCG, January 29, 1872, GCRUL.
31. WEG to MCG, January 29, 1872, GCRUL.
32. WEG to MCG, January 29, 1872, GCRUL.
33. Draft of letter, WEG to Murata, "12 mo. 9 day" [1871], GCRUL; this date corresponds to 18 January. WEG's Diary for January 16, 1872 contains an entry which says, messenger "returned with my letter to Muratta [sic], not having been able to get an audience of Muratta [sic], he being very busy with officers from other Hans, etc. Resolved, if hindered to go to Yedo, (alone even) Jan. 23rd." The following day (January 17) he described a meeting that he had with Murata culminating in his decision "that whether in honor or disgrace, alone or attended, I should set out for Yedo, overland, Jan. 23rd." He also revealed that he "Wrote a letter to Muratta [sic], in answer to his

official letter rec'd this evening 7 PM which was read and explained [to me]
to-day." The day after Griffis wrote this letter, he received a message from
the Fukui officials saying "All Right."

34.   See note 33.
35.   See note 33.
36.   See note 33.
37.   See note 33.
38.   See note 33.
39.   See note 33.
40.   See note 33.
41.   See note 33.
42.   See note 33.
43.   See note 33.
44.   See note 33.
45.   See note 33.
46.   WEG to MCG, January 22, 1872, GCRUL. See also Griffis, *The Mikado's Empire*, p. 540.
47.   WEG to MCG, January 22, 1872, GCRUL. See also Griffis, *The Mikado's Empire*, p. 540.
48.   WEG to MCG, January 22, 1872, GCRUL. See also Griffis, *The Mikado's Empire*, p. 540.
49.   WEG to MCG, February 4, 1872, GCRUL.
50.   WEG to MCG, February 4, 1872, GCRUL.
51.   WEG to MCG, February 4, 1872, GCRUL.
52.   WEG to MCG, February 4, 1872, GCRUL.
53.   Griffis, *The Mikado's Empire*, p. 550.
54.   WEG to MCG, February 4, 1872, GCRUL.
55.   WEG to MCG, February 4, 1872, GCRUL.
56.   WEG to MCG, February 12, 1872, GCRUL.
57.   WEG to MCG, February 12, 1872, GCRUL.
58.   WEG to MCG, February 12, 1872, GCRUL.
59.   WEG to MCG, February 12, 1872, GCRUL.
60.   WEG to MCG, February 19, 1872, GCRUL.
61.   Griffis, "Diary," February 12, 1872, GCRUL.
62.   Griffis, "Diary," February 13, 1872, GCRUL.
63.   Griffis, *The Mikado: Institution and Person*, p. 220.
64.   WEG to MCG, February 12, 1872, GCRUL
65.   Schwantes, *Japanese and Americans*, p. 187.
66.   WEG to MCG, February 26, 1872, GCRUL.
67.   Edward W. Clark to MCG, February 5, 1872, GCRUL. See also Griffis, "Extra Notes," May 11, 1872, GCRUL.
68.   Griffis, "Extra Notes," May 11, 1872, GCRUL.
69.   Griffis, "Extra Notes," May 11, 1872, GCRUL. This document also reveals that Griffis received a similar sword from a "Dr. Miyanaga" when he left Fukui for the capital.
70.   Edward W. Clark to MCG, February 5, 1872, GCRUL.
71.   WEG to MCG, March 18, 1872, GCRUL.
72.   WEG to MCG, March 22, 1872, GCRUL.
73.   WEG to Martha Griffis, April 15, 1872, GCRUL.

74.   WEG to Martha Griffis, April 15, 1872, GCRUL.
75.   WEG to Martha Griffis, April 15, 1872, GCRUL.
76.   WEG to MCG, April 21, 1872, GCRUL.
77.   WEG to MCG, April 21, 1872, GCRUL.
78.   WEG to MCG, April 21, 1872, GCRUL.
79.   MCG to Sisters, August 18, 1872, GCRUL.
80.   MCG to Sisters, August 18, 1872, GCRUL.
81.   MCG to Sisters, August 18, 1872, GCRUL.
82.   WEG to MCG, February 26, 1872, GCRUL.
83.   WEG to MCG, February 26, 1872, GCRUL.
84.   WEG to MCG, March 10, 1872, GCRUL.
85.   WEG to MCG, March 10, 1872, GCRUL. See also Schwantes, *Japanese and Americans*, pp. 53–54.
86.   WEG to MCG, March 10, 1872, GCRUL. See also Schwantes, *Japanese and Americans*, pp. 53–54.
87.   WEG to MCG, March 18, 1872, GCRUL.
88.   Griffis, "Diary," February 24, 1872, GCRUL.
89.   Griffis, "Diary," February 28, 29, and March 1, 1872, GCRUL.
90.   Griffis, "Diary," March 9, 1872, GCRUL.
91.   WEG to MCG, March 18, 1872, GCRUL.
92.   WEG to MCG, March 18, 1872, GCRUL.
93.   WEG to MCG, March 18, 1872, GCRUL.
94.   WEG to MCG, March 18, 1872, GCRUL.
95.   WEG to MCG, April 21, 1872, GCRUL.
96.   WEG to MCG, April 21, 1872, GCRUL.
97.   WEG to MCG, April 21, 1872, GCRUL.
98.   *Higher Education in Japan: Its Takeoff and Crash* (Tokyo: University of Tokyo Press, 1971), p. 22; hereafter cited as Nagai, *Higher Education in Japan*.
99.   Schwantes, *Japanese and Americans*, p. 157.
100.   Aoki Hideo, "The Effect of American Ideas upon Japanese Higher Education" (Ph.D. dissertation, Stanford University, 1957), p. 174.
101.   Griffis, *The Mikado's Empire*, p. 372.
102.   Griffis, *The Mikado's Empire*, p. 372.
103.   Harold S. Williams, *Foreigners in Mikadoland* (Tokyo: Charles E. Tuttle Company, 1963), p. 84.
104.   Williams, *Foreigners in Mikadoland*, p. 84. See also Griffis, *Verbeck of Japan*, p. 240.
105.   MCG to Sisters, September 21, 1872, GCRUL.
106.   "The Meiji Government and Foreign Employees," p. 77. See also Hazel Jones, "The Formulation of Meiji Policy toward the Employment of Foreigners," *Monumenta Nipponica* 23 (1968): 9–30.
107.   Nagai, *Higher Education in Japan*, p. 23, quoting Ogata Hiroyasu, *Seiyō Kyōiku inyū no hōhō* [*A plan for the introduction of western education*] (Tokyo: Kodansha, 1961), p. 142.
108.   An undated document in Griffis' hand in the Griffis Collection lists the following Nankō faculty: English Department—W. E. Griffis (Chemistry), P. V. Veeder (Physics), D. B. McCartell (Natural History), Horace Wilson (Mathematics), and Rev. J. A. Summers (Literature); French Department—

X. Maillot (Physics and Chemistry), G. Fontaine (Literature), and P. Fougue (Mathematics); German Department—[?] Ritter (Physics), E. Knipping (Mathematics), and C. Schenck (unknown subject).

This document obviously reflects the composition of the school's faculty at a particular point in time; other evidence (Aoki, "The Effect of American Ideas upon Japanese Higher Education," p. 174) indicates that men such as Guido Verbeck (Algebra and Moral Philosophy), Edward House (English) and others also graced its faculty, and at least some of the men on Griffis' list taught subjects other than those listed next to his name. For example, Griffis taught law in addition to science.

109.   WEG to MCG, March 18, 1872, GCRUL.
110.   WEG to MCG, March 18, 1872.
111.   WEG to MCG, June 6, 1872, GCRUL.
112.   WEG to MCG, June 6, 1872, GCRUL.
113.   MCG to Sisters, August 18, 1872, GCRUL.
114.   MCG to Sisters, September 28, 1872, GCRUL.
115.   MCG to Sisters, September 18, 1872, GCRUL.
116.   Ellen G. Johnson to WEG, October 19, 1872, GCRUL.
117.   Ellen G. Johnson to WEG, October 19, 1872, GCRUL.
118.   MCG to Sisters, October 30, 1872, GCRUL.
119.   WEG to Minister of Education [Tanaka Fujiro], September 3, 1872, GC-RUL.
120.   Griffis, "Diary," July 10, 1873, GCRUL.
121.   *Sensei* is a word difficult for a non-Japanese to comprehend fully. Literally, it translates as "teacher" or "master," but it has strong connotations of respect and esteem which go far beyond the typical western conception of a teacher-student relationship.
122.   Griffis, "Diary," June 6, 1872, GCRUL.
123.   Griffis, "Extra Notes," May 7, 1872, GCRUL.
124.   WEG to Sisters, December 23, 1872, GCRUL.
125.   Stewart Fraser, ed., *The Evils of A Foreign Education, or Birdsey Northrop on Education Abroad 1873* (Nashville, Tenn.: George Peabody College for Teachers, 1966), p. v.
126.   Samuel Lockwood to WEG, January 20, 1873, GCRUL.
127.   David Murray to WEG, August 14, 1872, GCRUL.
128.   David Murray to WEG, August 14, 1872, GCRUL.
129.   David Murray to WEG, August 14, 1872, GCRUL.
130.   "Dr. W. E. Griffis brings Message from the East," (unidentified newspaper clipping, probably 1911–1912), GCRUL.
131.   Sansom, *The Western World and Japan*, p. 197.
132.   Donald Shively, "Nishimura Shigeki: A Confucian View of Moderniza-tion," in *Changing Japanese Attitudes Toward Modernization*, ed. by Marius Jansen (Princeton, New Jersey: Princeton University Press, 1965), p. 197; hereafter cited as Shively, "Nishimura Shigeki."
133.   Shively, "Nishimura Shigeki," p. 209.
134.   Shively, "Nishimura Shigeki," p. 209.
135.   Papinot, *Historical and Geographer Dictionary of Japan*, p. 220.
136.   WEG to *New York Herald Tribune*, August 9, 1924, GCRUL.
137.   Okamoto Shumpei, *The Japanese Oligarchy and the Russo-Japanese War* (New York: Columbia University Press, 1971), pp. 26–27.

138.   Viscount Kuroda to WEG, April 12, 1915, GCRUL.
139.   William Elliot Griffis, "The Rise of the New Japan" (manuscript, n. d.), p. 14, GCRUL.
140.   Nishimura [?] to WEG, March 5, 1915, GCRUL.
141.   Karl Kasahara to WEG, May 1, 1916, GCRUL.
142.   MCG to Sisters, August 18, 1872, GCRUL.
143.   MCG to Sisters, September 4, 1872, GCRUL.
144.   MCG to Sisters, September 28, 1872, GCRUL.
145.   MCG to Sisters, September 28, 1872, GCRUL.
146.   MCG to Sisters, October 2, 1872, GCRUL.
147.   MCG to Sisters, October 2, 1872, GCRUL.
148.   MCG to Sisters, October 2, 1872, GCRUL.
149.   MCG to Sisters, October 2, 1872, GCRUL.
150.   MCG to Sisters, October 21, 1872, GCRUL.
151.   MCG to Sisters, October 30, 1872, GCRUL.
152.   MCG to Sisters, November 2, 1872, GCRUL.
153.   MCG to Sisters, November 17, 1872, GCRUL.
154.   MCG to Sisters, November 17, 1872, GCRUL.
155.   MCG to Sisters, November 17, 1872, GCRUL.
156.   MCG to Sisters, November 17, 1872, GCRUL.
157.   Schwantes, *Japanese and Americans*, p. 188.
158.   Schwantes, *Japanese and Americans*, p. 188.
159.   MCG to Sisters, September 21, 1872, GCRUL.
160.   MCG to Sisters, September 21, 1872, GCRUL.
161.   MCG to Sisters, September 28, 1872, GCRUL.
162.   MCG to Sisters, August 25, 1872, GCRUL.
163.   MCG to Sisters, August 30, 1872, GCRUL.
164.   MCG to Sisters, November 27, 1872, GCRUL.
165.   MCG to Sisters, December 5, 1872, GCRUL.
166.   WEG to Sisters, January 18, 1873, GCRUL.
167.   William Elliot Griffis, "The Teacher of Teachers" (galley proof of short article, no identification but probably appeared in a Japanese periodical, n. d.), GCRUL.
168.   Burks, "William Elliot Griffis," p. 95.
169.   Griffis, "Diary," March 3, 1873, GCRUL.
170.   Griffis, *Verbeck of Japan*, p. 222. Miss Bacon later wrote a useful book *Japanese Girls and Women* (Boston: Houghton, Mifflin and Company, 1892), in which she described the education of Japanese females.
171.   M. A. Linn to WEG, June 9, 1873, GCRUL.
172.   Griffis, "Diary," July 4, 1873, GCRUL.
173.   Griffis, "Diary," July 4, 1873, GCRUL.
174.   Griffis, "Diary," July 5, 1873, GCRUL.
175.   WEG to Sisters, July 29, 1873, GCRUL.
176.   Griffis, *Verbeck of Japan*, pp. 269–270.
177.   Griffis, *Verbeck of Japan*, p. 270.
178.   Griffis, *Verbeck of Japan*, p. 270.
179.   Charles E. DeLong to WEG, July 16, 1873, GCRUL. I have been unable to ascertain any details of the "cloud" in question.
180.   Letter, [signature and date illegible but probably William Y. Howell] to WEG, July 19, 1873, GCRUL.

118   GRIFFIS IN TOKYO

181.   Griffis, *Verbeck of Japan*, p. 271.
182.   Griffis, *Verbeck of Japan*, p. 271.
183.   WEG to Sisters, July 29, 1873, GCRUL.
184.   WEG to Sisters, July 29, 1873, GCRUL.
185.   WEG to Sisters, July 29, 1873, GCRUL.
186.   Tanaka Fujiro to WEG, August 16, 1873, GCRUL.
187.   Tanaka Fujiro to WEG, August 16, 1873, GCRUL.
188.   Tanaka Fujiro to WEG, August 16, 1873, GCRUL.
189.   Tanaka Fujiro, WEG, August 16, 1873, GCRUL.
190.   Tanaka Fujiro, WEG, August 16, 1873, GCRUL.
191.   Tanaka, Fujiro, WEG, August 16, 1873, GCRUL.
192.   "Sincere Pupils" (fourteen pupils of Griffis' First Scientific Class) to WEG, August 20, 1873, GCRUL.
193.   Students of Griffis' First Legal Class to WEG, August 20, 1873, GCRUL.
194.   Students of Griffis' Second Legal Class to WEG, August 22, 1873, GCRUL.
195.   Students of Griffis' Second Scientific Class to WEG, August 22, 1873, GCRUL.
196.   WEG to Iwakura Tomomi, September 11, 1873, quoted in Griffis, "Diary," September 11, 1873, GCRUL.
197.   T. S. Iwakura [son of Iwakura Tomomi] to WEG, September 19, 1873, GCRUL.
198.   For details see Hilary Conroy, *The Japanese Seizure of Korea, 1868–1910* (Philadelphia, Penna.: University of Pennsylvania Press, 1960) and Marlene J. Mayo, "The Korean Crisis of 1873 and Early Meiji Foreign Policy," *Journal of Asian Studies* 31, no. 4 (1972):793–819.
199.   Edward W. Clark to WEG, September 22, 1873, GCRUL.
200.   Tanaka Fujiro to WEG, October 10, 1873, GCRUL.
201.   WEG to Tanaka Fujiro and a certain Ban [Monbushō official?], October 13, 1873, GCRUL.
202.   WEG to Tanaka Fujiro and Ban, October 13, 1873, GCRUL.
203.   WEG to Tanaka Fujiro and Ban, October 13, 1873, GCRUL.
204.   WEG to Tanaka Fujiro and Ban, October 13, 1873, GCRUL.
205.   Griffis, "Diary," September 29, 1873, GCRUL.
206.   WEG to Sisters, September 23 [illegible], 1872, GCRUL.
207.   WEG to Sisters, September 23 [illegible], 1872, GCRUL.
208.   WEG to "Directors [of] K. S. G. [Kaisei Gakkō], November 24, 1873, GCRUL. See Appendix A.
209.   WEG to Guido Verbeck, December 5, 1873, GCRUL.
210.   Guido Verbeck to WEG, December 6, 1873, GCRUL.
211.   Letter [draft], Guido Verbeck to Tanaka Fujiro, December 5, 1873, GCRUL.
212.   Griffis, "Diary," December 19, 1873, GCRUL.
213.   Griffis, "Diary," December 19, 1873, GCRUL.
214.   Griffis, "Diary," December 22, 1873, GCRUL.
215.   David Murray to WEG, January 24, 1874, GCRUL.
216.   MCG to Sisters, January 8, 1874, GCRUL.
217.   MCG to Sisters, January 8, 1874, GCRUL.
218.   MCG to Sisters, January 8, 1874, GCRUL.
219.   MCG to Sisters, January 8, 1874, GCRUL.
220.   MCG to Sisters, January 8, 1874, GCRUL.
221.   MCG to Sisters, January 11, 1874, GCRUL.

222. MCG to Sisters, January 17, 1874, GCRUL.
223. WEG to Sisters, September 12, 1873, GCRUL.
224. Griffis, "Diary," March 20, May 27–29, and June 16, 1874, GCRUL.
225. Griffis, "Diary," June 16, 1874, GCRUL.
226. MCG to Sisters, February 15, 1874 and February 17, 1874, GCRUL.
227. Griffis, "Diary," March 11, March 20, and March 21, 1874, GCRUL.
228. Griffis, "Diary," July 10, 1874, GCRUL.
229. WEG to Sisters, February 11, 1874, GCRUL.
230. MCG to Sisters, March 29, 1874, GCRUL.
231. MCG to Sisters, March 29, 1874, GCRUL.
232. MCG to Sisters, April 5, 1874, GCRUL.
233. WEG to Sisters, February 11, 1874, GCRUL.
234. WEG to Martha Griffis, April 22, 1874, GCRUL.
235. MCG to Sisters, May 2, 1874, GCRUL.
236. MCG to Sisters, May 2, 1874, GCRUL.
237. MCG to Sisters, May 2, 1874, GCRUL.
238. MCG to Sisters, May 8, 1874, GCRUL.
239. MCG to Sisters, May 8, 1874, GCRUL.
240. MCG to Sisters, May 15, 1874, GCRUL.
241. MCG to Sisters, May 15, 1874, GCRUL.
242. Griffis, "Diary," May 14, 1874, GCRUL. For details of Capron's mission see Merritt Starr, "General Horace Capron, 1804–1885," *Journal of Illinois State Historical Society* 28 (July, 1925):276, 290–295.
243. MCG to Sisters, May 15, 1874, GCRUL.
244. MCG to Sisters, May 15, 1874, GCRUL.
245. Griffis, "Diary," July 17, 1874, GCRUL.
246. David Murray to WEG, July 17, 1874, GCRUL.
247. Griffis, *Sunny Memories of Three Pastorates*, p. 49.

Chapter 5

A Bridge Between East and West, 1874–1928

There was an element of the entrepreneur in the makeup of William Elliot Griffis, the man "on the make" for a reputation. Griffis' large ego and sense of self-importance were not often justified or satisfied for very long. His letters, diary, and writings—published and unpublished—all find Griffis working to dominate events. Countering these all too human failings, however, one notes the strong sense of duty and service that tempered and directed Griffis' life. He honestly saw himself as an instrument of a Christian God's will in introducing western science and ideas to the Japanese in Fukui and Tokyo during his years in Japan. He put forth substantial efforts outside his formal contractual obligations to assist the Japanese. These efforts took the form of having Japanese boys live with him, holding public evening classes on such topics as the American Constitution, popular science, etc., and "advising" Japanese officials on policy questions among other things.

Griffis conscientiously tried to do what was best for the Japanese and to advise them of their own best interests even when his advice conflicted with the desires of his fellow westerners. Griffis' open letter to Japanese Christians written shortly before his return to America in 1874 illustrates this. Introducing himself as "a fellow-Christian who has seen the dangers to the religion of Jesus in other lands," Griffis warned the Japanese Christians of Tokyo and Yokohama "of the great perils that now beset you and to try to show how you may be kept from them."[1] Western sectarianism was one such peril. "Some of your own religious teachers I hear, are beginning to cause division among you," because they "do not like the union movement."[2] Why they should find themselves pressured to embrace the peculiarities of a particular sect was a mystery to the Japanese converts. They failed to understand why the worship of the Christian God was not enough. Griffis attempted to lay bare the roots of differences among Christians.

> When the truth taught and lived by Jesus Christ was spread abroad . . .
> by his apostles . . . the Christian religion was greatly influenced by the
> peculiar kinds of mind in the various nations. Hence it was variously modi-
> fied, just as the same seed will be modified by various soils and climates.
> The people of Europe are not of the same origin, but are of different blood,
> and each national mind in Europe is somewhat different from the other,
> just as their languages are diverse.[3]

After recounting a simplified history of Christianity in the west through the Reformation, Griffis concluded that although unique historical reasons made sectarianism understandable in the west, this phenomenon should not be allowed into Japan.

> But let me warn you against introducing these sectarian dimensions into
> your country. There is no need of them. The Japanese people are not a mixed
> but a homogeneous people. There is no reason why Christianity in Japan
> should be divided. The people all speak one language and live in the same
> country. Do not allow these foreign sectarian divisions and doctrines to get
> a foothold on your soil. Let the missionaries teach you the gospel and make
> you Christians, but do not join their sects. Do not make any foreigner your
> pastor. Have your pastors chosen from yourselves.
>   The Japanese Christian Church is now like a child, a David, with a sling
> and a stone going out to fight the great Goliath of Paganism. Shall not the
> young church go forth trusting only in God? The great sects and missionary
> boards with their great strength are like Saul. They will try to get Daniel—
> the infant church—to put on their big helmet, and heavy coat of mail, and
> huge shield, which they are only too willing to furnish, but do not put these
> on. Let the limbs be free and the body unfettered, and let the heart of the
> native church be fixed on Jesus; let young David trust in the living God and
> the great giant Goliath of Paganism must fall. Now, to my mind, the sec-
> tarian doctrines are like the helmet and shield and armour of King Saul. They
> are useless to help us slay the giant of Paganism in Japan. I cannot believe
> that the special doctrines of the sects has [sic] anything to do with a man's
> personal salvation. If a man chooses to hold these opinions, I cannot say
> whether he is doing well or ill. This, I know, they have nothing to do with the
> religion of Christ, and the salvation of the soul.[4]

This letter, with its stress on the unity of Japanese Christians and its warning to beware of foreign religious leaders, did not sit well with the missionary representatives of the various Christian sects. Griffis, however, felt that the interests of the Japanese Christians were more important than those of western missionaries, and, therefore, he supported the Japanese.

Even before his arrival from Fukui in early 1873, Griffis had held this conviction. Once situated in the capital, he became immersed in the activities of the foreign settlement's Christian community and taught a Bible class of young Japanese men during his spare time. In addition, he played a role in the establishment of a Union Church in Tokyo and became one of its elders.[5] In 1872 Griffis attended a missionary convention in Yokohama which formulated "a plan of union, under the name of 'The United Church of Christ in Japan.' "[6] Griffis was firmly committed to the union concept and saw very little good coming from competitive sectarian conflicts over details of religious belief. He wrote, "It was a sad breaking away from a high ideal when the different sects, denominations and individuals began their divisions, and it helps largely to account for the comparative failure, or at least slow progress of organized Christianity in Japan."[7]

This sense of personal intellectual individualism exhibited in opposing the Christian missionaries remained a hallmark of Griffis throughout his career. Leaving Japan for the United States in 1874, Griffis left under circumstances that could have resulted in bitterness and animosity toward Japan and her people. He was disenchanted with the Japanese educational administrators in the Monbushō and the Kaisei Gakkō; Frances Helbig suggests, "he hated them."[8] Nevertheless, he was able to distinguish between the incompetent individuals with whom he had bad experiences and the Japanese people as a nation. He had a tremendous respect for the latter and returned to America determined to interpret Japan to the American people, the vast majority of whom were both uninterested in, and ignorant of, Japan.

THE WRITER AS TEACHER

William Elliot Griffis' formal teaching career came to a close the day he left Japan to return to the United States. Yet in a very profound sense, Griffis spent the remainder of his life teaching the American people about Japan and the Japanese. In books, newspaper and magazine articles, and in public lectures, his prolific pen produced a steady stream of words about the country and the people he loved. Although he never held an academic appointment in an American college or university, his "teaching" about Japan was far more influential than any professor's during the period from 1874 to 1926. Indeed, when thinking of this period, one is hard-pressed to identify American academics with a competency relative to Japan.

Assuming that a publisher can be persuaded to publish it, writing is probably the most efficient and effective way of reaching other people with one's ideas. Even the most moss-backed reactionary would be hard-put to defend the notion that all or even most teaching takes place in a classroom. Professor J. H. Hexter of Yale, in a recent defense of the concept of "publish or perish" for university teachers, identifies several common forms of formal "teaching"; classroom lectures, discussions, seminars, directed readings, etc.[9] At best, a teacher cannot be expected to have a teaching contact with more than several hundred students each year. Using his own career as an example, Hexter writes,

> I have been a classroom teacher since 1936. In that time, on a fair estimate I have taught about 5,000 students face-to-face. In the past three years [1966–1969] I edited one book, contributed a large section to another, and wrote a third. All are for the use of college students. The combined sales of the three are already more than 100,000 copies and the end is not yet in sight. Therefore, in the past three years I taught 2000 per cent more students by publishing than I have taught face-to-face in thirty-three; and I will be teaching many more.[10]

Granted that the analogy between Griffis and Hexter is not perfect, yet Griffis' *The Mikado's Empire*, as only one example, was first published in 1876 and went through a total of twelve editions through 1913! Surely, a very large number of people must have been buying and, presumably, reading the book to have it compile such an enviable record.

It might be argued that Hexter's 100,000 copies are textbooks and thus, his audience is a captive one. In any event, college students are notorious for buying books that they do not read.

> Besides the three publications directly aimed at college students and personal profit, I have over the years published several books and articles aimed at neither. They are all the sort of thing that the students, educationists, and muddy-minded reporters of educational news contemptuously refer to as mere scholarship or mere research. Through these publications I am sure I have taught better than I have in the classroom. They represent the most intense and precise effort I am capable of in that pursuit of the truth about the past, which is my calling. Unlike the publications aimed directly at undergraduates, which only gathered together knowledge retrieved by other historians, they explored areas not hitherto investigated or cleared up confusions left by earlier explorers. To some degree these works of scholarship improved and increased the available knowlege of the past. College teachers read such works and other scholars incorporate their findings in their own studies. Thus, scholarly efforts of this kind teach a host of students who will never have heard of the men who wrote them . . . . and it is in the publication of such works that those that publish well do their best and most important teaching.[11]

Hexter's arguments seem equally valid in the case of William Elliot Griffis. He too taught few students face-to-face but reached unknown thousands through the power of his pen. There is no way to measure his impact with any degree of precision, but it appears that Griffis also did "his best and most important teaching" via his publications.

GRIFFIS AS HISTORIAN

Griffis' best known and most lasting contribution was *The Mikado's Empire*, a labor of love which he began to draft almost as soon as he arrived in Japan. Indeed, he made a conscious and sustained effort to gather ideas and materials for the book during his entire sojourn in Japan. He read all that he could lay his hands on about Japan, he had several of his students read Japanese-language fiction to him, he traveled as often as possible throughout much of Honshu, he assigned his students to write papers on their home provinces, their families, etc. and he learned much through his contacts with the Meirokusha and its members, and through such friends and acquaintances as Fukuzawa Yukichi, Iwakura Tomomi, Matsudaira Shungaku, Guido Verbeck, John Black, Sir Harry Parkes, Algernon Mitford, Ernest Satow, William Aston, and many others.

As Helbig has pointed out in her interesting intellectual portrait of Griffis, much of his writing was derivative rather than original. Speaking of *The Mikado's Empire*, she suggested,

> Much of the material prepared for the book he worked up quickly and easily from prior periodical publication. Not only did this bring in some income, but it also softened up the reading public for *The Mikado's Empire*; Japan as a topic began to be coupled in people's minds with Griffis as an author.[12]

Helbig went on to describe most of Griffis' writing which led to *The Mikado's Empire* as dealing with "lightweight topics such as dolls, myths, various Japanese social customs, and travel in Japan."[13] The book is an easy mark for this charge. It should be noted, however, that this information was new to the American public and, lightweight or not, provided valuable source materials to social and cultural historians.

A more serious criticism of Griffis' writings, particularly *The Mikado's Empire*, was that the author failed to acknowledge fully the works of others from which he borrowed heavily. As Helbig points out, the only acknowledgement made in *The Mikado's Empire* appeared in the preface. There Griffis thanked a number of other researchers for their contributions. "This, he considered, freed him from citing specific sources of his material from these scholars."[14]

> The minor writers who were neither cited nor thanked . . . raised the loudest howl. Griffis thanked the editor of *The Japan Mail* and considers this

to include all the material therein including, as he notes, the papers of the Asiatic Society of Japan. The proprietors of *The Japan Herald* and *The Japan Gazette* were also thanked. This covered a lot of ground considering how much of a mother lode of facts, good history, interpretation and opinion these three papers offered, and that Griffis drew more heavily from them than his comments would indicate. Bear in mind here that most of these newspaper articles were written not by faceless scribes, but by real flesh and blood scholars and semi-scholars who were intensely proud of their contributions and jealous of their nameless use elsewhere.[15]

However, one of the book's real virtues was its fresh authenticity. Even the lightweight topics found richer meaning. As Griffis claimed, "I have not made this book in libraries at home, but largely on the soil of the mikado's empire."[16] Griffis' narrative contrasted sharply with what was probably the first account of Japan to be published in America. In 1855 Richard Hildreth, later a prominent scholar of American history, took advantage of "the increased popular interest in [Japan] after Commodore Perry's expedition."[17] Hildreth's biographer concludes that *Japan As It Is and Was* was "merely a compilation rather than a digested work of history."[18] In addition, Hildreth, unlike Griffis, had never been in Japan and wrote the book in the Boston Athenaeum, which was "his chief source of materials."[19]

Generally quite favorable reviews greeted the publication of Griffis' major work of history. A reviewer, writing in *Nation*, called it "undoubtedly the most important contribution that has appeared with regard to Japan."[20] *The Japan Gazette*, in commenting on the book, concluded,

> Probably the name of no modern writer on Japan is better known than that of Mr. Griffis. His writings upon the God-country have during the past few years been widely read. To great industry, the first requisite of a successful writer, he joins a power of observation, a retentive memory, a facility for clothing his thoughts in words, a talent for arrangement and classification, and an ornate style which is frequently highly poetical. These are advantages which more than counterbalance a certain want of profundity in his writing, and a not always logical train of reasoning.[21]

Thus, a major value of *The Mikado's Empire* came with the recognition that it stood alone as a vast storehouse of facts and opinions on Japan, spiced by Griffis' personal experiences, especially in the interior. Perhaps the strongest praise of the book lies in the fact that its popularity lasted for more than half a century. In 1891 the prominent Japanese scholar, Nitobe Inazō, discussed American writers on Japan, and concluded that *The Mikado's Empire* was "By far the best American work on Japan [for] the whole range of American (and in some sense of Western) authorship."[22] Nitobe conceded that Griffis "does not claim any originality of historical research or scientific investigation," but "no author has done more to present in attractive style the salient features of our [Japan's] tradition, history, manners and customs."[23] Most significant, however, "its worn-out condition in many a public library, attests how diligently and deservedly it is perused."[24]

One of our most distinguished contemporary scholars of Japan, Professor John W. Hall of Yale, has written that at least, "in the United States, up to World War I, probably the most popularly read book on Japanese history was *The Mikado's Empire* (1876) by William E. Griffis, an American teacher of science in Japan."[25] Most recently, Iriye Akira, after closely studying American writings on Japan, has concluded that *The Mikado's Empire* "remained the best book on Japanese history for decades."[26]

Although historians, both western and Japanese, have uncovered a great deal of new materials since Griffis' day and have advanced different interpretations than he proposed, *The Mikado's Empire* is still a very useful book for students of Japan. His firsthand account of life in Fukui during the last days of the feudal order gives one a dramatic sense of the turbulent times and the rapid changes of early Meiji Japan. In addition, Griffis was one of the first, if not *the* first, western writers to record "with fascination about what he believed to be the comparable features of European and Japanese feudalism."[27] This approach has "given rise to a large body of comparative literature" among historians in both Japan and the West."[28] There are signs of a revival of interest in Griffis in Japan today. In 1971 the Jiji Press of Tokyo reissued *The Mikado's Empire*, and, during the recent Meiji centennial anniversary, articles on various *yatoi*, including at least one on Griffis, have appeared.

What kind of a historian was William Elliot Griffis? In order to field a question of this sort, one must return to nineteenth-century standards. Like so many of his contemporaries, Griffis fares poorly when set against the standards of modern historiography. When he wrote *The Mikado's Empire* in 1876, for example, the historical monograph was not part of his experience. The style of history which was in vogue was the grand, cosmic history of George Bancroft. In several important ways, Griffis' narrative resembles that of Bancroft.

American nationalism permeated Bancroft's work; he saw the United States as the culmination of God's work and at least implicitly, a model for others. Griffis' work on Japan, especially *The Mikado's Empire*, also has this flavor although on a more muted scale. But it was apparent to the readers of his book that he clearly saw the United States as providing the best model for Japan to emulate. In speaking of the position of women in Japan, for example, Griffis wrote,

No one who is interested in the welfare and progress of the Asiatic nations can approach the question of female education without feelings of sadness as profound as the need of the effort is felt to be great. The American who leaves his own country, in which the high honor paid to women is one of the chief glories of the race to which he belongs is shocked and deeply grieved at beholding her low estate in pagan lands.[29]

Griffis was pleased to find women treated better in Japan than in other Asian lands. He took this to mean that the Japanese were, indeed, ready to progress. However, he continued, "what has thus far been done can not be looked upon as anything more than mere indications of the better time to come—the gray light before the far-off full day."[30]

Griffis shared with George Bancroft an unshakeable belief in the idea of progress. History, at least in the favored countries, was a chronicle of mankind working toward a life that was better and higher. For striving foreign countries the American record welcomed emulation. (America, meanwhile, advanced under its own engines of destiny.)

I can not but think that unless the modern enlightened ideas of government, law, society, and the rights of the individual be adopted to a far greater extent than they have been, the people be thoroughly educated, and a mighty spiritual force replace Shintō and Buddhism, little will be gained but a glittering veneer of material civilization and the corroding foreign vices, under which, in the presence of the superior aggressive nations of the West, Dai Nippon must fall like the doomed races of America.[31]

During the last two decades of the nineteenth century, the rise of American scientific history, enamored with Rankean objectivity and the search for a philosophy of history based on science, rejected the Bancroft approach to history. Like Bancroft, Griffis tended to make epochal statements and wrote in the literary style of the day. These characteristics became suspect in the last part of the century, and it is a tribute to Griffis' *The Mikado's Empire* that despite these distinguishing marks, the book remained valuable for such a long period of time.

GRIFFIS' VIEW OF JAPAN'S PAST

Like most historians who have been intimately involved with the country of their scholarly interest, or who attempt to write about a period of events through which they have lived, William Elliot Griffis was not always the objective scholar. Somewhat unfairly, however, Frances Helbig has charged Griffis with historical Manicheanism:

His was a world of bad guys and good guys where the bad guys were so bad they were devils. Yet so closely was he in tune with the American public that very few people noticed anything amiss. His prejudices were their prejudices.

Buddhism was the great religious villain; the Tokugawa shogunate was a hateful usurpation impeding progress; [Sir Rutherford] Alcock, "the apostle of murder and blind force" and "ever ready to shed blood," was a British devil. Instinctively playing upon popular prejudices and beliefs, he sometimes unmoored from his facts in the strong tide of emotional phrases.[32]

However, in his *Japan: In History, Folklore and Art*, Griffis saw Buddhism in positive terms.

Buddhism wrought a great change in both the court and the nation. Shrines, temples, and pagodas were built all over the country, and art and trades were greatly stimulated. Painters, carvers, and shrine-makers multiplied. Education, thought not yet national, grew to be more general. Books became less rare; manners and customs were improved. The priests were often real civilizers, making roads, sinking wells, maintaining schools, and softening manners.[33]

In another place, Griffis claimed, "Japanese history shows no other force comparable to Buddhism for the welding into one nation the various tribes of the archipelago."[34]

While it is true that Griffis did not have a high opinion of the Tokugawa system which he believed was "directly opposed to all progress and development,"[35] he was high in praise of Tokugawa Ieyasu, the founder of the dynasty, whom he credited with ordering much of the construction which transformed Tokyo from a backwater into an important metropolitan center.[36] Tokugawa Ieyasu, Griffis wrote, "spent the last years of his life . . . engaged in erasing the scars of war, securing the triumphs of peace, perfecting his plans for fixing in stability his system of government, and in collecting books and manuscripts."[37] In addition, Griffis offered high praise for many of the Tokugawas who, even prior to the Meiji Restoration, took concrete steps to improve the lot of their people. For example, he was consistently high in his praise of Matsudaira Shungaku, a member of the Tokugawa family, whom he described as making Fukui during the 1840s "a model of good government and an educational center for the advancement of science, morals and the manly arts of Bushido."[38] Clearly Griffis had an anti-Tokugawa bias, but he also openly applauded positive elements within the system. This was hardly the style of a Manichean historian.

Griffis' histories of Japan, backed by his more than three years' residence in that country, formed a double-edged literary sword. His readers found in him a man who understood and interpreted the Japanese on an affective as well as cognitive level.

It has been well said by a literary critic and reader of all the books on . . . [Japan] that to write a good history of Japan is difficult, not so much from lack of materials, but from the differences in psychology. This I realize. My endeavor, during the eight years' living contact with these people, has been, from their language, books, life and customs, to determine their mental parallax, and find out how they think and feel.[39]

Griffis went even farther. Wherever possible, he immersed himself in the local environment. When living in Fukui in the far interior of Japan, for example, his first abode was an old Japanese house.

I was glad that they had put me in this old mansion. It was full of suggestive history. It had been a home. Pagan, heathen, Asiatic—it mattered not; it was a home. Here in this garden the infant had been carried until a child— growing up, the playmate of the flowers and birds. . . . Here children played among the flowers. . . . Then as the boys grew up, they put on the swords, shaved off their fore-hair, and progressed in the lore of Chinese sages and native historians. . . . while the girls grew in womanly grace and beauty.[40]

Living in Fukui also enabled him to observe at close range the daily rhythm of Japanese life in an environment that was still feudal in many ways. He was also blessed with the opportunity of daily meetings with students, officials, and the common people unspoiled by earlier contacts with westerners. They were able to furnish him with firsthand accounts of various aspects of Japanese social and cultural life that the typical west- erner would not have discovered in Yokohama or Tokyo. This personal sense of involvement in the history that Griffis wrote, and particularly in that through which he lived, appealed to readers and may explain the popularity of his work to Americans of his day. It certainly contrasted sharply, for example, with Richard Hildreth's book on Japan which "smelled of the lamp," having been written exclusively from secondary materials.

On the other hand, this personal involvement with individuals who were literally making Japan's modern history sometimes colored Griffis' writing. Baron Komura, who represented the Japanese at the Portsmouth, New Hampshire negotiations which ended the Russo-Japanese War in 1905, was one of his former students in Tokyo. Griffis gave him high marks for his performance at Portsmouth and concluded that the Japanese at Portsmouth received "even more than she went to war for."[41] When news of the treaty's provisions reached Tokyo, however, the people were dis- illusioned and angry that Japan had not received "a full reimbursement from Russia for the expenses of the war" and took to the streets in violent protest.[42] Whether Komura could have negotiated a more favoable treaty under the circumstances is a matter of debate, but Griffis was uncritically satisfied with his former pupil's accomplishment. Some historians, how- ever, gave the Russian negotiator, Count Sergei Witte, credit for out-

maneuvering Komura in the battle for American public opinion. Okamoto Shumpei, for example, wrote that although the two diplomats had
agreed to a tight control over press releases, "Witte paid great attention
to the press and utilized it fully to influence American public opinion to
Russia's advantage . . . . Some believed that, because of Witte's skillful
use of the American press, the initially overwhelmingly pro-Japanese
public opinion in America gradually became pro-Russian."[43]

Beyond the level of personal loyalites, however, Griffis could hold his
ground. Griffis' interpretation of the Japanese past, for example, did not
always coincide with the conventional analyses of Japanese historians.
An excellent illustration of this is Griffis' treatment of the mythical origins of Japan. The traditional view as detailed in the early chronicles,
Nihongi [Chronicles of Japan] and *Kojiki* [Record of ancient matters],
held that the imperial family descended from the heavens and thus laid the
basis for the alleged divinity of the emperor. Griffis challenged this view.

> They [*Nihongi* and *Kojiki*] contain so much that is fabulous, mythical, or
> exaggerated, that their statements, especially in respect of dates, can not be
> accepted as true history. According to the *Kojiki*, Jimmu Tenno was the first
> emperor; yet it is extremely doubtful whether he was a historical person-
> age.[44]

Griffis' early interpretation of the importance of these chronicles is close
to the best of current historical views. Sir George Sansom, for example,
referred to these chronicles as including "a great deal of invention or
manipulation of both myth and history, and are full of inconsistencies."[45]
As Sansom later argued, Griffis suggested that these chronicles were not
completely useless; indeed, parts of them were undoubtedly historically
accurate. For example, he wrote,

> . . . the *Nihongi* details the history and exploits of these ancient rulers with
> a minuteness and exactness of circumstance that are very suspicious . . . .
> In the list there are many whose deeds, though exaggerated in mirage and
> fable, are, in the main, most probably historic.[46]

Griffis pointed out the dysfunction facing loyal Japanese brought up to
believe the chronicles as factual and then immersed in western rationalism
when they studied abroad. The jolting experience cost them their belief in
the emperor's divinity or the "truth of the *Kojiki*," but left them in no
position publicly to reject them. One student spoke for many: "It is my
duty to believe in them."[47] Reason became the serf of will.

Griffis' interpretation of Japanese history offered other interesting
facets. His treatment of both feudalism and the role of the emperor broke
new ground for historians. As mentioned earlier, John Hall credited
Griffis for his pioneering descriptions of "what he believed to be the com-

parable features of European and Japanese feudalism."[48] Griffis' first book, *The Mikado's Empire*, abounds in general portraits of Japanese feudalism as well as in specific anecdotes which breathe life into the accounts. For example, after describing the old Japanese mansion in Fukui which served as his first home, Griffis described his own retinue:

My interpreter, Iwabuchi, occupied a pleasant little house in the rear and within call, so as to be ready to assist me when visitors came, though most of them went first to Iwabuchi's house. I found that even in the kitchen the feudal spirit of grades and ranks was strictly observed. My cook had an assistant, who himself had a small boy, who often hired other small boys to do his work. My "boy" or body-servant, had another man to help him. Even the bettō, or groom, employed an underling to do all the actual manual work.[49]

Griffis' major contribution to western historiography of Japan, however, appears to be his focus on the emperor or, in his own term, the mikado. As far as can be ascertained, William Elliot Griffis was the first western historian to focus on the role of the mikado and its accompanying "mikadoism" as a key element in Japanese history. Like it or not, the mikado was squarely in the mainstream of Japanese history, and one could ignore this institution only at his own peril.

The student of this people and their unique history can never understand them or their national life unless he measures the mightiness of the force, and recognizes the place of the throne and the mikado in the minds and hearts of the people.[50]

Probably as a result of his own personal experiences in Tokyo, Griffis was particularly impressed with the young Meiji Emperor. As we have seen earlier, Griffis conducted scientific experiments at Nankō in the Emperor's presence, and Griffis was received, along with several other foreign teachers, by the Emperor on New Year's Day, 1873. These experiences reinforced Griffis' existing proclivity toward the Japanese institution. In the preface to his last major book on Japan, *The Mikado: Institution and Person* (1915), Griffis revealed that his audiences with the Emperor Meiji as well as an investigation of his life "lead me to place him among the really great men of our age. Without him, Japan could never have become what she is, and as the world recognizes her to-day."[51] Historical "if" questions are fraught with danger, but Griffis never shied away from them as this statement indicates. Without denying the important role of the Emperor, it seems simplistic to argue that his great talents were the sole, or even primary, reason for Japan's rapid advance from feudalism to modernity. Griffis' judgment, however, may be another case of the affective side of his nature overwhelming his cognitive powers due to his perceived personal connection with the Emperor. It might illustrate some attraction to "great man" theories of history. For whatever reasons, it is readily apparent that Griffis viewed the institution of the emperor as "the secret of Japanese unity," the cement that bound the Japanese nation together.[52] He pointed out that few of the emperors had been strong personalities or leaders, but that was not really important.

> . . . it is not so much the particular person who sat on the ancient mats or who sits on the modern throne, as it is the office or the descent incarcerated in him, which the Japanese consider divine. The "spirits of the Mikado's ancestors" are the spirits of the nation—which some day will be written with one word and with the greatest of all Names.[53]

Griffis recognized that even during the long feudal period, the emperors, although powerless, were treated with great respect and deference. After gaining power in 645 A.D., the Fujiwara family, for example, pursued a policy whose major objective was "to exalt the occupant of the throne to the 'shelf of the blue clouds,' making him . . . a 'god,' existent but absent from the people."[54] This policy allowed the secular powers to rule without the danger of a dysfunctional past.

During the last days of the Tokugawa era, the men who wished to topple that regime in favor of a restoration of imperial rule, according to Griffis, "felt that in the institution and person of the Mikado they had power by which, rightly utilized, they could reconstruct the nation of foundations older even than feudalism."[55] The "rightly utilized" power which the Meiji oligarchs wielded in the last quarter of the nineteenth century is the classic example of a traditional institution ("mikadoism") being used to execute radical reforms.

The new constitution, promulgated in 1889 as a gift from the Emperor to his subjects, was constructed around the principle of absolute imperial sovereignty. Griffis saw that this arrangement, in the light of Japan's past, made sense, but it also had some danger attached to it. On the one hand, he wrote,

> The Mikado is the living symbol of all that is glorious in the history of . . . Japan. He expresses to the sons of Nippon whatever is dearest in the present and auspicious in the future. He incarnates history and religion. His person embodies the nation's memory and the people's hopes.[56]

On the other hand, Griffis perceived potential danger.

> So long as the Throne of Nippon is based on mythology, and so long as things spiritual and temporal are mixed up in Japanese as in Russian politics, there is constant danger from the Government of violation of the Constitution, despite the strong language of this fundamental law, in favor of freedom of conscience . . . . When abused the doctrines of Mikadoism

have cramped the view and narrowed the intellect of the Japanese, both as individuals and as a nation.[57]

The above, written in 1915 and based on the experience of a series of "Peace Preservation" laws in the 1880s, illustrates Griffis' concern about the potential danger of the unique Japanese system which in less than a decade was to become a frightening reality.

As we have seen, Griffis was not adverse to speaking his own mind on controversial issues and John Ashmead's charge that he was nothing more than a mere "apologist for the Japanese" does not withstand close scrutiny.[58] Would an "apologist for the Japanese" write about his first days in the country as follows?

> I began to realize the utter poverty and wretchedness of the people and the country of Japan. It was not an Oriental paradise, such as a reader of some books about it may have supposed. I had only a faint conception of it then. I saw it afterward, until the sight oppressed me like a nightmare.[59]

Perhaps as a result of his contacts with his Japanese students at Rutgers, Griffis still maintained an affection for the Japanese despite this initial experience. In any event, he consciously attempted to describe Japan and the Japanese, warts and all.

> How pleasant it would be to mention in this book [*The Mikado's Empire*] nothing but the beautiful! How easy to let our glamoured eyes see naught but beauty and novelty! Why not paint Japan as a land of peerless natural beauty, of polite people, of good and brave men, of pretty maidens and gentle women? Why bring in beggars, bloody heads, loathsome sores, scenes of murder, assassin's bravery, and humanity with all nobility stamped out by centuries of despotism? Why not? Simply because homely truth is better than gilded falsehood. Only because it is sin to conceal truth when my countrymen, generous to believe too well, and led astray by rhetorical deceivers and truth-smotherers, have the falsest ideas of Japan, that only a pen like a probe can set right. No pen sooner than mine shall record reforms when made. I give the true picture of Japan in 1871.[60]

It is certainly true that Griffis' pen did not always draw a "true picture of Japan in 1871" or any other year, but the post-Bancroftean quest for historical truth has often been more arduous. Contemporary historians wince at such lack of diffidence. No historian, especially if he has participated in the grand events he writes about, whether he be a Bancroft or a Schlesinger, can be completely objective and flawless; he does not bring a blank mind to his research. He is rather the product of what Carl Becker referred to as a "climate of opinion." So it was with William Elliot Griffis. He was a mid-nineteenth-century American who grew up in pre-Civil War Philadelphia. He was both a nationalist and a devout Christian who shared the typical American's belief in the Puritan ethic and in the linear path of progress. His writings on Japan reflect all of these elements, but he was not a blind and unthinking "apologist" for Japan or even for Christianity.

Two final aspects of Griffis' history that deserve our attention revolve around the notion that historical events do not occur in a vacuum bounded by decision-making elites on the one hand and internal politics on the other. The historical processes which William Elliot Griffis saw at work in Japan also included important roles for both the common man and the foreign employee, or *yatoi*.

While it is true that Griffis consistently stressed the centrality of the mikado and "mikadoism" to any true understanding of the Japanese past, it is equally true that he strenuously advocated the study of both "the people" and the *yatoi*. Almost a century ago, he advocated a position that does not differ markedly from what many contemporary historians are recommending in 1972, that is, studying history "from the bottom up."

> What passes for history in the bland and dry native annals is the story of their conquerors, masters and tax-collectors. We see clearly outlined, however, the separation of classes . . . . Since 1868 all the grades below the samurai . . . have been fused into one class, the *hei-min*, or people . . . Heretofore "public opinion" has been the exclusive property of the samurai. "The People" in the modern, not to say American, sense, have not yet grown to consciousness. . . . Nineteen-twentieths of the inhabitants of Japan have been simply burden-bearers and tax-payers; now they are becoming "the people." . . . The people are now learning who and what they are.[61]

Much of Griffis' writings, particularly *The Mikado's Empire*, abounds in descriptions of the life and problems of the common man. Ironically, one of Frances Helbig's major criticisms of Griffis' history is that it consisted of many "lightweight" topics, that is, the "stuff" of the common man's life—family life, social customs, fairy tales, and children's games.

A constant theme in Griffis' interpretation of Japanese history was the role of the foreigner in helping the Japanese help themselves. It was a theme he pursued with a sense of mission throughout his career. His zeal was fired by his conviction that despite the *yatoi*'s importance, "I imagine that 'official' Japanese history will take no note of the 'yatoi.' "[62] He worked tirelessly in publicizing their role, writing biographies of Verbeck, Hepburn, and Brown in addition to numerous articles and public lectures on various aspects of this group. In his late years he began to set about collecting materials to write a comprehensive study of the *yatoi* in Japan, but he never completed this task.

That he did not complete the task was perhaps the greatest failure of his long life. The *yatoi* were significant to the development of Japan and in important ways were forerunners to the post-World War II foreign aid experts who still operate in much of the developing world. More important than this to Griffis, however, was the psychological bond which he felt to the work of the *yatoi*. After all, he had been a *yatoi*, a fact which he was enormously proud to recall at every opportunity, and considered himself as

> . . . the first of 5[000] or possibly 6000 of the yatoi (1868–1919) called out from a foreign country under the imperial oath to serve Japan, and the only one from America to go into the interior and live within the mysteries of feudalism.[63]

No man, particularly one with Griffis' strong sense of self-importance, wants to be forgotten by history. If the Japanese would not immortalize the *yatoi* (that is, Griffis), he would do the work himself. Although he did not complete his planned *yatoi* study, almost all of Griffis' works on Japan contain a strong dose of Griffis' role in the early Meiji period. In a review of Griffis' biography of Verbeck in the *American Historical Review*, C. Meriwether pointed this out with great clarity. Complaining that a defect of the book was Griffis' inability to keep himself out of the biography, Meriwether described the book as consisting of "something of Verbeck as a man . . . as a missionary . . . as a statesman, interlarded with a considerable something of Griffis." He charged, with a degree of justification, that the chapter, "The Biographer in Tokio," is "without structural purpose" except to place Griffis in the limelight, and no attempt is made at "any systematic design to show a complete Verbeck."[64] The same type of self-promotion is found in several of his other books on Japan, including *The Mikado's Empire*.

GRIFFIS IN AMERICA, 1874–1928

Upon returning to the United States in the late summer of 1874, Griffis visited briefly with his family and friends in Philadelphia and settled in New York City. Griffis selected his base of operations wisely. Then as now, New York was the center of the nation's literary life, and Griffis saw himself as part of this life. He immediately began to work seriously on his first book, *The Mikado's Empire*, and to seek a reputation as a Japan "expert." His sister Maggie had returned to Philadelphia to live with her sisters; in early September Griffis wrote her with some annoyance that the ship carrying Imadate Tosui from Japan had not yet arrived.[65] Imadate was a young Japanese scholar whom Griffis had arranged to come to America to attend college and also to help him in the preparation of *The Mikado's Empire*.[66] While awaiting Imadate's arrival, Griffis continued work on the book in an effort to have it published as soon as possible.

Two months later he informed Maggie that he had recently read a paper to the Oriental Society of New York on the subject of "Recent Literature of Japan." The audience, he wrote, consisted of about forty "of our greatest scholars [?] in Sanskrit, Hebrew, Arabic, Chinese, Assyrian . . . a fine gathering of tall foreheads."[67] The composition of the audience gives some indication of the state of the nation's knowledge of Japan. Griffis was uncharacteristically humble when describing how the *New York Times* "devoted half a column to it, calling it the 'most important paper of the meeting,' which I knew was simply because the reporter could understand it better than the others."[68] This modesty, however, offers an important key to Griffis' popularity as a historian. Many others were more erudite than Griffis, but few had either his personal experiences from which to draw and none wrote more lucidly.

Griffis spent a great deal of his time lecturing at various churches and other organizations interested in hearing about Japan from one of the few Americans who had actually lived in that still exotic country. Although this kept him busy, it put relatively little money into his pocket, and the money requests from his family that had been his bane in Japan kept turning up in his mailbox. When his lecturing was interrupted for the holiday season in 1874, he was not unhappy as it "will give me time to work on my book, which has been sadly interfered with by lecturing."[69]

His lecture agent was the American Literary Bureau, which he had contacted a few weeks prior to his departure from Tokyo. All his topics were variations on the Japan theme, and included "Inside Japan," "Street Life in Japan," and "Social Life in Japan."[70] Griffis delivered most of his lectures in the middle Atlantic states and in New England, with occasional ventures as far westward as Illinois and Iowa. His topics were timely and exotic, but even more impressive was the oratorical polish he appears to have brought to his lecturing. For a lecture he gave sometime in 1875 or 1876 in Pekin, Illinois, the earnest young Griffis received high praise. The local *Pekin Times* described his performance as "a treat that for instruction and literary excellence is seldom equalled." The *Times* reporter felt that Griffis was "a young man of great natural power and consumate education . . . . as a public speaker, he has few equals, both in regard to personal appearance and orational power." His "delivery is easy and graceful, his enunciation so clear and distinct that not a syllable is lost. His sentences are well rounded so that aside from the interest of the subject matter, the lecture as a literary work possesses great merit."[71]

At about the same time, Griffis delivered another lecture in Chicago, and the more cosmopolitan *Chicago Tribune* offered similar praise for his lecturing talents. On March 25, 1875, the *Tribune* informed its readers that Griffis "speaks without manuscript, and in a style that is at once picturesque and graphic. At times his sentences are exceedingly eloquent, and his manner full of impressive power . . . . he may be fairly ranked as the interpreter of Japan to the great Christian world."[72]

This initial success at the lectern pleased Griffis, and led to many offers to speak to groups of all kinds. During his first year in the United Staets alone, he gave a total of eighty-nine lectures on various aspects of Japan, and while attending Union Theological Seminary between 1876 and 1877, he spoke to groups on Japan more than one hundred times.[73]

Beginning in 1874, his output of newspaper and magazine articles increased from a steady trickle to a veritable torrent. In 1875 alone, for example, he published a total of fourteen articles on Japan in such organs as *North American Review, Lippincott's Magazine, Appleton's Journal, St. Nicholas, Overland Monthly,* and *New England Journal of Education.* His range of topics included politics, education, marriage, prisons, religion, and cities of Japan.[74] 1876 became an even more productive year for Griffis. He not only published the first edition of *The Mikado's Empire,* but at least three dozen articles, including eighteen entries in the *American Cyclopedia.* He had incorporated much of the substance of these articles into *The Mikado's Empire.*

As we have seen, from an early age Griffis had thought of entering the ministry and even justified going to Japan partly because he could pursue his studies there while gaining valuable experience and making some money. In the fall of 1876, he redeemed this promise and entered the Union Theological Seminary. Little is known about his life during the next two years except that "he studied under Drs. Schaff, Briggs, Adams, Hitchcock, and other religious leaders of the time. During his senior year there, he again served parttime at Knox Memorial Chapel . . . and was offered the pastorate there in April 1877."[75] At about the same time, he also received a similar offer from Spring Valley, New York, but refused both calls as they did not seem "sufficiently attractive" to him.[76] It seems that he was still considering the possibility of returning to Japan as a missionary, if he could find a suitable appointment within six months of his graduation.

Following graduation and ordination on May 31, 1877, he accepted a "sufficiently attractive" pastorate at the Dutch Reformed Church in Schenectady, New York. He toiled for nine years in Schenectady, where he met his future wife, Katherine Lyra Stanton, the brilliant daughter of a Union College Latin professor. In June 1879, the couple married and settled down to a quiet life.

While in Schenectady he continued his writing and turned his attention to local history—that is, the Dutch influence on upstate New York—and to Korea. His major publication during this period was undoubtedly *Corea, The Hermit Nation* (1882). George C. Noyes, reviewing *Corea* in

The Dial, judged it as "a volume . . . [that is] by all odds the best work on Corea which has ever been published in English."[77]

Griffis' life in Schenectady appears to have been a happy and fruitful one, and his long-time relationship with the Dutch Reformed Church exhibited no strains. Yet, "for reasons which are not clear," he left his Schenectady post in 1886 in favor of the pulpit of the Shawmut Congregational Church in Boston. He continued his writing and lecturing there, in addition to his pastoral duties. As a result of internal political maneuvering, however, Griffis decided in 1893 that his future did not lie in Boston. In that year he sought and won the pastorate of the Congregational Church in Ithaca, New York. There in 1898, after blessing him with two sons and a daughter, Griffis' wife Katherine died from what was probably leukemia.[78] A widower with three children, the lonely Griffis remarried in June 1900. His bride was Sarah Frances King of Pulaski, New York.

Stanton Griffis, Griffis' second child, described the 1890s life in the Griffis household in Ithaca. According to Stanton's autobiography, *Lying in State,* family life was characterized by "the calm regularity of Ithaca's Six Mile Brook, for father was the essence of careful habit." The daily routine started at 7:30 A.M. when all were roused from their sleep and after breakfast, gathered in their father's study "for a short reading of the Bible."[79]

The day started, and we scattered to our respective schools, while father took his regular walk to the post office and returned to work in his study on his sermons or books until the noon dinner of those days. The master of the household then slept for exactly fifteen minutes, no more, no less, and again retired to his study until supper; he made a second pilgrimage for the mail at 7:00; again he worked in his study, and at exactly 11:00, carrying his old-fashioned student lamp in one hand, he descended to the kitchen for his bottle of beer with cheese and crackers, inevitably toasting the cheese over the flame of the student lamp, much to the disgust of slavey.

Father eschewed electricity. He maintained that electric lamps were ruinous to the eyes, and while the household was at long last permitted this new-fangled development, his working light remained a student lamp until the end. He especially hated the telephone. We could always tell when he had been forced to use it for he inevitably left the receiver dangling from the hook as though he had fled in disgust. His method of household accounting was a modern miracle. When he received his bills he placed them carefully in the right-hand top drawer of his desk, and when some manna in the form of a check came in, he paid the top bills and left the older ones below in gentle oblivion. Walking up and down in the library dictating, or standing at work at an old-fashioned shelf desk correcting manuscripts with a stub pen, a gaunt figure with white mustachios, he will always remain in my memory as the picture of a contented, philosophical Christian man, not far separated from the spiritual world.[80]

Ten years of this ministerial and free-lance life in Ithaca began to wear on the elder Griffis. In 1903 he decided to retire from the ministry to devote the remainder of his life to literary and historical affairs. Although sixty years old, Griffis was in excellent health and at the height of his powers. "For years," he wrote, "I had set before myself, should God lengthen my days . . . the work of further interpreting Japan and liberty-loving Holland, in scholarly books."[81] Although Griffis was not a wealthy man, he determined to spend the rest of his life in a labor of love rather than duty. Perhaps however, the labor of love that he had set for himself was in a very real, if psychological sense, a duty. As we have seen earlier in this chapter, Griffis felt very strongly about the important role the *yatoi* had played in Meiji Japan and was convinced that the Japanese historians would ignore them in their writings. He could, on the other hand, redress this injustice by doing the task himself. In any event, it was about this time that he sent hundreds of letters and postcards to those *yatoi* whom he could identify in an attempt to acquire as much information as possible. His writing, beginning in 1900, also focused much more on the *yatoi*. Between 1900 and 1913, for example, he published biographies of

---

TO THE YATOI
(FOREIGNERS IN THE SERVICE OF THE JAPANESE GOVERNMENT)
1858-1900
OR THEIR CHILDREN, RELATIVES OR FRIENDS.

The undersigned; one of the **Yatoi** in Japan (1870-1874) would make a record of the services of those men and women from Western Countries, who, between the years 1858 and 1900, assisted the Japanese in Education in Civil, Mechanical, Mining or Electrical Engineering, in Finance, in Railway, Telegraph, Ship or Factory Construction, in the Naval or Military, Medical, Surgical, or Hygienic Sciences or Arts, or in any line of mental discipline, social improvement, commercial enterprise or phase of civilization. He respectfully seeks imformation as to their personality, accomplishments, previous record and preparation, services in Japan, and asks for an outline of their life and work. For the sake of accuracy and true history, let modesty give place to truth, and please answer if possible, as **fully** as may be desireable, the following questions. Send photograph also, if agreeable, and any available printed matter.
1. Date of Birth. 2. Education. 3. How appointed to Japan. 4. Date of Arrival and Departure from Japan. 5. Services to the Japanese. 6. Subsequent record and career, in outline. 7. Date of Decease, if not living. 8. Personal details as to wife and children. 9. Information as to other Yatoi.
The night cometh, and the living should be prompt to make record. Please Address :-

WILLIAM ELLIOT GRIFFIS, D.D., L.H.D.
(AUTHOR OF "THE MIKADO'S EMPIRE", "THE RELIGIONS OF JAPAN", ETC.)
ITHACA, N. Y., U. S. A.

---

three of the most important missionary/*yatoi* in Meiji Japan—Guido Verbeck (1900), Samuel Brown (1902), and James Hepburn (1913). In

addition a cursory glance at a bibliography of Griffis' writings clearly
shows a steady and growing trend in his output toward topics dealing
with Japan.

A GRATEFUL JAPAN HONORS ITS YATOI

William Elliot Griffis' reputation in Japan during his lifetime is relatively simple to assess; he was respected as an earnest, sincere friend of the
Japanese. He was highly regarded not only for his educational work
between 1870 and 1874, but also for his extensive efforts to explain Japan
and the Japanese to his sometimes skeptical countrymen. In 1908 he
received the Order of the Rising Sun, Fourth Class, from a grateful Japanese government. In expressing his appreciation, Griffis did not conceal
his preference for ideological and intellectual independence. He had in
fact thought his scholarship too independent to qualify for such an honor.
Thanking the Japanese Ambassador Takahira, Griffis expressed surprise
as well as pleasure, "for I have never ceased to criticize Japan and the
Japanese."[82]

> I have never flattered the Japanese or Have [sic] I defended them in a mere
> partisan spirit. In endeavoring to be an interpreter of the Orientals to the
> Occidentals I have proceeded in the spirit of the scientific student, my aim
> to break down the wall of prejudice, ignorance and bigotry whether ethnic,
> religious and social, and express the truth, without fear or favor. Hence I
> have criticized all things Japanese as freely and unreservedly as I should my
> own country and people.[83]

The highlight of Griffis' later years was undoubtedly his sentimental
return visit to Japan during 1926–1927 as a guest of the Japanese government. "The invitation to revisit Japan came from statesmen interested in
writing the official biography of the Meiji Emperor, who died in 1915.
. . . Dr. Griffis is to follow his new visit to Japan by writing a biography
of that monarch and a history of the New Japan."[84]

During this extended visit to Japan, Griffis not only revisited the scenes
of his earlier sojourn in Japan, but also Manchuria and Korea. On his
arrival in Tokyo, Griffis and his wife were "overwhelmed with honors,
gifts and attentions. During the six months that followed, he traveled
about the four greater islands of Japan, visited Korea and Manchuria, and
during the course of 2000 miles of journeying delivered some 250 addresses. His audiences ranged from princes to a colony of 500 lepers in
Korea."[85] Since the Griffises were guests of the government, a gentleman
traveling companion was provided, along with "the finest means of
conveyance."[86] Griffis later told reporters, "I was particularly delighted
with my reception in Fukui. . . . It consisted of four glorious days. The

whole town was decorated and more than ten thousand students were kind enough to come out to welcome me."[87] One newspaper report of this trip described his reception as of the type which "in the past have been given only to royal personages."[88]

On the eve of his departure from Tokyo in 1927, the government gave in his honor an official farewell ceremony. Twelve hundred people gathered at the Jiji Kaikan Hall in Ueno Park to do him honor. Several Japanese dignitaries, including the mayor of Tokyo, Viscount Kaneko and Prince Tokugawa, eulogized Griffis and his contributions to Japanese-American understanding. In his turn, Griffis eloquently returned the compliments and went on to praise the Tokugawa family's role in Japanese history.[89]

> Now if we judge the Tokugawa family by modern circumstances and customs we might be doing it a great injustice. In my opinion, after the long wars which Japan had been through, the work done by Ieyasu approached nigh to human genius, and his successor and other men whose memory I recall led me to believe that under a system of government which was necessary for Japan at that time—the feudal system—it could not have been better governed.[90]

The nation that he had known so intimately more than a half century earlier had experienced a remarkable transformation, and Griffis was well pleased with what he saw in 1926–1927.

> I was particularly impressed with the remarkable strides that Japan has taken since my last visit 50 years ago. Everywhere I noted changes, changes in the physical appearance of the people, changes in hygiene, in cleanliness of the cities. On my last visit, houses had tile roofs made of highly inflammable material making them easy targets for devastating fires. Now these are being fast replaced by tin and other uninflammable roofing. Then I noticed the disappearance of small pox which used to ravage Japan as it did England 200 years ago, and social diseases which were quite prevalent are all being rapidly wiped out.
>
> I was especially impressed with the educational system . . . [which] is wonderfully well established comparing favorably with educational systems in the most advanced countries with its institutions for the finest training of industrial and professional men.[91]

He received a favorable impression during this trip and earnestly believed that the Japanese and American peoples' long-time friendship was too broad and too deep to allow difficulties between them to get out of hand. Responding to the many speculations of the day regarding the possibility of the United States and Japan going to war with one another, Griffis argued that "all the hostile war spirit is on this side of the Pacific Ocean, and is manufactured, in my opinion, by American munition makers."[92] Fortunately, he did not live to see this statement undermined.

Shortly after returning to the United States from his long and arduous journey, Griffis traveled to his winter home in Florida where, on February 5, 1928, he died after a brief illness. As one of his last achievements before he died, he completed a study, "Reminiscences of the Meiji Tenno," which, his second wife wrote, "he was permitted to offer to the Japanese nation in recognition of the unbounded hospitality and honor shown to him."[93] Exactly one month before his death, on January 5, 1928, at a formal dinner attended by 1,100 guests of the Japan Society, Griffis presented the study to Ambassador Matsudaira, a relative of the old Fukui daimyō who had originally brought Griffis to Japan in 1870.[94] It was a fitting end to a long and fruitful life devoted to the two countries he loved and respected.

SUMMING UP

William Elliot Griffis was a man both common and unique. He was a typical American of his time in the attitudes and values that were part of him, but he was also unusual in that he saw himself as not only a "helper" of Japan in her quest for a "better time," but also a conscious interpreter of that country to his fellow citizens. As a bridge between the two cultures, he attempted to teach the Japanese the best in his native culture so that they could enjoy its fruits. At the same time he tried to pass on his love and affection for Japan and her people to the American people, whom he knew were ignorant of the realities of the East. As the *New York Evening Post* put it in commenting on his death, Griffis' experiences in Japan "enabled . . . [him] to interpret Japan with peculiar insight. . . . He was one of a little band of early visitors to the country that gradually made Japan known to the West."[95]

Griffis' Japan experiences are also instructive for the kinds of intercultural problems he faced between 1870 and 1874. His solutions to them were unique, but they did foreshadow many of those that have become the focus of governmental and academic concern in the days of Peace Corps, Point Four, and AID.

A prolific author of books, journal articles, and newspaper pieces, and a powerful lecturer and propagandist in the best sense of that often misused word, William Elliot Griffis was one of the first, and most effective, writers to help shape American attitudes about Japan. His career is neatly summarized in the description of a Japanese reporter writing in 1926:

> Dr. William Elliot Griffis, author of "The Mikado's Empire" and other works, is one of the few who is credited with having placed Japan on the intellectual and artistic map of the world. Had he no other claim to bril-

liance than his "The Mikado's Empire," that alone would entitle him to front rank, for, in it Dr. Griffis saw in Japan, long before she had become one of the great Powers of the world, the making of a great nation.[96]

Any man could be proud to have as much said about his life.

NOTES

1. Letter, WEG to "Dear Christian Brethren in the bonds of Christ in the Churches of Tokio and Yokohama," January 21, 1874, GCRUL. A slightly edited version is also found in Griffis, *Sunny Memories of Three Pastorates*, pp. 43–48.
2. Griffis, *Sunny Memories of Three Pastorates*, pp. 43–48.
3. Griffis, *Sunny Memories of Three Pastorates*, pp. 43–48.
4. Griffis, *Sunny Memories of Three Pastorates*, pp. 43–48.
5. Griffis, *Sunny Memories of Three Pastorates*, p. 42.
6. Griffis, *Sunny Memories of Three Pastorates*, p. 42.
7. Griffis, *Sunny Memories of Three Pastorates*, p. 42.
8. "William Elliot Griffis: Entrepreneur," p. 72.
9. J. H. Hexter, "Publish or Perish—A Defense," *The Public Interest*, No. 17 (Fall, 1969): 64; hereafter cited as Hexter, "Publish or Perish."
10. "Publish or Perish," p. 71.
11. Hexter, "Publish or Perish," pp. 71–72.
12. "William Elliot Griffis: Entrepreneur," p. 83.
13. Helbig, "William Elliot Griffis: Entrepreneur," p. 83.
14. Helbig, "William Elliot Griffis: Entrepreneur," p. 84.
15. Helbig, "William Elliot Griffis: Entrepreneur," pp. 84–85.
16. Griffis, *The Mikado's Empire*, 9th ed., 1: 7.
17. Donald E. Emerson, *Richard Hildreth* (Baltimore: Johns Hopkins Press, 1946), p. 152; hereafter cited as Emerson, *Richard Hildreth*.
18. Emerson, *Richard Hildreth*, p. 153.
19. Emerson, *Richard Hildreth*, p. 153.
20. *Nation* 23 (November 23, 1876): 317.
21. Review of *The Mikado's Empire*, by William Elliot Griffis, n.d. [probably late 1876 or early 1877], pp. 3–6, quoted in Helbig, "William Elliot Griffis: Entrepreneur," pp. 86–87.
22. Nitobe Inazō, *The Intercourse between the United States and Japan: An Historical Sketch* (Baltimore, Md.: Johns Hopkins University Press, 1891), p. 145; hereafter cited as Inazō, *The Intercourse between the U.S. and Japan*.
23. Inazō, *The Intercourse between the U.S. and Japan*, p. 145.
24. Inazō, *The Intercourse between the U.S. and Japan*, pp. 145–146.
25. *Japanese History: New Dimensions of Approach and Understanding*, (2d ed. Washington, D. C.: Service Center for Teachers of History, A Service of the American Historical Association, 1966), p. 4; hereafter cited as Hall, *Japanese History*.
26. Iriye Akira, *Across the Pacific: An Inner History of American-East Asian Relations* (New York: Harcourt, Brace & World, 1967), p. 21.
27. Hall, *Japanese History*, p. 31.

28.   Hall, *Japanese History*, p. 31.
29.   Griffis, *The Mikado's Empire*, p. 551.
30.   Griffis, *The Mikado's Empire*, p. 552.
31.   Griffis, *The Mikado's Empire*, p. 578.
32.   "William Elliot Griffis: Entrepreneur," p. 88.
33.   (Boston: Houghton, Mifflin and Company, 1892), pp. 70–71.
34.   William Elliot Griffis, *The Japanese Nation in Evolution* (New York: Thomas Y. Crowell & Co., 1907), p. 130.
35.   Griffis, *The Japanese Nation in Evolution*, p. 267.
36.   Griffis, *The Mikado's Empire*, 1: 280–281.
37.   Griffis, *The Mikado's Empire*, 1: 284.
38.   Griffis, *The Mikado: Institution and Person*, p. 68.
39.   Griffis, *The Mikado's Empire*, 9th ed., 1: 7.
40.   Griffis, *The Mikado's Empire*, p. 437.
41.   Griffis, *The Mikado's Empire*, p. 710.
42.   Griffis, *The Mikado's Empire*, p. 710.
43.   Okamoto, *The Japanese Oligarchy and the Russo-Japanese War*, p. 157.
44.   Griffis, *The Mikado's Empire*, 1: 39–40.
45.   George Sansom, *A History of Japan to 1334* (Stanford, Calif.: Stanford University Press, 1958), p. 29.
46.   Griffis, *The Mikado's Empire*, 1:60.
47.   Griffis, *The Mikado's Empire*, 1:59.
48.   Hall, *Japanese History*, p. 31.
49.   Griffis, *The Mikado's Empire*, p. 440.
50.   Griffis, *The Mikado's Empire*, 1:187.
51.   Griffis, *The Mikado: Institution and Person*, p. vi.
52.   Griffis, *The Japanese Nation*, p. 101.
53.   Griffis, *The Japanese Nation*, p. 102.
54.   Griffis, *The Mikado: Institution and Person*, p. 39.
55.   Griffis, *The Mikado: Institution and Person*, p. 188.
56.   Griffis, *The Mikado: Institution and Person*, p. 15.
57.   Griffis, *The Mikado: Institution and Person*, p. 17.
58.   John Ashmead, "The Idea of Japan, 1853–1895: Japan as Described by Americans and Other Travelers from the West," 2 vols. (Ph.D. dissertation, Harvard University, 1951), 2:399.
59.   Griffis, *The Mikado's Empire*, p. 416.
60.   Griffis, *The Mikado's Empire*, p. 361.
61.   Griffis, *The Mikado's Empire*, pp. 608–609.
62.   Griffis, *Verbeck of Japan*, p. 219.
63.   William Elliot Griffis, (draft of an unfinished manuscript, *circa* 1919), GCRUL.
64.   C. Meriwether, review of *Verbeck of Japan*, by William Elliot Griffis, in the *American Historical Review* 6 (July, 1901): 829–830.
65.   WEG to MCG, September 5, 1874, GCRUL.
66.   College Department, University of Pennsylvania, "Extract from History Class of 1879," Pennsylvania, 1899, n. p. (Typescript.)
67.   WEG to MCG, November 4, 1874, GCRUL.
68.   WEG to MCG, November 4, 1874, GCRUL.
69.   WEG to MCG, December 22, 1874, GCRUL.
70.   Helbig, "William Elliot Griffis: Entrepreneur," p. 83.

71.   *Pekin Times*, n.d., n.p., in William Elliot Griffis, "Tokio Scrapbook," p. 73, GCRUL.
72.   *Chicago Tribune*, March 25, 1875, n.p., in Griffis, "Tokio Scrapbook," n.p., GCRUL.
73.   Yamamoto Masaya, "Image-Makers of Japan: A Case Study in the Impact of the American Protestant Foreign Missionary Movement, 1859–1905" (Ph.D. dissertation, The Ohio State University, 1967), p. 161.
74.   Helbig, "William Elliot Griffis: Entrepreneur," Appendix A, "Preliminary Bibliography of W. E. Griffis's Published Works," n.p.
75.   Helbig, "William Elliot Griffis: Entrepreneur," p. 98.
76.   Helbig, "William Elliot Griffis: Entrepreneur," p. 98.
77.   George C. Noyes, review of *Corea, The Hermit Nation*, by William Elliot Griffis, in *The Dial*, 3 No. 32 (1882): 167.
78.   Helbig, "William Elliot Griffis: Entrepreneur," p. 99.
79.   Stanton Griffis, *Lying in State* (New York: Doubleday and Company, 1952), p. 22. Griffis' second child Stanton, born in Boston in 1887, turned out to be a very different man than his father both in his attitudes and in his calling. Young Stanton graduated from Cornell University before experimenting for "a short period as a farmer in Oregon; a dive into Wall Street, interrupted by by service in the First World War. Then a few years of money grubbing, specializing in industrial reorganizations, and later the show business period covering the organization of the Katherine Cornell Productions, purchase of control of Madison Square Garden, and finally some years as Chairman of Paramount Pictures" (page 10). Stanton Griffis also served in government during World War II with the OSS and the Red Cross. Following the war, he served as American ambassador to Poland, Egypt, Argentina, and Spain in the Truman Administration.
80.   Stanton Griffis, *Lying in State*, p. 23.
81.   Griffis, *Sunny Memories of Three Pastorates*, p. 270.
82.   WEG to Ambassador Takahira, May 7, 1908, GCRUL.
83.   WEG to Ambassador Takahira, May 7, 1908, GCRUL.
84.   "Japan's Teacher on Way Back Here," n.d., n.p., GCRUL.
85.   "Japan's Teacher on Way Back Here."
86.   "Dr. Griffis Is Much Impressed," n.d., n.p., GCRUL.
87.   "Dr. Griffis Is Much Impressed."
88.   "Japan's Teacher on Way Back Here."
89.   "Dr. Griffis Is Much Impressed."
90.   "Griffis in Farewell, Pledges to Interpret Japan to U.S.," n.d., n.p., GCRUL.
91.   "Dr. Griffis Is Much Impressed."
92.   Clipping, "Japan Pays U.S. Teacher High Honors," *San Francisco Chronicle*, July 17, 1927, n.p., GCRUL.
93.   Frances King Griffis to Imadate Tosui, March 1, 1928, GCRUL.
94.   Frances King Griffis to Imadate Tosui, March 1, 1928, GCRUL.
95.   "Obituary," *New York Evening Post*, February 7, 1928, n.p., GCRUL
96.   "Dr. William Elliot Griffis Tells of His Early Days in Japan," n.d., n.p., GCRUL.

Appendix

Griffis outlined a three-year course of study which he described as "similar to that of the best Polytechnic schools in Europe and America." After the beginning students had "earned the elements of Inorganic Chemistry," he suggested that their future work follow this pattern:

1ST TERM OF THE YEAR 1874

Organic Chemistry lectures by the Prof. and recitations by students. One term of five months, 80 recitations and lectures, 2 hours a week for forty weeks.
Chrystallography, forty recitations and lectures, one hour per week.

Blowpipe Analysis

80 exercises, two each week of two hours each, occupying one term of five months.
The remaining one hour a week being devoted to Hooker's Chemistry [textbook].

2ND TERM OF THE YEAR 1874

Qualitative Analysis

80 exercises of two hours each. Two exercises of two hours each per week.

Determinative Mineralogy

80 exercises. Two exercises of one hour per week.

General and Practical Chemistry

How to work with gases, to handle instruments, glass-blowing, use of reagents, etc. 80 exercises of two hours per week.
The expense for a class of students in Qualitative Analysis, will be about $300 for a class of 24 students. The expense for a class in General and Practical Chemistry will be about the same.

1ST TERM OF THE YEAR 1875

Qualitative Analysis

80 exercises in the laboratory of two hours each, four hours per week.

Applied Chemistry

Lectures by the professor, and recitations by the students; 80 exercises of two hours each, four hours per week.

Geology, Metallurgy, etc.

The expense of a class in Qualitative Analysis will be about $500 for a class of 24 students.
In applied Chemistry, about $200 for the Professor's use will be needed.

2ND TERM OF THE YEAR 1875

Applied Chemistry

80 recitations of two hours each, four hours per week.

Quantitative Analysis

80 recitations of two hours each, four hours per week.

Assaying, Geology, Metallurgy

1ST TERM OF THE YEAR 1876

Applied Chemistry
80 exercises of two hours each.

Quantitative Analysis
80 exercises of two hours each.

Assaying, Geology, Metallurgy

2ND TERM OF THE YEAR 1876
Drawing of Furnaces, Machine apparatus, etc.

Essays or theses on chemical and scientific subjects.
Projects of chemical works, etc.

Wm Elliot Griffis.

Bibliography

Books

Bacon, Alice M. *Japanese Girls and Women*. Boston, Mass.: Houghton, Mifflin and Company, 1892.

Barr, Pat. *The Deer Cry Pavilion: The Story of Westerners in Japan, 1868–1905*. New York: Harcourt, Brace & World, 1968.

Black, Cyril E. *The Dynamics of Modernization: A Study in Comparative History*. New York: Harper and Row, 1966.

Black, John. *Young Japan: Yokohama and Yedo; A Narrative of the Settlement and the City from the Signing of the Treaties in 1858, to the Closing of the Year 1879, with a Glance at the Progress of Japan during a Period of Twenty-one Years*. Vol. 2. Yokohama: Kelly & Co., 1883.

Blacker, Carmen. *The Japanese Enlightenment: A Study of the Writings of Fukuzawa Yukichi*. Cambridge: Cambridge University Press, 1964.

Bush, Lewis. *77 Samurai: Japan's First Embassy to America*. Tokyo: Kodansha International, 1968.

Carey, Otis. *A History of Christianity in Japan*. Vol. 1. New York: Fleming H. Revell, 1909.

Churchill, Sir Winston. *A History of the English Speaking Peoples*. Vol. 3: *The Age of Revolution*. London: Cassell and Company, 1957.

Clark, Edward Warren. *Life and Adventure in Japan*. New York: American Tract Society, 1878.

Conroy, Hilary. *The Japanese Seizure of Korea, 1868–1910*. Philadelphia, Penna.: University of Pennsylvania Press, 1960.

Demarest, Richard. *A History of Rutgers College, 1766–1924*. New Brunswick, N.J.: Rutgers Press, 1924.

Dore, Ronald P. *Education in Tokugawa Japan*. Berkeley and Los Angeles, Calif.: University of California Press, 1965.

Dubois, W. E. G. *The Philadelphia Negro: A Social Study*. New York: Shocken Books, 1967.

Dulles, Foster Rhea. *Yankees and Samurai: America's Role in the Emergence of Modern Japan.* New York: Harper and Row, 1965.

Earl, David. *Emperor and Nation in Japan: Political Thinkers of the Tokugawa Period.* Seattle, Wash.: University of Washington Press, 1964.

Emerson, Donald E. *Richard Hildreth.* Baltimore, Md.: Johns Hopkins University Press, 1946.

Fairbank, John K.; Reischauer, Edwin O.; and Craig, Albert M. *East Asia: The Modern Transformation.* Boston: Houghton Mifflin Company, 1965.

Fraser, Stewart, ed. *The Evils of a Foreign Education, or Birdsey Northrop on Education Abroad 1873.* Nashville, Tenn.: George Peabody College for Teachers, 1966.

Griffis, William Elliot. *A Maker of the New Orient, Samuel Robbins Brown, Pioneer Educator in China, America and Japan, The Story of His Life and Work.* New York: Fleming H. Revell, 1902.

————. *America in the East: A Glance at Our History, Prospects, Problems and Duties in the Pacific Ocean.* New York: A. S. Barnes, 1899.

————. *Dux Christus, An Outline Study of Japan.* New York: Macmillan and Company, 1904.

————. *Hepburn of Japan and His Wife and Helpmates: A Life Story of Toil for Christ.* Philadelphia, Penna.: The Westminster Press, 1913.

————. *Honda the Samurai, A Story of Modern Japan.* Boston: Congregational Publishing Society, 1890.

————. *In the Mikado's Service: A Story of Two Battle Summers in China.* Boston: A. W. Wilde Company, 1901.

————. *Japan: Its History, Folklore and Art.* Boston: Houghton Mifflin and Company, 1892.

————. *The Japanese Nation in Evolution: Steps in the Progress of a Great People.* New York: T. Y. Crowell and Company, 1907.

————. *John Chambers: Servant of Christ and Master of Hearts, and His Ministry in Philadelphia.* Ithaca, New York: Andrus and Church, 1903.

————. *Matthew Calbraith Perry: A Typical American Naval Officer.* Boston: Cupples and Hurd, 1887.

————. *The Mikado: Institution and Person; A Study of the Internal Political Forces of Japan.* Princeton, N. J.: Princeton University Press, 1915.

————. *The Mikado's Empire.* 2 vols. 9th ed. and 12th ed. New York: Harper and Brothers, 1900, and 1913.

————. *Millard Fillmore: Constructive Statesman, Defender of the Constitution, President of the United States.* Ithaca, New York: Andrus and Church, 1915.

————. *The Religion of Japan from the Dawn of History to the Era of Meiji: Shinto, Buddhism and Confucianism.* New York: Charles Scribner's and Sons, 1895.

————. *Rutgers Graduates in Japan.* New Brunswick, N.J.: Rutgers College, 1916.

————. *Some of Japan's Contributions to Civilization; Direct and Indirect.* New York: Japan Society, 1928.

————. *Sunny Memories of Three Pastorates.* Ithaca, New York: Andrus and Church, 1903.

————. *Townsend Harris: First American Envoy in Japan.* Boston: Houghton Mifflin and Company, 1895.

————. *Verbeck of Japan: A Citizen of No Country.* New York: Fleming H. Revell, 1900.

———— and Byas, Hugh. *Japan: A Comparison.* New York: Japan Society, 1923.

Griffis, Stanton. *Lying in State.* New York: Doubleday and Company, 1952.

Hall, John W. *Japanese History: New Dimensions of Approach and Understanding*. 2d ed. Washington, D.C.: Service Center for Teachers of History, American Historical Association, 1966.

Higham, John. *Strangers in the Land*. New Brunswick, N.J.: Rutgers Press, 1955.

Iriye, Akira. *Across the Pacific: An Inner History of American-East Asian Relations*. New York: Harcourt, Brace and World, 1967.

Issacs, Harold. *Scratches on our Minds*. Cambridge: The M. I. T. Press, 1958.

Jansen, Marius, ed. *Changing Japanese Attitudes Toward Modernization*. Princeton, N.J.: Princeton University Press, 1965.

————. *Sakamoto Ryōma and the Meiji Restoration*. Princeton, N.J.: Princeton University Press, 1961.

Kiyooka, Eiichi, ed. *The Autobiography of Fukuzawa Yukichi*. Cambridge: Cambridge University Press, 1964.

Maclay, Arthur C. *A Budget of Letters from Japan: Reminiscences of Work and Travel in Japan*. New York: A. C. Armstrong & Son, 1886.

Nagai, Michio. *Higher Education in Japan: Its Takeoff and Crash*. Tokyo: University of Tokyo Press, 1971.

Nitobe, Inazō. *The Intercourse between the United States and Japan: An Historical Sketch*. Baltimore, Md.: Johns Hopkins University Press, 1891.

Okamoto, Shumpei. *The Japanese Oligarchy and the Russo-Japanese War*. New York: Columbia University Press, 1971.

Papinot, E. *Historical and Geographical Dictionary of Japan*. Tokyo: Charles E. Tuttle, 1972.

Pyle, Kenneth B. *The New Generation in Meiji Japan: Problems of Cultural Identity, 1885–1895*. Stanford, Calif.: Stanford University Press, 1969.

Sansom, Sir George. *A History of Japan to 1334*. Stanford, Calif.: Stanford University Press, 1958.

————. *The Western World and Japan: A Study in the Interaction of European and Asiatic Cultures*. New York: Alfred A. Knopf, 1950.

Scharf, J. Thomas, and Walcott, Thompson. *A History of Philadelphia*. 2 vols. Philadelphia, Penna.: L. H. Everts Company, 1884.

Scheiner, Irwin, *Christian Converts and Social Protest in Meiji Japan*. Berkeley and Los Angeles, Calif.: University of California Press, 1970.

Schwantes, Robert S. *Japanese and Americans: A Century of Cultural Relations*. New York: Harper and Brothers, 1955.

Shively, Donald, and Craig, Albert. *Personality in Japanese History*. Berkeley and Los Angeles, Calif.: University of California Press, 1970.

Spence, Jonathan. *To Change China: Western Advisors in China, 1620–1960*. Boston: Little, Brown and Company, 1969.

Wainwright, Nicholas B., ed. *A Philadelphia Perspective: The Diary of Sidney George Fisher Covering the Years, 1834–1871*. Philadelphia, Penna.: Historical Society of Pennsylvania, 1967.

Warner, Sam Bass. *The Private City: Philadelphia in Three Periods of Its Growth*. Philadelphia: University of Pennsylvania Press, 1968.

Williams, Harold S. *Foreigners in Mikadoland*. Tokyo: Charles E. Tuttle, 1963.

————. *Shades of the Past or Indiscreet Tales of Japan*. Tokyo: Charles E. Tuttle, 1960.

————. *Tales of the Foreign Settlements in Japan*. Tokyo: Charles E. Tuttle, 1958.

Yazaki, Takeo. *Social Change and the City in Japan*. San Francisco: Japan Publications, 1968.

Articles

Many articles cited in this section are clippings saved by William Elliot Griffis and therefore often do not reveal important information about their publication. Usually all that can be ascertained from them are the name of the publication and its date. Wherever possible, however, I have endeavored to provide as much other information as possible.

Burks, Ardath. "William Elliot Griffis, Class of 1869." *The Journal of the Rutgers University Library* 19, no. 3 (1966): 91–100.

"Extract From the History Class of 1879." Philadelphia: University of Pennsylvania, College Department, n.d., n.p.

"Griffis, William Elliot." *Appleton's Cyclopaedia of American Biography.* 1st ed., Vol. 3.

Griffis, William Elliot. "American Relations with Japan." *Magazine of American History* 27 (1892): 449.

——. "Britain and America in Africa." *Landmark* 7, no. 10 (1925): 613–616.

——. "British and American Cooperation in Asia." *Landmark* 7, no. 9 (1925): 553–556.

——. "Chemical Laboratories in Japan." *Nature* 6 (1872): 422.

——. "Coercion in Japan." *Nation* 46 (February 16, 1888): 129–131.

——. "The Department of Education in Japan." *American Education Monthly* 10 (May, 1873): 217–218.

——. "Education in Japan." *The College Courant* 14 (May 16, 1874), n.p.

——. "First Glimpses of Japan." *The Christian Intelligencer*, March 2, 1871, n.p.

——. "The Games and Sports of Japanese Children." *Transactions of the Asiatic Society of Japan* 2 (1874):125–141.

——. "Griffis' Laboratory of Physical Science in Fukuwi." *Nature* 6 (1872):352.

——. "In the Heart of Japan." *The Christian Intelligencer*, April 27, 1871, n.p.

——. "Introduction of Chemistry into Japan: An Appreciation of the Service of Charles William Elliot as a Chemist." *Chemical Age* 3, (April 17, 1924), n. p. [galley proofs]

——. "Japan As I Knew It and Know It." *Home Progress* 4, no. 4 (1914):642–650.

——. "Japan At the Time of Townsend Harris," in Griffis, William Elliot, and Byas, Hugh, *Japan: A Comparison.* New York: Japan Society, 1923, pp. 5–29.

——. "Japan, Child of the World's Old Age: An Empire of Mountain Islands, Where People Constantly Conquer Harsh Facts of Land, Sea and Sky." *National Geographic* 63 (March, 1933):257–302.

——. "Japanese Ambassador." *Outlook* 94 (February 27, 1910):473–475.

——. "Japanese Peace Commission." *Outlook* 80 (July 22, 1905): 711–714.

——. "The Japanese Students in America." *Japanese Student* 1 (October, 1916):8–15.

——. "Japan's First Ambassador to the United States." *Outlook* 80 (January 27, 1906): 164–166.

——. "Man Who Rules Japan." *Harper's Weekly* 49 (January 21, 1905):92–93.

——. "Millard Fillmore's Forgotten Achievements." *Harper's Magazine* 122 (May, 1911): 943–949.

——. "Nature and People in Japan." *Century* 39 (December, 1889): 213–239.

——. "New World of Books in Japan." *Critic* 47 (August, 1905): 128–133.

——. "Our Navy in Asiatic Waters." *Harper's Magazine* 97 (October, 1898): 738–760.

——. "Personality of the Mikado." *Outlook* 68 (July 6, 1901):559–569.

——. "Pioneering in Chemistry in Japan." *Industrial and Engineering Chemistry* 16, no. 11 (1924):1165.

———. "The Recent Revolution in Japan." *North American Review* 120 (April, 1875): 281–315.

———. "Roosevelt and Japan." Letter to *New York Herald Tribune*, August 9, 1924, n.p.

———. "The Streets and Streetnames of Yedo." *Transactions of the Asiatic Society of Japan* 1 (1873):18–26.

———. "Takahira: Student and Ambassador." *Outlook* 88 (January 25, 1908):213–215.

———. "Why Russia and Japan Should Shake Hands." *Outlook* 80 (August 19, 1905): 961–964.

Hexter, J. H. "Publish or Perish—A Defense." *The Public Interest*, no. 17 (Fall, 1969): 60–77.

Jones, Hazel. "The Formulation of Meiji Policy Toward the Employment of Foreigners." *Monumenta Nipponica* 23 (1968):9–30.

Lannie, Vincet P., and Diethorn, Bernard C. "For the Honor and Glory of God: The Philadelphia Bible Riots of 1840 [1843]." *History of Education Quarterly* 8, no. 1 (Spring, 1968):44–106.

Mayo, Marlene. "The Korean Crisis of 1873 and Early Meiji Foreign Policy." *Journal of Asian Studies* 31, no. 4(1972): 793–819.

Meriwether, C. Review of *Verbeck of Japan: A Citizen of No Country*, by William Elliot Griffis. *American Historical Review* 6 (July, 1901): 829–830.

Nakamura, Takeshi. "The Contributions of Foreigners." *Journal of World History* 9, no. 2 (1965):294–319.

Noyes, George C. Review of *Corea, The Hermit Nation*, by William Elliot Griffis. *The Dial* 3, no. 32 (1882):167.

"Obituary." *Nation* 126 (February 22, 1928):199.

"Obituary." *New York Evening Post*, February 7, 1928, n.p.

Rezneck, Samuel. "The Social History of an American Depression, 1837–1843." *American Historical Review* 40, no. 4 (July, 1935): 662–687.

Shively, Donald. "Nishimura Shigeki: A Confucian View of Modernization." *Changing Japanese Attitudes Toward Modernization*. Edited by Marius Jansen. Princeton, N.J.: Princeton University Press, 1965, pp. 193–241.

Starr, Merritt. "General Horace Capron, 1804–1885." *Journal of Illinois State Historical Society* 18 (July, 1925):276–295.

Wilson, George. "The Bakumatsu Intellectual in Action: Hashimoto Sanai in the Political Crisis of 1858," in Craig, Albert, and Shively, Donald, *Personality in Japanese History*. Berkeley and Los Angeles, Calif.: University of California Press, 1970, pp. 234–263.

Unpublished Materials

Aoki, Hideo. "The Effect of American Ideas Upon Japanese Higher Education." Ph.D. dissertation, Stanford University, 1957.

Ashmead, John. "The Idea of Japan, 1853–1895: Japan as Described by Americans and Other Travelers from the West." 2 vols. Ph.D. dissertation, Harvard University, 1951.

Burks, Ardath. "Reflections on 100 Years of Cultural Exchange." Paper presented at the Japan Society's "Meiji Centennial Lectures" series. Rutgers, the State University, November 13, 1967.

Hall, Ivan. "Mori Arinori: A Reconsideration." 3 vols. Ph.D. dissertation, Harvard University, 1969.

154   BIBLIOGRAPHY

Helbig, Frances Y. "William Elliot Griffis: Entrepreneur of Ideas." M.A. thesis, University of Rochester, 1966.

Johnson, Katherine. "Paternal and Maternal Ancestors and Relatives of William Elliot Griffis." GCRUL.

Jones, Hazel. "The Griffis Thesis and Meiji Policy toward Employment of Foreigners." Paper presented at the Rutgers-Japan Conference, Rutgers, the State University, April, 1967.

———. "The Meiji Government and Foreign Employees, 1868–1900." Ph.D. dissertation, University of Michigan, 1967.

Kanai, Madoka. "Fukui, the Domain of a Tokugawa Collateral Diamyō: Its Tradition and Transition." Paper presented at the Rutgers-Japan Conference, Rutgers, the State University, April, 1967.

Motoyama, Yukihiko. "The Education Policy of Fukui Han and William Elliot Griffis." Paper presented at the Rutgers-Japan Conference, Rutgers, the State University, April, 1967.

Yamamoto, Masaya. "Image Makers of Japan: A Case Study in the Impact of the American Protestant Foreign Missionary Movement, 1859–1905." Ph.D. dissertation, The Ohio State University, 1967.

Manuscript Collections

Rutgers, the State University. Library, Department of Special Collections, William Elliot Griffis Collection.

Edward R. Beauchamp is Associate Professor of Education at the University of Hawaii. He has had a long-standing interest in the role of American advisors in Asian countries and has published several articles on this theme. During 1975–1976 he was Fulbright Lecturer in American Studies and Comparative Education at International Christian University, Keio University, and the University of Tokyo in Japan.

Asian Studies at Hawaii

Orders for Asian Studies at Hawaii publications should be directed to The University Press of Hawaii, 2840 Kolowalu Street, Honolulu, Hawaii 96822. Present standing orders will continue to be filled without special notification.

No. 1 *Bibliography of English Language Sources on Human Ecology, Eastern Malaysia and Brunei.* Complied by Conrad P. Cotter with the assistance of Shiro Saito. Two parts. September 1965. (Available only from Paragon Book Gallery, New York.)

No. 2 *Economic Factors in Southeast Asian Social Change.* Robert Van Niel, editor. May 1968. Out of print.

No. 3 *East Asian Occasional Papers (1).* Harry J. Lamley, editor. May 1969.

No. 4 *East Asian Occasional Papers (2).* Harry J. Lamley, editor. July 1970.

No. 5 *A Survey of Historical Source Materials in Java and Manila.* Robert Van Niel. February 1971.

No. 6 *Educational Theory in the People's Republic of China: The Report of Ch'ien Chung-Jui.* Translation by John N. Hawkins. May 1971. Out of print.

No. 7 *Hai Jui Dismissed from Office.* Wu Han. Translation by C. C. Huang. June 1972.

No. 8 *Aspects of Vietnamese History.* Edited by Walter F. Vella. March 1973.

No. 9 *Southeast Asian Literatures in Translation: A Preliminary Bibliography.* Philip N. Jenner. March 1973.

No. 10 *Textiles of the Indonesian Archipelago.* Garrett and Bronwen Solyom. October 1973.

No. 11 *British Policy and the Nationalist Movement in Burma, 1917–1937.* Albert D. Moscotti. February 1974.

No. 12 *Aspects of Bengali History and Society.* Edited by Rachel Van Baumer. 1975.

No. 13 *Nanyang Perspective: Chinese Students in Multiracial Singapore.* Andrew W. Lind. June 1974.

No. 14 *Political Change in the Philippines.* Edited by Benedict Kerkvliet. November 1974.

No. 15 *Essays on South India.* Edited by Burton Stein. 1975.

No. 16 *The* Caurāsī Pad *of Śrīhit Harivaṁś.* Charles S. J. White. 1976.

No. 17 *An American Teacher in Early Meiji Japan.* Edward R. Beauchamp. 1976.